SAILING
in PARADISE

SAILING
in PARADISE

Yacht Charters Around the World

Rod Heikell

ADLARD COLES NAUTICAL
LONDON

Acknowledgements

Thanks to everyone who helped with this book. Special thanks to Lu, my wife, for checking things over and taking lots of the photos. Thanks also to Barry Nielsen, Graham Sewell, Willie Wilson and Imrays, John Kaye and Nigel Wadlow all those years ago, Andy O'Grady, Joe Charlton and Frank Whelan. Finally the crew at Adlard Coles Nautical, Janet Murphy, Liz Piercy and Hannah Leech, who turned my text and photos and odd scribbles into the book you hold in your hands.

Photography Credits

Lorraine Harris (www.lorraineharris.com) for photo on p. 187.

Rod Heikell for photos on pp. 13, 17, 19, 32, 46, 54, 66, 77, 80, 86, 91, 94, 100, 112, 134, 157, 175, 193, 194, 201 and 208

Lu Michell for photos on pp. 10, 25, 31, 35, 41, 44, 63, 75, 88, 99, 106, 124, 125, 135, 149, 152, 153, 177 and 204.

Andy O'Grady for photos on pp. 47, 55, 68, 72, 73 and 215.

Robert Ronnbom for photo on p. 208.

Sailing Holidays for photos on pp. 4, 9, 37, 43 and 104.

This edition published by
Adlard Coles Nautical
an imprint of A & C Black Publishers Ltd
36 Soho Square, London W1D 3QY
www.adlardcoles.com

Copyright © Rod Heikell 2009

ISBN 978-14081-0951-9

The right of the author to be identified as the author of this work has been asserted by him in accordance with the Copyright, Designs and Patents Act, 1988.

A CIP catalogue record for this book is available from the British Library.

This book is produced using paper that is made from wood grown in managed, sustainable forests. It is natural, renewable and recyclable. The logging and manufacturing processes conform to the environmental regulations of the country of origin.

Printed and bound by C&C Offset Printing Co Ltd, China.

CONTENTS

PREFACE

In our fast paced world, there is something quite magical about stepping on board a boat and entering a different space and time afloat. It's a feeling I never tire of and I've done an awful lot of it! I've been lucky enough to sail to many parts of the world on my own boat and though I'd like to think I've seen a lot, it takes only a cursory glance at a map of the world, a conversation over a beer with other fellow voyagers, a quick flick through *National Geographic*, to make me realise this world is a big place and there are just too many places to get to in my lifetime. Like everyone else I need to work, allot time to other things, and somehow survive it all. Ergo, the only way to get to sail around these places, a few of the 1001 places to sail before you die, is to charter a boat there.

In 1977 I fell into yacht charter in Greece. I'd sailed down to Greece in an old 20-footer and I needed to work to top up the kitty. By the next year I was setting up a new flotilla sailing operation, which meant buying the boats and the equipment and getting everything down to Greece, to work there. Things were very different in those days and we had to make do to keep the boats going. Spares came out with new charterers and repairs to the boats were carried out as best we could. When a mast broke we swapped it for the one on the lead boat and had to motor around with the fleet for two weeks until a new mast was shipped out.

Over the intervening years I've kept in touch with many of the people who were involved with yacht charter in those early days and have kept tabs on the world of charter. Many of those old friends are still involved in running charter companies, skippering yachts in various parts of the world and running yacht service companies. Lots of these people have provided valuable insider information for this book.

A sailing holiday doesn't have to cost as much as you might think. After all, you are like a snail carrying your own home around with you, and most excursions are done under your own steam. You can cook on board or treat yourself to a meal ashore depending on your whims and your budget. And all around you will be the biggest swimming pool in the world.

I hope this book answers some of your questions or at least points you in the right direction. More than that, I hope this book fires you up to go sailing somewhere in the world. If there is one thing that hasn't changed through all the years I've been sailing, it is the sheer joy all of us feel from sailing a boat in foreign climes. There is something about hopping on board a boat and sailing off into the blue that cannot be duplicated. If this book smoothes your way, I've done my job.

Rod Heikell
South Pacific & London
2009

INTRODUCTION

Chartering a yacht is never going to save your life, but it can certainly provide breathing space, far from the incessant buzz of information that continuously assails you. It doesn't have to be perfect, nor the holiday of a lifetime...it just needs to offer a way out for a little time at least.

People go on a yacht charter holiday for all sorts of reasons. For the simple pleasure of getting away from terra firma. For that sweet magic when the sea and the wind click in to give you the sail of a lifetime. For evenings ashore and nights afloat. For the parties. Some go chartering to become human again after a stressful time at work. Or to re-establish some sort of contact with a wife or partner and children. Some just can't do without it for no good reason they can put their finger on.

If chartering is to be an enjoyable process, a little initial research and planning will go a long way in making it as hassle free as possible. Finding the right company to book with, the type of yacht to suit your needs and a destination that meets your sailing skills and inclinations, is not always straightforward. In this book I'll hopefully guide you through the whole business as gently as possible.

One thing is certain. Sailing holidays can be addictive, and the pleasure of waking up on board after the first night is something that may grace your dreams for years to come. Every time I get on a boat, some strange chemistry afflicts my neurones and turns me from western schizoid man into a human being with a bit of time to think about things which don't revolve around timetables and diary appointments. Conrad once said something along the lines of ... 'a boat is not a slave, give her your all, your love, your skill and she will carry you for as long as she is able'. On a yacht charter, you can capture some of that magic.

Captain Cook Bay on Moorea

GOING ON CHARTER

Basically you need a boat, a destination, a date, and crew. Like most good ideas it sounds simple and for the most part it is. When planning the trip, some details will be fixed: school holidays, a limited budget, limited experience or an area you just have to visit whatever anyone says. Wherever you go remember this is a holiday you are on and it should be fun.

WITH WHOM

Families
Friends
Pot luck
Sailing schools

Families

Many people will choose to charter with the family, ergo the crew is ready made. A family holiday should be just that, a holiday for all the family and not some arduous voyage you are intent on making.

It is necessary at the beginning to get some idea of what members of a family want to do on a holiday afloat. The most common mistake is to try to achieve too much. Any timetable made for a foreign cruise should have lay days built into it and a short circuit so that you can cut out part of the itinerary and get the boat back comfortably on time.

If you are going on a skippered charter, find out if there is enough to occupy children on board for the duration of the cruise.

Friends

A yacht charter with friends as crew can either cement friendships through the shared experience or destroy a life-long relationship in a short time. It is essential that friends sailing together talk about the location, the boat, the route, and tasks on board before you put a deposit on a yacht charter. Those who have not been sailing before should endeavour to see a similar boat to the one they will be living on for two weeks or so. Non-sailors should be given some time for trips ashore and at the beginning of the cruise start slowly so they can get accustomed to sailing and overcome any initial fear of being on the water in a fragile plastic tea-cup. You may have to change an itinerary if the spectre of seasickness puts in an appearance.

All these things need to be discussed beforehand so that the cruise is a shared experience, not an enforced Bligh-like voyage of endurance. You want your friends to come on future yacht charters, don't you?

Pot luck

For those who cannot find friends eager and willing to go sailing with them, there are several options available. Most of the flotilla companies run pot-luck boats (also called stowaway, share-boat, share a yacht, berth sharing, or a similar name) where you will be put on a yacht with other singles or couples.

The flotilla companies require that at least one of those on board has sailing experience and he or she will then assume the role of skipper. If there is more than one would-be skipper on board then some sharing of the role is advised. Other inexperienced sharers fit into whatever role they are best suited to.

If flotilla is not for you then scan the internet forums or the personal column of the yachting magazines for others looking for crew for a yacht charter or post a forum question or advertise yourself.

You may come across advertisements for crew or single berths on owner operated boats cruising in an area or on yacht deliveries. These can offer some exotic locations, long passages, and the company of a skilled captain and navigator who knows his boat backwards, but it will not give you much scope for command or even partial command of your own. Better to approach it as a learning experience and the chance to do some unusual sailing. Remember though that you will not have the bonding of an established company and arrange adequate insurance for flights and any mishaps that might happen along the way.

Sailing schools and other institutions

For those wanting to learn to sail or to hone basic skills in yacht racing, old-timers or specific boats, there are many opportunities for either single or group participation. Most sailing schools, whether offering courses for basic skills or more advanced courses, will take either singles or groups and mix-and-match as appropriate.

WHEN

> • Charter seasons: High and low seasons
> • Weather
> • School holidays are peak season

Most areas have a time of the year when the charter season closes down. In the Mediterranean there are really no charters during the northern winter. In the Caribbean there are few charters (sensibly) during the hurricane season from June to October. In the Pacific Islands the hurricane season from November to May likewise delimits the time of the year when charter boats operate. In somewhere like Thailand, there is a 2–3 month period at the height of the rainy season in the summer when it is just too hot and humid to do anything.

The charter season itself is usually chopped up into a low season either end of the high season. Naturally enough the high season is the best time to go and is consequently the most expensive period and the most popular. The low seasons on either end are a bit more of a lottery when it comes to wind (too much or too little) and weather, although you can have wonderful conditions with a bit of luck. Some people prefer the low season in some areas on the basis that the high season is too hot and too crowded.

In the Mediterranean, spring or autumn can be wonderful times to go sailing as fewer people are around afloat and ashore. The possible wet and unsettled weather may however keep you in harbour. In the Tropics, parts of the summer season can mean wonderful sailing and in some months there is little chance of hurricanes, even if it is still officially the hurricane season.

In the second half of the book on charter areas, the different charter seasons are given along with the sort of weather you can expect. Remember that weather is more critical for a holiday afloat as opposed to a land-based holiday so tailor the time to your experience and the expected conditions. Remember too that all weather is statistical and you can get a high season holiday when it blows above or below average and rains all the time, even though the odds are against that. Likewise a low season holiday may have perfect high season conditions, but likely will not.

For many, at least those who have school-age children, the dates for a holiday afloat are locked into the school holidays. There is no escape from this and inevitably this is when charters cost the most. It is sometimes possible to organise a low season yacht charter with children by running a few days over Easter or a mid-term break to fit into a one- or two-week slot. Most parents think that the foreign experience more than makes up for the few days the children have missed at school – but check with the school if it is OK.

Those with allergies or certain medical problems need to do some checking on conditions at different times of the year. Hayfever sufferers should avoid seasons when pollen counts are high. Hot countries can have very high pollen counts at certain times of the year. Those who suffer from heat rash should also avoid the height of summer or the hottest times in the Tropics and anyone who has a severe allergic reaction to mosquito and midge bites needs to avoid some areas at certain times. Consult with your doctor and the charter company if you are unsure.

Flotilla sailing is a good option for families

WHERE

> - Choose destinations you are unlikely to sail to yourself
> - Try an area you think you might want to sail to
> - Think of what it will be like for those going with you and tailor holiday plans to their plans as well

For most, the 'where to go' question is the one that gets the juices going. Thumbing through brochures with all those wonderful photos of yachts tied up outside a taverna in Greece, in a translucent coral fringed anchorage in the Virgin Islands, under sheer limestone cliffs covered in jungle in Thailand, in St Tropez next to a rock star's floating home, on the waterfront in Sydney with that extravagant opera house in the background, in fact almost anywhere except where you are right now conjures up visions of you in another world at the helm of your own yacht.

And why not? Even if you own a yacht, the logistics of getting it to that place are impossible for most and the cost may be prohibitive. A week or two on a charter yacht makes a lot of sense in our busy world and it also makes sense to go to paradise and have a look at it just in case there are a few things you don't like about it. Considering the interests of those you are going with is key. Try also to tailor your choice of location to your level of experience.

IN THE END...

... it is the planning at the beginning which goes some way in determining whether a yacht charter is a dream come true or a nightmare not to be repeated. If there seems to be a lot of negative advice in the foregoing it is not meant to put you off yacht charter, just ensure you get the maximum enjoyment from it. In truth a very small percentage of those who go on a yacht charter would not repeat it and the majority plan to repeat it the next year and forgo the new kitchen or new car. Some will choose a different company because once they have been in an area they get to look at other boats.

TYPES OF CHARTER

- Flotilla sailing
- Bareboat
- Skippered charter
- Sailing schools
- Ashore and afloat
- Leaseback
- Delivery cruises
- Ocean passages
- Sail-dive
- Racing
- Corporate charter
- Sailing for the disabled
- Adventure charters
- Expedition charter
- Hitchhiking

There are basically three types of yacht charter available and a number of other options related to yacht charter or to just getting on the water for a holiday afloat. The basic types of charter are flotilla sailing, bareboat, and skippered charter, although there are a lot of variations on the themes.

FLOTILLA SAILING

Also called sailing in company.

> For inexperienced sailors who want to get some experience, usually in a warm climate, and have a holiday at the same time
> For experienced sailors who want a relaxing holiday
> Good social life with others for kids in the school holidays
> Experienced lead boat crew to help you berth, share local knowledge and tell you about that special restaurant or bar

Flotilla sailing started in Greece over 35 years ago and has proved enduringly popular ever since. A lot of nonsense and a sort of snobbery revolves around the idea of flotilla sailing, but many of those who go on flotilla return again. It is not solely for those with little sailing experience; often experienced sailors who own a yacht choose to take the flotilla option.

On flotilla you sail in company with a group of yachts (typically 10–12) and a lead boat on which there is a skipper and hostess and sometimes an engineer. The skipper is in overall charge of the fleet and is responsible for the care and repair of boats and clients alike. He will brief the new arrivals on the ins and outs of their boats and will provide pilotage and general navigation briefings each morning. The engineer is responsible for the maintenance of the yachts, making sure the engines, plumbing, electrics and rigging are in good order. In his other capacity he usually supervises the preparation of the punch served at barbecues. The hostess looks after day-to-day life on board and advises on facilities ashore – where to shop, restaurants, doctors and dentists, and excursions inland. She is usually a dab hand at minor first aid.

With a lead boat around in radio contact with the fleet, much of the apprehension of a new sailing area and a strange boat to cope with is removed and you can get on and enjoy the sailing and the scenery. Should you get into difficulties the lead crew is there to help you. Their experience means you get local knowledge on harbours and anchorages, a guide to the best restaurants, and immediate help to fix the loo or get the engine going.

Although yachts sail together as a fleet, this doesn't mean you have to sail in line astern behind the lead boat. In most areas you leave a harbour or anchorage in your own time, stop off for lunch in a bay somewhere if you are so inclined, and finally end up in the next bay or harbour for the evening. Depending on the area, on a two-week flotilla you could get anything from three to eight days independent sailing where you can go off and explore an area before rejoining the flotilla towards the end of the cruise. Flotilla options with a lot of independent sailing days are effectively a 50-50 mix of flotilla and bareboat, though with the added advantage that when you are off sailing independently, you can always call up the lead crew should you have any problems.

Flotillas score highly for the social side of things. A fleet of identical boats means there are lots of opportunities for a bit of impromptu one design racing. On flotilla you will make a lot of friends and some will forge lifelong friendships.

Flotilla holidays are generally two-week affairs and typically cover anything from 100 to 200 miles in easy stages. The degree of experience needed depends on the area and the distance covered. Most flotilla companies will give you a good idea of the qualifications needed for a particular flotilla and may advise you to go on a short familiarisation course if they feel your experience is a bit on the light side. In general, flotilla qualifications start at those with dinghy experience for the easier flotillas and work up to previous flotilla experience or small-craft owners for the more arduous flotillas.

BAREBOAT

For semi-experienced to experienced sailors depending on the location

Plan your own adventure and set your own pace

Choose the sort of sailing options you want and sail to places other options might not get to

Bareboat basically means you charter a boat and sail independently in a given area. Most companies require you to return the boat to the home base but many now offer a one-way cruise from one base to another. Bareboats are not bare, but come with everything you need, except the provisions. In fact many companies can arrange to provision your boat should you desire it, though you can have a lot of fun trying to buy marmite in Thailand or bacon in Turkey.

If you are going bareboat, it is important that you take some time choosing a charter company. Pick your fellow companions carefully and put some thought into planning the cruise.

When choosing a charter company check on what is included in the inventory. What safety equipment is there? What anchors, chain and warp is supplied? What navigation equipment is provided? What charts and local pilots? Ask about backup in case any problems occur. Most bareboat companies require that you have some experience handling, sailing and navigating something larger than a dinghy. The degree of experience depends on the location and likely conditions you will encounter. Depending on the local regulations, charter companies may require an official bit of paper saying you are qualified to skipper, although this can often be a basic qualification. Perversely in some countries, the RYA International Certificate of Competence, which you can get with a Day Skipper certificate, is preferred in some countries to an RYA Yachtmaster qualification because it has the word 'International' on it.

Some companies may suggest that you take a brush-up course or even go on a flotilla holiday first. This is in the interests of safety and should not be ignored.

All bareboat charter companies require a security deposit or a premium on insurance for damage for the boat and gear. At the end of the holiday, any gear that has been lost or damaged and any damage to the boat will be deducted from the deposit or your premium is used. They may also require that you have personal insurance including adequate medical insurance. If you return the boat late there are various penalties that can be invoked by the company which usually means a certain amount deducted from your security deposit or a payment for each day you are overdue. There will also be penalties for not returning the yacht to the charter base because bad weather prevented you from getting back.

All of these penalties are covered by the security deposit or short-term insurance (read the fine print) and until the company is satisfied the boat has been returned at the appointed time and place and in good condition, it is up to you to do so or lose all or part of the deposit or make a payment.

Force majeure applies only in exceptional circumstances to bareboat charter.

SKIPPERED CHARTER

- For inexperienced crew at base level
- For anyone at skipper and crew level
- Do as little or as much hands-on as you want
- The skipper will often have detailed knowledge of out-of-the-way spots and the best restaurants ashore

Skippered charter encompasses everything from small bareboats where a skipper is engaged to look after the boat, up to superyachts with not only skipper but a full complement of crew. On a large yacht the crew will often outnumber the guests and on this sort of charter, service is expected to be the equal or better than a five star hotel.

At the bottom level, skippered charter equals bareboat plus skipper. Charterers of a bareboat may take on a skipper if they are short on experience or occasionally because the charter company has suggested they do so. Sometimes this will work on the basis that the charterers take a skipper for one week and then take over themselves on the second week when they feel more confident about things. At this level, the skipper is responsible for the operation and maintenance of the boat although he will require help from the charterers when reefing, berthing and anchoring. He or she will not expect to cook, clean, entertain or guide you ashore although it is very likely he will do some of these things. This sort of arrangement for bareboats will often extend up to 50–60 footers depending on the boat and how easy it is to handle.

Most skippered charter is in the mid-range on yachts 45–80 foot which will often be run by a couple. Usually this means he is skipper and ultimately responsible for all things nautical and some things social and she is cook, crew, sometimes child-minder and the balance of things social. Many of these couples are a well accomplished act whose service to charterers goes well beyond any job description they might have. Many people will return to the same skipper and hostess almost irrespective of their command because in the end it is their contribution to the charter which has the greatest impact.

At superyacht level there will be not only skipper and hostess, but usually another two to eight crew depending on size and the level of luxury catered to. This sort of operation comes at a price and it is essential that a reliable broker with a track record is engaged or reliable personal recommendations taken up.

MOTORBOATS

It has to be said that most of the charter options talked about here are for sailing boats. In all the options there are possibilities for motorboat charter although, with the exception of skippered charter, there are fewer possibilities than for sailing boats. A few bareboat options are available in some areas. Skippered motorboat charter is the most popular option and in most charter areas there are numerous possibilities available ranging from trawler type motorboats from around 50 feet up to superyacht level.

SAILING SCHOOLS AND 'LEARNING TO SAIL' COURSES

- For novices and beginners wanting to brush up on their skills
- For sailors wanting to learn unfamiliar techniques like berthing Mediterranean style
- Acquiring qualifications

The two are not quite the same thing. Sailing schools usually work towards a recognised qualification and put you through a syllabus to obtain a qualification such as the RYA Competent Crew certificate or Yachtmaster qualification. Such courses may not teach you unfamiliar techniques found in foreign cruising areas or the skills relating to sailing there.

There are now numerous sailing schools offering qualifications like the RYA Yachtmaster or even higher commercial qualifications which are taught all over the world. Some of these will involve learning in home waters and then an ocean passage to rack up the miles needed for these 'Fast Track' qualifications. In this sense they are less yacht charter and more like work, albeit pleasant work.

Learning to Sail courses are not usually geared to a qualification but have the aim of getting you on the water and familiarising you with techniques and procedures you will use on a charter yacht. Sometimes the two will be combined and you get a qualification and learn other stuff as well. Often they will be on the same yacht used on charter and they may be in the same country where you intend to charter. Inexperienced crew who wish to take a flotilla or bareboat yacht may be asked, in the nicest possible way, to take one of these courses by the charter company. They vary from one-day brush-up courses to three- to seven-day courses teaching you nearly everything you need to know. These courses are useful in so far as they familiarise you with techniques that might otherwise prove stressful during the first few days of a charter and allow you to get on and enjoy the sailing.

ASHORE AND AFLOAT

> Called variously Villa Flotilla, Stay and Sail, or Club Holidays
> Usually aimed at novices or families where one half wants to go sailing and the other half wants a relaxing time ashore

These holidays are generally two weeks split 50–50 between one week in a villa or apartment ashore and one week on board a charter yacht. The holiday ashore will often have access to dinghy sailing, board-sailing,

or may include a relaxed introduction course to flotilla sailing with instruction on board the same sort of boat you will be using in the second week.

This sort of holiday leads a spouse (him or her) and children towards a sailing holiday in a relaxed and easy fashion without everyone being dumped on board in a foreign country and left to get on with it. It also includes the opportunity for avid dinghy and board-sailors to get out by themselves and experience some exhilarating sailing while the other half relaxes around the pool with a cold drink.

One variation on the theme is where you simply stay ashore and get the use of sailing dinghies and boards to go out sailing. There is no charter yacht involved. A number of these club holidays have the latest hot dinghies and boards for customers and expert tuition on hand to get the most out of them.

LEASEBACK

> Your own yacht with a charter company which you get to use for nominated periods
> Can often use other yachts from the same company in different charter destinations

Under this arrangement you front up with around one-quarter to one-third of the purchase price of the sort of boat used by one of the charter companies and the company leases it back from you over a period of years, usually three to five years, with the charter fees paying off the balance or a part of the purchase price. The charter company contracts to maintain the boat, and you, the future owner, get the use of the boat for certain periods of the charter season.

The arrangement has the primary advantage of paying off the balance of the boat over the agreed period of years and letting you have the use of it at certain times over that period. It also means that the ongoing upkeep of the boat is out of your hands until the boat is paid off. Thus

On a bareboat charter you are on your own

you can scheme to go off cruising in the Mediterranean or the Caribbean in your own yacht after a number of years having spent time aboard getting used to it out there anyway.

If the arrangement has any pitfalls it revolves around the charter company which operates the leaseback system. Some companies have not maintained the boat at all well and at the end of the lease period the boat has been turned over to the owner in an awful state.

You also need to guard against the company going bust and your yacht being seized as part of the assets of the company. Most companies arrange it so that you are the owner from the time you sign the contract. Give the contract to your solicitor to check over, but even if it is watertight in the country where the contract is signed, in practice you may have difficulty extracting the yacht from the country it is chartered in if the company goes under. It is not unheard of for yachts under leaseback schemes to be seized in the country it is chartered in and this can entail a good deal of expense and time for you to extract it. The best bet is to go with a company that already has a good track record operating a leaseback system and, if possible, check out an insurance scheme to cover the risks.

DELIVERY CRUISES

> For experienced crew only
> Get in some sea miles and see other parts that most charter yachts don't go to

Charter companies will often move yachts between bases at the beginning or end of a charter season and sometimes move them to a new location. These delivery cruises cover longer distances under more arduous conditions than the normal charter routes and you should not necessarily expect them to be a slightly longer version of flotilla or bareboat sailing in the season. The trips vary between slightly longer legs within an area say from one charter area in Greece to another, or long delivery cruises with extended offshore passages transatlantic or from the Mediterranean to somewhere like Thailand. Anyone undertaking one of these delivery cruises should be fit and experienced for the trip, something the charter company usually tries to make sure of when vetting applicants.

On a more casual basis you can often pick up delivery trips from advertisements in the classified columns or by word of mouth. On some of the pitfalls encountered on this sort of trip, see the section on *Hitchhiking*.

OCEAN PASSAGES

> For experienced sailors looking to build sea miles
>
> For adventurous types who want to experience the raw excitement of sailing long distance

A number of events like the Atlantic Rally for Cruisers and the Bluewater Rally Antigua will have participants who advertise berths on their boats. Some of these will be on a shared expenses basis and others will expect a more substantial charter fee for the berth. Some private individuals crossing on their own will also advertise berths on a shared expenses basis and some of the 'Fast Track' sailing schools have boats doing ocean passages. Berths for an ocean passage can be found on various internet sites that have pages for 'crew wanted' or in the classifieds in yachting magazines.

It is important that you meet the owner/skipper before you take on one of these places and any responsible skipper will ensure that he sees you.

Stuff to dream of...

Take a look at the *Hitchhiking* section in this chapter.

SAIL-DIVE

> For those learning to dive on PADI courses
>
> For keen divers who want to go sailing as well

In parts of the world with good diving over coral there are yachts which combine a cruise with a circuit of the good dive sites in the area. Most of these yachts are 40 feet plus and all are skippered cruises. Most of these charters are one-man bands who are keen divers and also like sailing. The yacht will be equipped with all dive gear and the skipper will usually be a qualified dive instructor. This means you get to potter around an area and can stay overnight at dive sites without wasting time going back to shore-based accommodation.

Most of the areas offering sail-dive charter are in tropical or semi-tropical areas. The Red Sea, the Caribbean, the Seychelles, Maldives, Thailand, the Great Barrier Reef in Australia, and the South Pacific Islands all have sail-dive charter available.

RACING

> For semi-experienced to experienced
>
> Learn how to really sail

Racing charter encompasses everything from fun events to arduous round-the-world races to training sessions by professional racing skippers.

Most racing charter revolves around fun events like Marmaris Race Week in the Mediterranean and Antigua Race Week in the Caribbean. As anyone who has been racing there knows, the competitive urge is only just under the skin in most of us and the racing is fiercely competitive. The parties afterwards can be just as competitive for the amounts of alcohol consumed.

The following established race series will have charter boats or berths available though this list is in no way definitive.

Race series

UK

The Round-the-Island Race	A one day affair with numbers of charter yachts racing around the Isle of Wight.	June.
West Highland Yachting Week		July–August.
Falmouth Race Week	Features many classic yachts.	August.

France

La Niourlague	A week of racing out of St Tropez featuring classic yachts and state of the art racing machines.	September–October.
Brest and Douarnenez Week	A week of festivities celebrating traditional sailing craft with races. Places often available on the boats.	Biennial July.

Greece

Ionian Regatta	One-day short race involving mostly flotilla yachts in Levkas.	September.

Turkey

Marmaris Race Week	A week of racing involving a large number of charter yachts from Marmaris in Turkey.	October–November.
Bodrum Race Week	A week of racing.	October.
Göcek Race Week	A week of racing.	November.

Caribbean

Grenada Sailing Festival		February.
Heineken Race Week at St Maarten		March.
Rolex Cup at St Thomas USVI		April.
BVI Spring Regatta		April.
Antigua Race Week	A week of racing renowned for its *après mer* parties. Bareboats and skippered charter.	April–May.
Angostura Tobago Race Week	A week of relaxed racing with bareboats and skippered charter.	May.
Martinique Regatta		June.
Carib Cup		July.

Malaysia

Raja Mudra	A week of racing up the west coast of Malaysia from Port Kelang to Langkawi.	November.

Thailand

Kings Cup	A week of racing from Phuket. Bareboat charter available.	

There are also lots of smaller race series where charter boats will be available so check race calendars and the internet and classified advertisements.

Round-the-world races

Round-the-world races are for those wanting a serious injection of adrenaline and are arduous affairs for the committed only. Crews are selected after a series of trials and the costs are not inconsiderable both in actual monetary terms and the time off required for the selection and training as well as the race itself. There is only one round-the-world race as such for amateurs at present.

- **Clipper Race** Robin Knox-Johnston's Clipper Race in 68 foot identical GRP yachts. Paying berths with professional skipper.

There are also several round-the-world rallies which although not strictly racing nonetheless have a bit of a competitive element amongst some of the yachts participating. Some of the yachts on these rallies have paying crew.

- **ARC Atlantic Rally for Cruisers** Has paying berths on racing and cruising boats. It joins up with the Round the World Rally below.
- **ARC Round the World Rally** One and a half year rally around the world via the Cape of Good Hope. Starts and finishes in St Lucia. Yachts can start after the Atlantic Rally for Cruisers. Private entries with no ratings. Berths available on some of these yachts.
- **Bluewater Rally** A two-year rally around the world via the Red Sea. Starts and finishes in Gibraltar. Private entries with no ratings. Berths available on some of these yachts.

For anyone wanting to gain experience either for a fun weeks racing or more serious stuff there are a number of courses available with professional crew. These can vary from a one-day refresher picking up a few tips to a full week's instruction with some actual racing thrown in. These courses are not intended to be relaxing and are more akin to teaching courses than holidays.

CORPORATE CHARTER

Involves a company or group of people who work together under a professional association or the like chartering a yacht or several yachts as a reward for bonuses achieved and targets met, for entertaining clients, or for the nebulous thinking that uses a yacht charter for character building, group bonding, or other vaguely titled matters.

SAILING FOR THE DISABLED

A number of companies operate yacht charter for the disabled. Most charter is on specially modified boats to provide all the facilities needed, but it may be possible to go on a bareboat or flotilla holiday depending on the mobility and requirements of a disabled person.

Of course there will be those who need the specialist skills and equipment installed on boats designed for the disabled. Personally I favour the approach where a disabled person comes along with everyone else on charter including late nights in the local bar.

ADVENTURE CHARTERS

In some of the remote parts of the world adventure charters are offered depending on experience or physical fitness. These trips operate in remote regions like Tierra del Fuego, Antarctica, lesser known Pacific islands, Alaska and the Arctic and offer the opportunity to sail in parts of the world few others get to. The sailing can be arduous and life in the extreme cold testing on even experienced adventurers. The trips are always on a skippered and crewed yacht and may include other activities such as climbing mountains or sub-aqua diving on remote reefs.

EXPEDITIONS

A number of charter berths are often offered on scientific or quasi-scientific expeditions looking at anything from the migration routes of whales to the flora and fauna of remote locations. Some of these expeditions can be arduous and you need to be committed to the project for some of the

Moorea. The 'where to go' question is the exciting one

hardships you will undergo. Others are comparatively comfortable affairs with all mod cons on board and frequent visits to 'civilisation'. Expedition charter is always on a skippered and crewed basis with costs ranging from expenses for food and drink to full luxury charter rates.

HITCHHIKING

Not really a form of charter, more a cheap way of getting on board a yacht and crewing for the pleasure on a pleasurable voyage. If you turn up at popular jumping off spots for yachts on passage it is sometimes possible to help crew from one place to another. Obviously you will have to be in the right place at the right time.

There are a number of websites around that advertise for crew. You usually log-in and then contact the owner/skipper through the website and then by e-mail and phone. The only problem with crewing websites is that it is hard to gauge the condition of the boat and the character of the skipper until you get there. Don't be shy of asking pertinent questions about the boat, the itinerary and your duties.

Some care is needed when hitchhiking your way around on a boat. You should

carry full medical insurance for the countries you are going to and indeed some owners will insist on it. Most owners have pretty strict rules about no drugs, no illegal items like firearms, and for some no smoking. Some owners will also insist on you putting up a bond (usually around US$500) which will be returned to you at the end of the voyage.

It pays to make thorough enquiries about the boat and skipper before you leave.

- For the Atlantic try Gibraltar and the Canary Islands (especially Lanzarote and Gran Canaria) between October and January
- For getting to Panama and through to the Pacific, try Florida, the Virgin Isles, St Martin or the ABCs for passage to Panama and possibly onwards between January and April
- For the Pacific try San Francisco, Los Angeles or San Diego in April or May and Panama February to May
- In the South Pacific it is possible to hop through some of the Pacific Islands depending on your luck. Some of the better places are Tahiti, Tonga and Fiji
- For the Indian Ocean try Darwin or Phuket

CHOOSING A COMPANY

- Cost
- What you get with flotilla, bareboat and skippered charter
- Tips on reading a brochure or website
- Company guarantees
- Staff
- Getting more information
- The internet
- Yacht charter brokers

Once you have decided to book a holiday there remains the choice of company to book with. The internet can be a valuable source of information for charter locations, types of boats, local attractions etc. Equally yachting magazines and brochures are helpful starting points when researching the best company for you.

Some will have heard of a company by word of mouth or through recommendations from a yacht club or travel agent. Boat shows are another source of information and here you will probably meet some of the staff who work at the charter base or as flotilla crew and you can ask all the questions you want about the boats and the area.

COST

Flotilla costs
Bareboat costs
Skippered charter costs

Cost is an important consideration for many and one which can considerably narrow down the options. It is important that you establish either from the brochure or over the phone what additional costs there will be.

The following sections will give you some idea of what to expect:

FLOTILLA

A flotilla sailing holiday is virtually an all-in package. A flotilla holiday should include the following:
- Flight from the specified airport included. There may also be flights from other airports subject to supplements.
- The transfer to and from the destination airport to the charter base.
- The yacht and a specified inventory.
- Some companies will include fuel, gas, and water. Others don't.
- Paperwork with the relevant authorities when not sailing independently.
- The services of the lead crew.

This is the bare minimum and many companies will offer better equipped yachts with CD players and outboards, tempting additions to the inventory like snorkelling gear and cockpit cushions, and the shared use of equipment like sailboards.

It usually does not include:
- Airport taxes and visa charges in the destination country.
- Security deposit or a damage/loss excess waiver fee.
- Your food and entertainment.
- Harbour dues.
- Additional equipment like an outboard motor for the tender, gennakers or spinnakers, personal use of a sailboard, although some companies now include these.
- Travel insurance though most add it on with the initial deposit.
- Yacht cleaning.

BAREBOAT

Most bareboat holidays are not all-in packages although many companies can arrange travel and other requirements at extra cost. The holiday usually includes the following:
- The yacht and a specified inventory. The

inventory is usually of a higher specification than that of a flotilla boat.

- Initial paperwork with the relevant authorities to get you away.
- The services of the charter base staff.

This is the bare minimum and again many companies offer much more.

It usually does not include:

- The flight or other transport to and from the charter destination.
- Airport taxes and visa charges in the destination country.
- The transfer to and from the destination airport to the charter base.
- Security deposit or damage/loss excess waiver fee.
- Fuel, gas and water for the whole charter.
- Additional equipment such as an outboard motor for the tender, spinnaker, and sailboard, although some companies will include these free of charge with the yacht.
- Paperwork with the relevant authorities and harbour dues en route.
- Your food and entertainment (some companies supply a small free starter pack).
- Travel insurance though most add it on with the initial deposit.
- Yacht cleaning.

CREWED

Most crewed charters take considerable care to look after you and cosset you from the burdens of local paperwork, finding your way around, and choosing a restaurant. It usually includes the following:

- Yacht and specified inventory. On larger yachts the inventory may include toys like sailboards, jet skis, and a tender suitable for water-skiing.
- The services of a skipper and, depending on the size of the yacht or your requirements, cook and crew.

It does not include:

- The flight or other transport to and from the charter destination.
- Airport taxes and visa charges.

- The transfer to and from the charter base although many skippers will meet you at the airport if it is not too far away.
- Fuel, gas and water for the duration of the charter.
- Harbour dues en route.
- Your food and entertainment. Remember it is only politic to entertain your skipper and crew occasionally.
- Travel insurance.
- Tips for the skipper and crew, a customary courtesy although considered mandatory in some areas.

Clearly the extra costs you have to add in increase as you move from flotilla to bareboat to skippered charter. Between flotilla and bareboat the cost can work out much the same if you shop around for flights and take a little care over costs on the water. Many of the bareboat companies can arrange flights for you and some of them do very good deals indeed. If you are not satisfied with the price of flights from a bareboat company or agent, a quick perusal of budget and charter airlines on the internet should turn up a selection of competitive prices.

COMPANY GUARANTEES

Some companies offer various guarantees if you lose some or all of your holiday due to a breakdown. Some will put it in the fine print of the brochure and if it's not there then it's worth asking the company anyway. To a large extent this relies on the staff on the ground being able to carry out the promised guarantee. (You can just hear the company director: 'I don't care if its Force 9 and the ferries aren't running, get another yacht down there yesterday'.) But it does at least give you some guarantee of fulfilling the sailing part of the holiday rather than sitting around in a bar wondering when a mechanic or a new sail is going to turn up. Usually these guarantees will promise that for sailing time lost due to no fault of your own, typically an engine breakdown or rig or sail failure, they will do one or several of the following:

- Provide an equivalent or larger replacement yacht.
- Provide a credit towards another sailing holiday with them.
- Make a monetary payment.

There are usually provisos to the guarantee along the following lines:

- Normally the lost time must be one day or more although some charter companies stipulate as little as four hours' lost time before they credit you with a discount or extra days.
- Some companies restrict the area where you can make this claim.
- You must obtain written evidence of the lost time, usually from shore or flotilla staff.

You should have this guarantee in writing, including the amount of money offered towards another holiday or paid ex gratia. You will find most companies want your custom again and will provide adequate compensation.

I must add here that charterers who act irresponsibly with their charge and damage craft through their own negligence, either by mooring badly, paying too little attention to their navigation and encountering underwater objects, keeping too much sail up in strong winds and damaging the rig and sails, or through not following engine checks cause damage to the engine, are themselves liable to pay the charter company or lose the whole or part of the security deposit.

STAFF

What you get from flotilla, bareboat and skippered charter staff

The crew on flotilla, the shore-based staff of bareboat companies, and the skipper and crew on skippered charter are the backbone of any charter company. They are in the end the ones who can make or break your holiday.

Flotilla crew

Flotilla staff brief you at the beginning of the flotilla on the boats and area, repair engines, sails and toilets, and facilitate your forays ashore. Their relationship with you and yours with them is an important ingredient in the success of a flotilla. If you can meet them at a boat show or talk to one of them in the winter you will get some idea of the quality of the crew employed by a company.

Bareboat staff

While you will see less of them than flotilla crew, the quality of shore-based bareboat staff is just as important to your holiday. They are the ones who maintain your yacht, fix any minor niggles, and get you quickly and efficiently on your way. You need to check the inventory with them, correct or note any deficiencies, get some idea of the cruising area and suggested itineraries, note any recommended restaurants, collect the paperwork and be on your way.

More importantly you need to know that in the event of a breakdown they can get someone to you to fix things or authorise someone locally to do so. The biggest problem on a bareboat charter is undoubtedly a breakdown away from the charter base and you should seek assurances from a company that they will dispatch staff if necessary or authorise work locally.

Skippered charter

At the beginning check what the skipper thinks are his obligations and duties. A single skipper on a 45 foot or 50 foot yacht is not going to be skipper AND nanny, cook and cleaner all rolled into one. This means you need to be reasonable in your expectations of what a solitary skipper on board can do. If you get a hostess and another crew member as well then you do get the nanny, cook and cleaner as well as the skipper.

A sympathetic skipper and crew are the essential ingredient for a successful, efficient and enjoyable skippered charter.

Staff are an essential part of the equation for a successful charter

GATHERING INFORMATION

Reading a brochure or website

Brochures only want to show you the 'best' for an area. The same applies to websites in terms of style and content not entirely reflecting the truth. There are however some yacht forums on the internet which provide frank discussions of areas, companies and boats plus some brochures have started to introduce a more down-to-earth description of an area with some indication of what the reality is like, which is rather more helpful for the reader.

The best solution is as usual to talk to someone who has been on a holiday with that company. Failing that ask for some interpretation of the brochure at a boat show or on the phone.

OTHER SOURCES OF INFORMATION

There are a number of other options although they have their pitfalls:
- Boat shows enable you to meet staff and ask some nitty gritty questions about the company and its boats. Many of them run videos of charter holidays and some will let you have a copy of the DVD if you leave a deposit for its safe return. Magazines, newspapers and television travel shows sometimes run features on yacht charters and if you read between the lines a bit, you can pick up some information from these. Remember that magazines and newspapers rely on advertisers so it is unlikely an article is going to criticise a yacht charter unless it was seriously flawed.
- Yacht clubs and associations sometimes have a mini-lecture and slide show on yacht charter holidays and these can be a good way of finding out just what a company was like.
- Yacht charter brokers will rarely be used other than for bareboat and skippered charter. A reputable broker will not have unsatisfactory boats on his books and will often have been to the area and should have visited the boat and crew.

CHOOSING A BOAT

- What type of boat
- Number of berths versus a comfortable number of people
- Equipment – what to expect and the extras
- A few questions you should ask

To some extent the choice of boat is determined by the choice of company although it also works in reverse in that the sort of boat you want may determine the company you choose to book with. This chapter refers only to flotilla, bareboat or skippered bareboat charter. Skippered and crewed charter on larger yachts tend to be such a mixture of craft that it is really impossible to give a general idea of the sort of boat to expect. However, the literature for crewed charters should be liberally sprinkled with photographs and descriptions of what you get and from this you will have to make a choice.

TYPE OF YACHT

What sort of boat to expect

Flotilla and bareboat yachts up to around 50 feet are pretty much interchangeable these days. Flotilla companies do not offer craft much over 35–40 feet and to get on a larger craft you will be looking at a bareboat charter. Some companies offer a 'cruising in company' formula with bigger yachts where a small group, usually three to six yachts, cruise around together.

Most charter yachts tend to be stable forgiving craft with few vices. They are not intended to be greyhounds but they are generally not plodders either. When choosing a boat there will obviously be some differences in performance and characteristics although for the most part

not a lot. If you want performance then something like a Swan or a Danish X-boat will be quicker than a standard Beneteau, Jeanneau or Bavaria.

These two French boat-builders, Beneteau and Jeanneau, and the German boat-builder Bavaria, dominate the charter yacht market with a range of yachts which can be had as charter versions. The charter version offers more cabins than owner or racing versions and so affords more privacy for charterers.

A number of other boat-builders also produce charter yacht versions, but these three companies have the lion's share of the market and so figure prominently in charter fleets. What that means is that your chances of getting something that goes a bit faster are limited and the chances are that you will get a yacht from either Beneteau, Jeanneau or Bavaria. A number of other boat-builders like Dufour, Hunter, Feeling, Gib Sea, and the catamaran manufacturers, principally the Lagoon series, Leopards and Fontaine Pajot, also figure prominently in charter fleets as do a number of locally produced yachts in various countries which have been designed specifically for the charter market.

Unless you are looking specifically for something which has go-faster knobs and whistles, most charter yachts provide more than enough speed and thrills from the standard range available. Most have been designed with charter in mind and have had numerous modifications made for comfort during your holiday. All these comforts, bigger watertanks, biminis, roller reefing genoas and mainsails, barbecues, air conditioning and lots of other things enhance the enjoyment of a charter far too much to worry about how performance has been degraded.

NUMBER OF BERTHS

All charter prices are based on the boat, either directly or indirectly. For a bareboat the price is X amount per week irrespective of how many people will be aboard. For a flotilla boat the price is per person with a price band that decreases with the number of people aboard. It is a mistake to think that everyone will be able to live comfortably on board if the maximum number of berths are utilised. There will be little privacy, insufficient stowage space, queues for the heads, insufficient water capacity and an overcrowded cockpit when sailing. If cost is the prime concern and you just can't afford not to fill every berth then that is the way it has to be. If you can manage it, restricting the number on board will go a long way towards the enjoyment of the holiday for all on board.

It is important to remember that in hot climates ventilation is important. If it is possible to sleep in the cockpit or on deck this can provide some relief from the heat, it can even feel cold at times, and for those who enjoy sleeping under the stars, this is a wonderful option.

EQUIPMENT

What to expect and the extras

Charter yachts now are much better equipped than they were in the early days. Most of the refinements and additions to equipment cater for the comfort of those on board, especially in a hot climate. On most flotilla and bareboat yachts you can expect to find the following as standard equipment over and above the standard trim of the yacht.

Standard equipment

- Inflatable dinghy, or RIB
- Roller reefing genoa and mainsail
- Fold down swimming ladder on the transom
- Bimini
- Windscoop for the front hatch
- Basic instrumentation and basic navigation equipment to include charts and a yachtsman's pilot
- VHF radio
- Fridge
- Masks and snorkels

Many of the yachts also have the following as standard depending on size.

- Electric anchor winch
- Autopilot
- Radar
- Mobile phone
- More extensive instrumentation
- CD player and radio
- DVD player and flat screen
- Transom shower
- Transom barbecue
- RIB and outboard motor

Check what equipment comes with the boat

have boats less than five years old. A few companies have boats less than three years old. Companies with older boats may operate a policy whereby boats are banded by age with older boats costing less to charter than newer, better-equipped boats.

What are the maintenance schedules? A new boat gets a hard life on charter and it is important that maintenance of the equipment is carried out every year. In this context an older boat that has been constantly maintained can be a better bet than a one- or two-year old boat that has not been properly maintained in the off-season. Constant maintenance during the charter season is important if basic things like the engine and batteries are going to be reliable. Unless regular oil changes are made to an engine through the season and a full winterisation programme carried out it will give trouble. Sails should be properly valetted and repaired in the off-season. Are spare sails available? Does the company operate a compensation policy for gear that is missing or not working?

Most of the charter companies offer extras at an additional cost. These extras are commonly items that are frequently damaged on charter such as outboards which get dunked in the sea after a heavy session ashore and cruising chutes or spinnakers which are left up a little too long in a rising wind and come down on the deck shredded. Other extras like mobile phones, an autopilot and a GPS are additional to standard equipment on the basic bareboat and are considered to be a 'luxury' of sorts. Some of the larger yachts in some fleets will have some of these 'extras' as standard equipment.

In the charter area the yacht operates in there must be a certain standard of safety equipment and depending on the country and the licence this will include DSC VHF, lifejackets, horseshoe buoy(s), liferaft, fire extinguishers, a first aid kit and flares. It may also include safety harnesses, a Danbuoy, a more extensive medical kit and additional flares.

For all equipment it is important to realise that the maintenance of gear is crucial given the hard use it gets on charter. Again word of mouth can provide welcome reassurance on the reliability of different companies.

What spares are available? Good charter companies should have a fairly extensive store with those items that constantly give trouble readily available to replace the troublesome items. Some companies carry a complete spare engine ready to pop into a yacht should there be terminal problems with an existing engine. Spare sails should be stocked. Some stock a spare mast. If there are problems not of your own making, can another yacht be made available and what is the company's policy on that?

Is there a company engineer available on call-out? Some flotillas have an engineer on board the lead boat and other flotilla companies and bareboat operators will have a shore-based engineer available to deal with any problems. If there is not and local skills are relied upon, try to get some opinions on how well the company has coped with problems in the past.

A FEW QUESTIONS

What is the age of the boat? Most of the bigger yacht charter companies will only

BOOKING A HOLIDAY

- How charter companies work
- Payment and cancellation charges
- Paying by credit card
- Booking flights (for bareboat and skippered charter)
- Security deposits
- Compensation claims
- Legal considerations

HOW CHARTER COMPANIES WORK

The charter company that sells you a sailing holiday can operate in different ways. These are as follows:

- Most of the larger charter companies and some smaller ones own and operate the boats you will be using.
- They manage the boats. The company either leases or contracts to operate the boats for a set period. Although the boats are not owned by the company they will usually employ the staff who run the charter fleet.
- They are the sole agent. The company has the exclusive rights to charter the boat for the owner. A large number of companies selling bareboat holidays as well as many crewed charter yachts are sold this way.
- They are the agent or broker or one of several agents who can sell a flotilla, bareboat or crewed yacht holiday. A broker is pretty much like an insurance broker and will source hard-to-get charters or review charter options.
- They are small owner-operators. They usually advertise in the classified columns and own and operate the boat, with friends or family organising the booking of the boat.

In practice many companies are a combination of these categories. Remember that deciding who to charter with is based on a number of factors and not just how well known a company is.

PAYMENT AND CANCELLATION CHARGES

Payment for a yacht charter holiday is usually along the following lines:

- 25% deposit to secure a booking.
- 25% or the balance 90 days prior to departure.
- Balance if 25% stipulated at 90 days.
- Travel insurance is taken out from the first booking date.

There are many variations on this but what it basically means is that you pay most of the holiday cost well before departure. While this may seem unreasonable to some, in fact charter companies need to operate like this as it is next to impossible to dispose of unwanted boats during the season. Unlike land-based holidays where accommodation can be disposed of relatively easily, expensive yachts usually just lie idle if they are not booked.

Cancellation fees are also fairly stiff and it is for this reason that most charter companies insist on travel insurance being taken out when the deposit is paid so you will be covered for the cancellation fee losses if they fall within the remit of the insurance policy. The cancellation penalties are usually something like the following:

- 90 days prior to departure you lose your deposit or a smaller cancellation fee may be levied.
- 45 days prior to departure you lose 50% of the total holiday cost or a smaller cancellation fee may be levied.
- 15 days prior to departure you lose 75% of the total holiday cost.
- Less than 15 days 100% of the holiday cost is forfeit.

Again there are many variations on this and there is some room for leeway if you are a regular client with the company or if you intend to book again the following year.

PAYING BY CREDIT CARD

Paying for your holiday with a credit card means that the credit card company (Visa or Mastercard) are responsible for the debt if a holiday company does not satisfactorily fulfil its contract to you or goes bankrupt and cannot provide for its contracted services at all.

Under the Consumer Credit Act you can claim compensation for amounts over £100 from both the charter company and the credit card company. You will not get two settlements but what will happen is that the credit card company will put pressure on the charter company or the insurance company to settle your claim quickly. In the absence of a quick settlement it may make a temporary credit to your account until it is settled by other means or it will front up with the money itself.

To claim from a credit card company:

- Write a letter of complaint to the company or make a claim to the insurance company. Send a copy of the letter to the credit card company with a covering letter telling them you are holding them jointly liable with the charter or insurance company.
- If no action is forthcoming from the charter or insurance company write asking for a settlement from the credit card company.
- Keep copies of all correspondence and in the last instance take the charter company to arbitration and complain to the banking ombudsman about the credit card company. In most instances the credit card company will act responsibly.

Given the additional protection (under the Consumer Credit Act) that paying by credit card gives, it is well worth paying for your whole holiday in this way.

BOOKING FLIGHTS

Most companies booking a bareboat or skippered charter for you can also book flights. Most of the companies know where to get the best deals on flights at the time of year you are going, but in case they do not take some time looking around yourself.

There are a number of options available to you when booking flights:

- Full fare flights. These can be booked at any travel agent or by phone or on the internet and offer the most flexibility. Dates can be changed with a small re-booking charge.
- APEX fares. These are basically the same seats as at full fare economy class but must be booked at least two weeks prior to departure. They offer significant savings (often 50% and more) over the full fare economy ticket but are totally inflexible. These tickets can be booked through a travel agent, over the phone or on the internet.
- Budget airlines. Many European destinations have budget airlines with no-frills flights (EasyJet and Ryanair are the two biggest, but there are others) flying to them on a regular scheduled basis. Many of these flights can only be booked on the internet or by phone as a last resort. Low cost airlines work by selling off the first 10% of seats at rock bottom prices, the next 10% slightly higher, and so on. If you book early you can get remarkable deals. Once the plane is nearly full the price is comparable with a regular airline price.
- Charter flights. These are the cheapest flights going and can often be 60–70% cheaper than the standard full fare. They are non-refundable and cannot be changed. There are a number of agencies who specialise in these flights or you can go on the internet and look at the prices available for any charter airline.

Buying tickets at cut-rate prices from bucket shops and small agencies used to carry some risk but these days most of that risk has been eliminated with the bonding requirements that have been brought in.

SECURITY DEPOSITS

All charter companies ask for a security deposit. The amount varies depending on the size and value of the yacht, the equipment on board, and the duration of the charter. The actual amounts and method of payment vary as follows:

- A security deposit in cash or travellers cheques deposited at the charter base where you pick up the boat.
- A security deposit in either cash, travellers cheques or a blank credit card or charge card slip signed by the charterer and deposited with the charter company from whom you booked the boat. Cash and travellers cheques as above and a credit or charge card slip up to the total borrowing amount plus or minus your balance.
- A non-refundable insurance premium paid to the charter company from whom you booked the boat.

By far the best option is to pay the non-refundable insurance premium. This covers every contingency including major damage or total loss of yacht equipment which can easily exceed the total of a cash or other security deposit. It is also one less thing to worry about at the end of your holiday.

Security deposits in cash, travellers cheques or a blank credit or charge card form will normally be redeemed at the end of the yacht charter once the yacht and inventory have been inspected by the charter base staff. Most companies do not make deductions for minor breakages or losses such as cutlery and crockery, the odd fender, a winch handle, boat hook or similar. Deductions will be made for damage to the hull, stanchions and lifelines, sails, shaft and propeller, and for major losses like the dinghy, outboard motor, liferaft, anchor(s) and chain, warps, sun awning, etc. Many companies also employ a diver to go down and take a peek underwater for any damage there.

Problems arise mostly from assessments of damage by the charter base staff. Damage to yachts, even when it appears minor, costs a good deal more to repair than most customers think.

Most charter companies are fair about assessments for damage to a yacht but there are cowboys around who have kept the whole security deposit without good cause. The problem for the charterer is how to get his money back. If it is lodged at a charter base overseas there are really no avenues open to you to get a refund. Talk to the company with whom you booked the charter. Take photographs and make a report on the damage before you leave the boat. Try to get an independent assessment of the cost of repairing the damage before you leave the boat. In the end it really boils down to your word against that of the person from the charter base who made the assessment.

If you have a security deposit lodged with a charter company in the country in which you live then take your evidence to them if a deduction is made which you believe to be unreasonable. If you think your case is strong enough and you get no satisfaction from the company then you can start proceedings against them. This is really a last resort as it is not only costly, but even if you have a judgement against a company you still have to extract the money from them.

The moral from the foregoing is clear. Paying an insurance premium instead of putting up a cash or other deposit is by far the preferable method of making a security deposit. Failing that, leave the security deposit with the company in your own country. The last option is to leave it with the charter base where you pick up the yacht. In truth a very small number of problems arise over security deposits given the numbers who go on yacht charters.

COMPLAINTS

Most of the larger companies have an established complaints procedure should you feel that there were problems with the boat or the organisation of the charter. If you have a complaint the following advice will help get redress.

- Before you leave make a written report of problems with the boat or the conduct of staff. For boat problems take photographs if possible.
- Get an independent assessment on the spot if possible.
- Give a copy of the report to the charter base staff and inform them you are going to make a complaint.
- As soon as you arrive back from your holiday send a copy of the report to the charter company.
- Most of the large charter companies arrange for an independent arbitration body to look at your complaint if they decide not to settle outright.

COMPENSATION

What do you do when you arrive if the boat is not available or unsafe or unusable? What do you do if the boat becomes unusable during the charter for reasons which have nothing to do with you?

Most of the established companies now spell out unequivocally in their brochures and booking terms what your redress is should a boat be unavailable, in unsafe condition or should it be out of commission for a certain period during the charter.

The fact that companies are prepared to make these promises effectively means that they will do their utmost to avoid getting into this situation.

Most compensation clauses are along the following lines:

- The company will find an equivalent or larger yacht for your charter holiday should the exact yacht you booked be unavailable.
- Should a yacht be out of commission for more than a day the company will credit you with extra sailing days, give you a credit for another sailing holiday with them, or make a cash refund to you. The details vary from company to company.

- There are also exception clauses which will rule out compensation. Compensation will not be paid for not sailing in the defined charter area, anchoring where you have been specifically told not to by the charter base staff, and not taking care with the charter yacht under your command.
- Should a yacht be considered unseaworthy by a charterer then the procedure outlined under 'Complaints' above should be followed if it cannot be sorted out at the charter base. If you can sort it out this is by far the best thing to do as getting redress can be difficult afterwards.

For companies that do not spell out compensation clauses in their brochures or booking conditions you will have to negotiate on the ground or when you get back over compensation for unsuitable substitute yachts or a yacht being out of commission for reasons beyond your control. Make sure you obtain any promises in writing from the charter staff or the company itself. If you get no satisfaction then make a complaint with adequate documentation as outlined above.

LEGAL CONSIDERATIONS

The legal status of charter varies from country to country and in a good number of countries no difference is made between yacht charter and big ship charter under law. This is an entirely different matter to your agreement with the charter company. It is impossible to untangle the ramifications of the legalities involved with yacht charter in different countries, but in general the following points should be borne in mind. Most of the following applies to bareboat charter and not to skippered charter where the skipper/owner is responsible for the boat. Flotilla sailing can be assumed to fall under the bareboat category for these legal points as well.

- The charterer is considered to be responsible for the operation and safety of the vessel and its crew and other

Catamarans are a popular option in many charter areas

people on board. This means others in the party or an insurer can sue the charterer of the vessel for injury, material loss, etc.

- The charterer must ensure that the vessel remains fit and safe under the regulations of the country chartered in. He/she will be liable for any damage or the loss of the craft if it is illegally modified in any way. An example of this may be over-tightening the standing rigging causing loss of the mast or vessel.
- The skipper/master may be held accountable for the safe operation of the vessel and will be responsible for any damage or death caused by failure to operate safely. This usually means third party actions.
- A charterer may not use the vessel for illegal purposes such as carrying drugs, contraband or aliens within a country.
- In a number of countries the charter

agreement specifically names those in the charter party and this may not be added to on an ad hoc basis.

- The skipper/master will be at all times governed by the maritime law of the country and is responsible for enforcing it. One example is that the skipper is responsible for illegal spills and discharges (for example from toilets, holding tank, diesel tank etc.) and any penalties must be paid by him or her.
- A bareboat can be seized by the authorities and be forfeit for illegal activities even though it is chartered and the owner is not on board.

In practice this muddled area of legal points rarely affects people on yacht charter, but it needs to be mentioned. It is also worthwhile checking up on how much legal and third party cover your insurance provides for.

PLANNING A CRUISE

- Talking to others – the pleasure principle
- Charts and guides
- Children
- Documents and money

TALKING TO THE OTHERS

In the first chapter I talked about the would-be Captain Blighs of this world who organise a yacht charter assault course for their family and friends who come on the charter. It is important when you sit down with those who are going on charter with you that you consult them about their needs, wants, preferences and dislikes and it is important that these are built into an itinerary and not over-ruled by you. Remember what happened to Bligh.

The following suggestions for involving family and/or friends may sound a bit soppy to crusty old salts, but in the end it will enhance the enjoyment for all:

- If possible some other member of the crew, whether wife, lover or drinking buddy, should know the rudiments of how to sail and handle the boat under power. Like teaching a person to drive a car, it is best done by someone else. There are numerous one-day or weekend courses run by sailing schools to teach the rudiments of sailing and boat handling and some of the larger companies offer courses specifically aimed at new flotilla or bareboat charterers, often on the same sort of boat that will be chartered on the holiday.
- Everyone going on the charter should, if possible, be involved in the planning of a cruise. Buy a chart that covers the area, pilot or travel guides, and let everyone put something into the cruise. When planning the cruise ensure there are sufficient laydays so that you and the crew can lie around doing not a lot except swimming, reading, sitting in bars or whatever.
- Make sure on a bareboat charter that you allot plenty of time to get the boat back to the charter base. Lots of bareboat holidays are ruined by the last couple of days because too little time has been left to cover a lot of distance and the boat must be thrashed back against the prevailing winds.

CHARTS AND GUIDES

Although charter companies provide all the charts you need on board, or should do, it is still worthwhile buying a chart or perhaps two of the area you will be chartering in so that you can more easily plan the cruise. It will also acquaint you with the area so it is not all frighteningly new when you arrive. Charts for all the areas are fairly easily found at any large chandlers or in many cases the charter company you book with will be able to suggest a source or may even supply the charts themselves.

For most of the popular charter areas there are sailing pilots or guidebooks available. Again the charter company will be able to help you out or refer to the second section of this book where a list of the popular guides will be found for the various areas. Admiralty pilots to areas not covered by yachtsman's pilots are pretty hard going for cruise planning purposes and it is best to ask the charter company if they have any other material you can use for that purpose.

It is also worth buying a general guide-book for your charter destination so that some planning for land-based trips can be carried out. There are general guidebooks to all charter destinations with very few exceptions. Try the *Rough Guides*, *Lonely Planet* series, *Footprint Handbooks*, or *Blue Guides* depending on your taste. These or other popular series are not necessarily the best guides, but give you a head start in the absence of detailed knowledge of the literature covering a country.

CHILDREN

The age at which children go on a yacht charter is solely the choice of the parents as they are the ones who will deal with the tantrums and tears. For popular destinations like the Mediterranean and the Caribbean, babies of less than a year old have been taken on charter and appear none the worse for it.

For young children, it is worth considering if it makes sense to take a young child to an exotic destination when the child hardly knows if you are in the Mediterranean or the Caribbean. In the Tropics the heat and humidity, not to mention the mosquitoes and runny tummy, can make a small child's life intolerable. Really it is up to the parents to decide if the enjoyment they get out of an exotic destination is worth the hassle of having unhappy children around them.

Older children may also find that going on a yacht charter holiday with their parents is just a chore rather than the exciting adventure their parents have told them about.

Some companies split the children up into groups with different activities for different age groups and it is worth thinking about this sort of watersports holiday if you are taking children along. Often it is possible to split a sailing holiday 50/50 between a land-based watersports holiday and a sailing yacht and in this way parents and children both get an equal enjoyment out of the overall holiday.

It is rarely wise to inflict your own children on friends in the confines of a small yacht. Again parents can deceive themselves that really their friends do love the eccentric ways of their children and seem blind to any subtle hints that this is not always the case.

DOCUMENTS AND MONEY

Whatever documents you need should be planned well in advance. Anyone in the group who doesn't have a passport or who has a passport that will expire soon should attend to this. Children may need to be added to your passport or to get one of their own. Any visas you need should not be left until the last minute. For some countries it may take up to two weeks to get a visa after application and at busy times it can take longer. In the gazetteer covering charter areas there is a section dealing with documentation including visas. EU nationals should remember that although you can travel freely through EU countries, you are still required to have either a passport or identity card on you for all countries.

Additional documentation such as a certificate of competence showing you can skipper a yacht or that you are a competent crew is needed in some cases and if you are going on a course then get it all over and done with well before departure.

Most charter companies can give you some idea of how much money you will need on the holiday although your spending habits may be more or less than the norm. In the gazetteer of charter destinations there is some advice on the relative cost of destinations although this information is subject to variations from year to year depending on the economy of the country you are going to and to the sort of places you visit.

What form you take your money in depends on the destination. There are few countries now where you cannot get cash out of a hole-in-the-wall machine (ATM) with a credit/debit card (Visa or Mastercard) and few countries where at least some of the restaurants and shops will not take a credit card in payment. For this reason at least one member of the group should have a credit card (with some credit left on it) in case it is needed.

WHAT TO PACK

- Clothes
- Jewellery and valuables
- Protection from sun and sea
- Navigators kit
- Still and video cameras
- Communications
- Music
- Essential treats
- Miscellaneous checklist

CLOTHES

Most people take too much and the old maxim for back-packing applies equally to sailing: pack your bag with the bare minimum and then take it all out and halve it. For most destinations like the Mediterranean and the Caribbean you will be wearing very little most of the time. When sailing, a swimsuit is the normal attire or at most shorts and a T-shirt. You will want a few shore-going clothes but not a change of outfit for every occasion. Amongst the things you should pack are the following:

- A swimsuit or two, towel(s), several T-shirts, several pairs of shorts, a couple of sweatshirts or light pullovers and light cotton underwear.
- A wide-brimmed hat or two with ties. The peaked visors that tennis players used to wear are also useful as they do not restrict peripheral vision as much as a hat. A neck scarf to keep the sun off your neck.
- A light cotton long-sleeved shirt and light cotton long trousers for protection from the sun in the first few days. In some areas a 'rash top' to prevent UV damage is useful.
- A light anorak or wet weather jacket for hot climates and heavier wet weather gear for less temperate destinations.
- Sailing shoes and some tough form of footwear for walking around rocks and coral. 'Crocs' work well.
- Loose clothing for the flight to and from the charter destination.

Everything should be packed into soft sailing bags that can be easily stowed once you have unpacked on board. There is no room to stow suitcases on board a yacht and no rigid bags should be taken.

JEWELLERY AND VALUABLES

Jewellery such as rings, gold chains and bracelets, expensive watches and any other bodily adornments should be left at home. This is not because you are likely to be mugged for them, but because they are dangerous on a yacht and liable to be lost. If a rope or part of the boat gets entangled with items of personal jewellery it can be dangerous. Fingers have been lost because a ring snagged on the anchor chain or injured because the ring hooked onto wood trim. Likewise hands and necks can be injured if a necklace or chain gets snagged by a rope or a bit of the boat.

Most items will be covered by the insurance you have taken out, but the insurance doesn't cover the attachment to personal jewellery that was given to you by a husband, wife or lover. Better to leave those bits of sentiment at home where you can safely reclaim them when you get back.

PROTECTION FROM SUN AND SEA

In Australia the catchy 'slip, slop, slap', slip on a shirt, slop on sun protection cream, and slap on a hat, cannot be bettered for encapsulating what you need for protection from the sun. Out on the water the reflected sunshine greatly increases the chance of sunburn and sun damaged skin. Make sure hats, sun block cream of factor 15, 20 or 30 (the systems seem to vary), and light shirts are taken for everyone in the group. Do not rely solely on sun block cream as although it cuts down on harmful rays reaching the skin, it does not eliminate them and even with waterproof varieties, still gets washed off to some extent. If you are snorkelling make sure you wear a T-shirt or 'rash top' at least part of the time as it is easy to underestimate the amount of sun reaching your body when it is partially cooled by the sea. And if you have very fair skin take a pair of loose long trousers to keep the sun off. And don't forget to take lots of moisturising cream for après-sun application.

Fair skinned souls should take along a scarf or bandana to stop wind-burn when beating to windward. Spray and wind can soon set your cheeks burning and cause tender lips to chap. Take along lots of lip salve to keep those lips tender and moisturising cream for glowing cheeks.

In most of the warmer charter areas no waterproof gear is required for short day-sailing legs or at most just a light anorak or jacket. However, if you are going to be sailing at night it is surprising how cool it can be even in the Mediterranean or the Caribbean once a bit of spray has come aboard. The further away you are from the equator the more likely it will be that warmer wet weather gear is required. Check with the charter company and consult the tables for temperatures in the section on the different cruising areas, always remembering that these are averages and everyone knows what they say about statistics.

NAVIGATOR'S KIT

While flotilla and bareboat yachts will be equipped to a certain level, it can be useful to bring along a few items of your own.

As I have mentioned previously, it is useful to buy a chart or two and a yachtsman's pilot so that you can familiarise yourself with an area. Bring these along as while charts are always provided, they can sometimes be a bit scrappy and may not be of the type you are used to. Yachtsman's pilots can be old editions or may be sheets cobbled together by a company.

If you have useful portable items – a portable GPS is probably the most useful

item – then bring them as well. A lot of flotilla and smaller bareboat yachts do not have GPS fitted and really do not need them. Even if a GPS is fitted you will be familiar with the operating system on your own portable GPS and this will save time and effort getting to grips with some other operating system. With a bit of planning you can have a number of useful waypoints plugged in for use on the holiday. Remember that chart datums can vary and importantly that the accuracy of charts varies greatly in different areas. A lot of modern metricated charts are still in truth old 19th century surveys.

A hand-bearing compass can be useful to have along as some of those provided by charter companies are not the best units around. Other useful items you might think about bringing are a pair of binoculars and silly little things like a couple of pencils and a rubber. The latter always seem to go missing from chart tables.

One item which you may think does not strictly fall into the category of an aid to navigation is a good pair of polarised sunglasses. I mean polarised, not UV resistant, photochromatic or whatever else manufacturers of sunglasses like to stick on the lenses. Polarised lenses allow light through on one plane only and by cutting down on the reflected light off the water allow you to pick up shallow patches, rocks, coral reefs or anything under the water with a good deal more clarity than other sunglasses can. It can be one of the most important aids to navigation you have when eye-balling through a tricky channel or close to navigational dangers.

CAMERA AND VIDEO

On any charter boat it is unusual if there is not one camera around and the chances are there will be several. If you have a full blown single lens reflex camera and a bag full of lenses then my advice is to leave it at home. Bring along a compact digital and if you don't have one it may be worth getting one for the trip.

Weatherproof and waterproof cameras are somewhat more expensive than the base camera they are derived from. On holiday you rarely need anything more than a weatherproof camera if you are going to be out taking pictures with spray coming on board or beach shots.

Digital camcorders (I mean simple ones with AVI or MPEG formats) are now relatively cheap for basic models and on a boat it's worth thinking about a basic model. More expensive models should be left at home because the salty environment on a boat just doesn't do them any good. To recharge batteries you will either need a cigarette lighter plug adapter for 12 volts if there is a socket on the boat or a small inverter if no cigarette lighter charger is available. Failing that, buy an adapter plug so that you can inveigle someone ashore to charge the batteries. A couple of fully charged batteries will give you a pretty good run until you find somewhere to recharge them, but once a battery is flat take the first offer to re-charge it that comes along. If you eat ashore at a restaurant ask them if you can plug the charger in and remember to leave a good tip for their benevolence in letting you do so.

Digital camcorders are particularly susceptible to a salty atmosphere and especially to salt water damage. You need to be careful about when you use them and to keep it out of the way of any spray coming on board.

COMMUNICATIONS

Digital cellular phones with GSM (Global System for Mobile Communications) capacity work in most countries with just a few exceptions. If you go to your service provider's website you can find out if there is coverage in the country you are going to. Your service provider will need to have an agreement with a service provider in that country and you will need to have the 'roaming' facility enabled on your account. In practice the system is seamless and your phone will register with a provider when you turn it on in the country you are in.

Remember that as well as charges for making calls, there are fairly hefty charges for receiving calls as well.

Some of the larger bareboats and skippered charter will have a phone on board you can use but you will be charged for calls. Some charter companies will hire a phone out at an extra charge. This facility should be mentioned in the inventory and equipment list.

While you can get phones which access the internet in your own country, you will often find that the country you are going to does not offer this service or only offers it in the larger urban areas. In more remote cruising areas you will likely not be able to receive internet data on your phone and quite possibly will not be able to use it at all if you are sailing in waters that land-based masts do not cover.

E-mail resources ashore are surprisingly common, either wi-fi in some cafés or in dedicated internet cafés. If you are really keen you can take your laptop with you and somewhere along the line you should be able to log-on if you really have to, although it seems to me a bit of a paradox that some folk want to take their work with them when they are on holiday ostensibly getting away from it all. Land-based internet cafés also mean that you can use VOIP programmes like Skype to communicate cheaply – if you have to.

MUSIC

Many charter yachts are now equipped with CD players and some will have DVD players as well. Take a small selection of your favourite music to cover ghosting along, beating hard to windward, romping downwind, and sitting quietly at anchor. If there is one thing you don't need to do, it is inflict on your neighbours or the natives your own taste in music at volume.

ESSENTIAL TREATS

In most parts of the world you can find, if not the exact 'can't do without' nibbles, spreads, sauces or breakfast cereal, then at least a passable substitute. If you really feel you have to take along a certain brand of sauce, a certain textured cereal or only brand X peanut butter, do so. My advice is that you should not take anything if you use a little flexibility when shopping. Moreover you will discover all sorts of wonderful home-grown treats in the country you are going to. Part of the joy of going to another country is discovering the food there.

Diabetics, those with a wide range of allergies and anyone on a strict diet regime for whatever reason should bring along a small selection of foodstuffs that they can dip into if necessary. Vegetarians will have few problems in most countries. Vegans should not find things too difficult in hot climates where few dairy products are used,

but should not expect their dietary needs to be commonly understood.

In the alcoholic beverage line you should need little other than a bottle of your own choice of duty-free. Nearly everywhere you will find mixers for your own particular potion and besides there is the local hooch. In Greece there is ouzo, in the Caribbean you'll find rum, in France there are excellent wines at bargain prices and in Thailand there is local whiskey which is, well, passable with soda or another mixer. In most countries there will be a lager type beer which is always quaffable and often very good. Experiment with the local hooch and you will be surprised at how well it slips down even if you are none the wiser in the morning.

Miscellaneous checklist

❖ **Spectacles** If you wear spectacles, take a spare pair. There is nothing worse than being blind for part of a holiday because you misplaced your specs, sat on them in the cockpit, or dropped them overboard. To avoid the latter get a spectacle chain or, in the spirit of the holiday, one of those bright coloured stretch bands that slip over the ends to hold them securely on your head. Contact lenses have a magical way of disappearing during high-spirited barbecues so take spares and all the kit you need for washing them.

❖ **Fishing** If you like to go fishing don't bother to take a rod. It is bulky and awkward to carry and for trolling you don't really need it. Take just the reel if you are keen, plus a couple of stainless jubilee clips to attach it to the pushpit rail. Otherwise a straight hand-line is sufficient. *Rapallo* lures made in Finland are the favoured brand for trolling, but if you are into fishing you will no doubt have your own favourite. In tropical waters take a stainless wire trace or bigger fish will just bite the lure off.

❖ **Linen** Most charter companies supply everything you need in the way of linen, duvets or sleeping bags and pillows. For some home waters charter, a few small operators will want you to supply these. Check beforehand to see if this is so. Most provide shower towels but prefer you to bring a beach towel.

❖ **A small flashlight** of the *Mag-Lite* variety is useful for getting back to the boat at night. And a multi-tool or boat penknife if you want to feel nautical. Just remember to pack them in your hold luggage before you get on the plane.

Take fishing lines and you may just catch supper

HEALTH AND SAFETY

- Safety equipment at sea
- Vaccinations
- Malaria
- Unwanted visitors
- AIDS
- Marine perils
- Potions, lotions and pills
- Seasickness
- Water

SAFETY EQUIPMENT

All charter companies must have a certain level of safety equipment on board according to the regulations of the country they operate in. In most countries this level of equipment varies according to the stated use of the boat, usually how many miles it is permitted to go from the coast, the number of berths, and the type of charter with some exceptions made for small flotilla yachts over bareboat and skippered charter.

Most charter yachts will have a bare minimum as follows. The maximum number of people on board a yacht is usually determined by reference to the number of berths on the yacht, though not in every case.

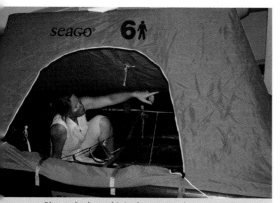

Please don't try this in the water unless you really have to

- **Lifejackets** For the maximum number on board. Some countries stipulate an additional one or two lifejackets. Children's lifejackets may or may not be part of the regulations, but most charter companies will supply them anyway. Check with the charter company and take your own along if unsure. This may be a good idea anyway if you have a lifejacket with integral harness for a toddler, though you will need to check with the airline to see if the cylinders for gas-inflated jackets will be allowed on board the plane.

- **Life harness** Varies from country to country and often the specification is for two or three harnesses on a yacht depending on the size. These will usually be lifejackets with an integral harness. There will often be insufficient harness points around the yacht and jackstays are not common. In truth there are few destinations where you will need a harness, but check with the charter company and take your own along if worried.

- **Safety flares** All countries specify a minimum number of in date authorised safety flares. Find where they are stored and how they operate.

- **Life-buoy** All countries specify a life-buoy and in some cases two. A life-buoy light is also usually specified. Dan-buoys are specified only in some countries.

- **Certified liferaft** Most countries specify a liferaft for the maximum number on board. In some countries a life-float capable of supporting the maximum number of people on board may be specified for yachts under 30 feet or so which have a limited range from the coast.

- **VHF radio** Just about all countries specify a VHF radio and even if not specified, it is more than likely one will be fitted. It will almost certainly be a DSC VHF. Some yachts will also have a hand-held VHF.

- **Fire extinguishers** Certified fire extinguishers depending on the size of the boat. Many boats will also have a fire blanket.

In all charter destinations there are fairly rigid safety equipment specifications and an annual check on equipment plus spot checks in some countries. On the whole, charter companies are concerned about safety on board and this is reflected in the comparatively few accidents that have occurred in the last 30 years. Many of the accidents that have occurred have been through negligence on the part of the charterer and not a safety equipment failure.

Most accidents on charter boats have involved fire. Anyone who has attempted to use a fire extinguisher on a fire will know just how pathetic these things are. If possible try to smother a fire on board either with a fire blanket if provided or with anything like a blanket, duvet, coat – whatever can be quickly grabbed. Depriving a fire of oxygen is the best way of putting it out. Check if your charter yacht has a fire blanket and if not suggest to the company that for a modest investment it can save lives. Safety precautions over gas and petrol stowage should be rigorous. Keep cigarettes out of range when changing gas bottles or filling an outboard and always turn the gas off at the regulator when you have finished using it. Do remember that the number of incidents of fire is relatively low and probably no higher than for privately owned yachts.

Always keep an eye on anyone, particularly children, in the water, not just in case they get into difficulties, but also to ensure morons on waterbikes or powerful RIBs do not stray too close to them.

VACCINATIONS

For many charter destinations no vaccinations are required over and above ensuring that tetanus and polio jabs are in date. Tetanus and polio jabs last ten years so you need to be within this period until the end of your holiday. For other areas,

particularly tropical areas such as some of the Pacific Islands, Thailand, and parts of the Caribbean, some additional vaccinations may be necessary. In the gazetteer there are details on recommended vaccinations for the different charter areas although you should always consult with your doctor.

- Hepatitis A is only a moderate risk but Hepatitis B is on the increase. Hepatitis B is only transmitted by sexual contact or contaminated blood. For Hepatitis A gamma globulin is not now widely used and the only effective vaccination is the new Hepatitis A (Havrix) vaccine. Havrix can be given in conjunction with other vaccinations.
- Dengue fever is on the rise in some Pacific islands and other tropical destinations. Transmitted by mosquitoes so see Malaria entry below.
- Japanese encephalitis is on the increase in a few tropical areas. Effective vaccines are available.
- Typhoid is a risk only in a few areas. Injectable or oral vaccines last three years only so check with your doctor.
- Cholera is low risk in most areas. As the vaccine is only 60% effective and lasts for only 3–6 months it is not normally recommended. If there has been a recent cholera outbreak in an area you are going to your doctor will be able to advise you if vaccination is useful.
- Rabies. Not normally recommended as the incidence is extremely low.
- Tuberculosis (TB). Children should be immunised at any age.

Advice on vaccinations can be obtained from your doctor, the charter company, or some internet sites.

MALARIA

The risk of malaria is nil or low in most charter destinations with just a few exceptions. In some of the Pacific Islands, Thailand and Malaysia there is a possible risk in some areas although usually not in the coastal regions. Check with your doctor for up-to-the-minute details since malarial areas can shift and the risk of malaria can recur in areas which were once free of it.

While malaria is transmitted by mosquito bites, it is only transmitted by the anopheles mosquito, so whilst mosquitoes are common in most parts of the world, the majority of species do not transmit malaria. Because there are mosquitoes around does not mean you are at risk and in fact anopheles normally come out in the evening and at dawn only.

The choice of treatment is between the old fashioned prophylactic regime of two Proguanil (commonly Paludrine) a day and two chloroquine a week (commonly Nivaquine or Avloclor) or the newer treatments which usually involve a smaller number of pills but may have side effects for some people.

The best protection against malaria is to prevent mosquito bites. Some boats have mosquito screens fitted, but unless you are going to stay below on balmy evenings this is not much of a help. In the following section on dealing with unwanted visitors there are suggestions for keeping mosquitoes (and other aerial visitors) at bay.

UNWANTED VISITORS

In warmer climes by day, you can be visited by flies, wasps, bees, flying ants and an assortment of other creatures depending on where you are. For stings take an antihistamine cream or something like Waspeze in an aerosol can which contains a mild local anaesthetic as well as an anti-histamine.

In the evening and early morning mosquitoes and midges are a problem in many charter areas. Midges come in different varieties including the tiny variety called variously no-no's or nosee'ums. In the Caribbean, Australia, some Pacific Islands, Thailand and places like Alaska, Scandinavia and Scotland, midges can be a real problem. They are not disease carriers but can inflict an irritating bite out of all proportion to their size. Mosquitoes in most areas are not malaria carriers, but the bite is

irritating and some poor souls have an allergic reaction to the anticoagulant the mosquito injects and which causes the irritation. If you know that mosquitoes or midge bites cause an allergic reaction take whatever medication is necessary.

In the evenings cover yourself up with a long sleeved shirt and long baggy trousers. Use a reliable mosquito repellent. Those that contain DEET are the most effective but in some people they cause an irritable reaction on the skin and they will also dissolve some plastics including watch straps and the like. Use vapour coils if these do not suffocate you and if the boat has a cigarette lighter adapter it is possible to purchase 12 volt tablet 'cookers' which plug into lighter adapters similar to the ones which plug into 220V mains sockets.

AIDS

- Avoid unnecessary medical or dental treatment and situations which may make this necessary
- Avoid having casual relationships but if you have sex with someone new, always use a condom
- Don't inject drugs or share needles and syringes
- Remember alcohol and drugs affect your judgement
- Avoid having a tattoo, acupuncture or your ears pierced unless sterile equipment is used

The incidence of AIDS in the world still increases dramatically and nowhere more so than in popular tourist destinations. The TravelSafe code from the Department of Health should be followed at all times.

MARINE PERILS

Not sharks or conger eels which you will rarely encounter, but the more common perils of jellyfish, sea urchins and coral cuts.

Jellyfish stings are the most common injury encountered in the marine world. All

Portuguese man-o-war

jellyfish sting as that is the way they immobilise their prey and is also their defence against predators. They will only sting if you bump into them or inadvertently become entangled in their trailing tentacles. There are various treatments although none are 100% effective.

Those likely to have a violent reaction should use antihistamine creams and something like Waspeze. Other treatments are dilute ammonium hydroxide, neat alcohol, vinegar, lemon rubbed on the sting, and even meat tenderiser which is said to break down the protein base of the venom. One tip is to wear gloves when hauling up an anchor as jellyfish tentacles can become wrapped around it and will still sting you even if detached from the body of the jellyfish.

Sea urchins are a problem when wandering around rocky areas if you tread on one and get the spines embedded in your foot. Always wear shoes or sandals when walking in shallow water around rocky areas and watch where you put your feet. The spines themselves are not venomous but are difficult to remove and may cause an infection.

Coral cuts are common when you go swimming or walking around reefs and for some reason take an age to heal. Coral does sting mildly, but this is not the cause of cuts taking a long time to heal. Any cuts should be washed with an antiseptic solution and

then the cut kept dry. If necessary put a plastic bag on the foot with a rubber band around the ankle when going ashore in a dinghy or anywhere else the foot is likely to get wet.

Ciguatera is not a well known disease but does claim a number of victims every year. Though it is seldom fatal its effects can be long term. It is caused by eating certain types of fish, usually reef fish, although others higher up the food chain have been implicated, which for some reason become infected and pass the infection on to humans when eaten. The problem is that the disease affects fish which are normally edible and there is no way of knowing whether a fish is infected or not. It only affects tropical fish and has been associated with fish living around coral that has been damaged in some way. If you have been fishing around a reef ask the locals if the fish is OK to eat.

There are other things lurking in the sea that can cause injury, but in truth you are unlikely to come across them. If you have some sort of morbid interest in the subject then get hold of *Dangerous Marine Animals* by Halstead, Auerbach and Campbell or *Cruising in Tropical Waters and Coral* by Alan Lucas.

POTIONS, LOTIONS AND PILLS

There are a few basic items you need to take with you.

- Most important is sun block creams of Factor 15–50 to keep delicate skin from sun damage. Get a waterproof type as it tends to rub off less easily out of the water as well as in it.
- Take adequate supplies of a good insect repellent and antihistamine or other creams to treat insect bites. A small first aid kit with the basics like aspirin, antacid tablets, a few waterproof sticking plasters, mild medication for the runs, like Dio-calm, and heavier treatment for diarrhoea, like Lomotil or Enterosan. All charter yachts will carry basic first aid kits and many provide telephone numbers for doctors and hospitals along

Are the fish safe to eat? Ask the locals

the way. On flotilla the lead boat will carry a more comprehensive medical kit and crewed charter yachts also carry full medical kits.

- Stock up on any special medication you are on (for high blood pressure, angina, diabetes, etc.) for the duration of the trip. Asthma sufferers should ensure they take adequate refills for inhalers and any other necessary medication. Hayfever sufferers should take whatever medication they need.

SEASICKNESS

Most people suffer at some time or other from seasickness, some more chronically than others. If you know that you are susceptible take your preferred remedy with you. In most charter areas the relatively short day passages in sheltered waters and the warm weather can have remarkable curative effects on even long term sufferers. If you are new to the water a number of remedies are listed below.

- **Tablets** A number of tablets are on the market, commonly Avomine, Dramamine, Marzine RF, and Stugeron. Of these, Stugeron is widely accepted as the most effective. They all cause drowsiness to some extent, though Stugeron is reported to do so to a lesser extent than the others. The tablets should be started prior to going sailing, sometimes as much as a day before-hand. Other tablets such as

Phenergan, Kwells and Sereen contain hyoscine hydrobromide which has a sedative effect and leaves the sufferer drowsy.

- **Patches** A small elastoplast patch is stuck on the body, usually behind the ear, and releases the sedative slowly into the bloodstream. This has the advantage of a small continuous dosage as opposed to the instant dosage in tablet form and thus is less likely to cause drowsiness. Commonly contain hyoscine hydrobromide. Young children cannot use this system and it does have side effects on some people, usually drowsiness, although a few souls have experienced mild hallucinations.
- **Homeopathic cures** A number of homeopathic treatments are available: Nux Vomica, Cocculus Indicus, and Ipecac. Other natural remedies are ginger, glucose and Vitamin B12. Ginger appears to come out favourite. Try crystallised ginger, ginger biscuits or even ginger ale.
- **Sea bands** Elasticised bands with a small knob sewn into them. When slipped over the wrist the knob is supposed to press on the nei-kuan pressure point that reduces nausea. The problem is hitting exactly the right point – something an acupuncturist spends years learning to do.

In general someone who is seasick should be kept warm but should stay in the cockpit if possible. Watching the horizon seems to have a curative effect and giving them something to do like steering, if they are able, seems to take the mind off the nausea. Any odours from diesel, gas, cooking smells and the like will aggravate the nausea. When seasick try to eat something like crackers or dry bread and drink plenty of water as vomiting causes dehydration.

WATER

Water is a tricky issue and staying clear of waterborne diseases or complications cannot be solved by drinking bottled water. In any of the charter destinations you go to you will come into contact with it by virtue

Messing around in the sun is great fun but don't get burned

of eating ashore. Salad vegetables and fruit will be washed in it, local ice and ice-cream will be made from it, cooking and other utensils will be washed and rinsed in it, and you will wash and clean your teeth in it. Even the most fastidious amongst you will not be able to avoid contact with it in one way or another unless, Howard Hughes-like, you cocoon yourself from everything which hardly seems like much fun.

In most places the water is safe to drink. At worst it may contain local micro-organisms which in themselves are not dangerous, but may cause a minor case of upset tummy and the runs until your digestive system adapts to them. Otherwise my advice is to drink the local water as you will inevitably come across it in one way or another.

For infants and children it is probably best to use bottled water for their needs as these micro-organisms initially cause a good deal more distress for them. You can use water purifying tablets for infants. Ashore there is not a lot you can do except to get the kids to drink bottled water.

One last plea. Dispose of used water bottles in recycling or garbage containers. There are too many plastic water bottles littering the seas and beaches of the world and none of us should add to this very visual form of pollution.

Papeete market

WHEN YOU ARRIVE

- Finding the boat
- Stowing gear
- Inventory and boat checks
- Familiarisation
- Boat papers
- Provisioning
- Water and fuel

FINDING THE BOAT

Not as silly as it sounds. You may think that because you have booked a Beneteau 35 called *Crazy Horse* that finding it in Kalamaki Marina will be a cinch. By the time you have walked around looking at 600 boats in the dark, including at least 20 charter white Beneteau 35s, none of which is called *Crazy Horse*, you finally locate someone from the charter base who tells you the boat is now in Poros and you need to get a ferry there, except the ferries don't run until the morning.

One of the things that can make or break a charter holiday is how efficiently transfers are carried out and how caring charter base staff are.

For flotilla holidays and bareboat charters from companies who arrange transfers, a lot of hassle is taken out of getting the sailing holiday off to a good start. You will be met at the airport, shepherded onto the coach or a minibus, get snippets of information fed to you en route about what to expect when you arrive and be able to get answers from the representative on just where you can change money tomorrow and how much the local beer costs.

Many bareboat companies and most skippered and crewed charters will arrange for a member of the crew or the charter base staff to meet you at the airport and arrange transport to the boat. If this is an option, take it or at least arrange for the

company to have a trusted taxi driver to meet you at the airport.

If you are going to find the boat on your own get explicit instructions from the charter company on how to get to the marina or harbour, what the going rate is for whatever transportation is available, where exactly the boat is located, and a local contact telephone number. Give the charter company a ring just before you leave home to see if there have been any last minute changes. Get the name, address and telephone number of a hotel nearby – just in case you need it.

STOWING GEAR

Boats are comparatively small environments and it is essential that things are stowed away properly for the safety of all the crew. When you arrive everyone should have a locker (or two) allotted to them and some space in the hanging locker. You also need to allot space for a booze cabinet (teetotallers excepted) and for bits and pieces like sun protection creams, sunglasses and the novel you picked up at the airport.

Everything should have its place on a boat and everything should be in its place when you set off.

INVENTORY AND BOAT CHECKS

Once you are settled in on board the inventory of boat gear and other items on board must be checked. The company will supply you with a checklist sheet and this should be ticked off against the items on board. It is inadvisable to assume from a quick glance around that all items are there. The inventory should be meticulously checked off or it may be that missing items overlooked by the charter base staff from the last charter group will have to be paid for by you. The inventory is usually divided up into categories along the following lines:

- **On deck** Includes life-buoy and liferaft, sails, anchors, chain and warps, fenders, awning and bimini, transom barbecue, boathook, and other sundry items. Check the liferaft has a valid in-date certificate. Check the sails are in good condition with no tears or badly chafed seams. Check warps to ensure there are no badly chafed spots. Make sure fenders are an adequate size and there are at least six of them. Make a note of any missing equipment and a note of any wear and tear or damage, especially to sails.

- **Cockpit and lockers** Dinghy (if not rigid or already inflated), outboard, dinghy pump and oars, water and fuel jerry cans, winch handle(s), warps, gas bottles, funnels, masks and snorkels, cockpit cushions and other sundry items. Check the dinghy for wear and tear as it gets a hard life on charter. Make sure the outboard works and the fuel can is full. Check the gas bottles are full and get any empties filled before you leave. List any missing equipment – winch handles are a favourite.

- **Galley** Cutlery, crockery, glasses, pots and pans, tea towels, fire extinguisher and fire blanket, cleaning materials. Check all burners on the stove work. Check the fridge works. Check there is a bottle opener and a corkscrew. Make sure there are sufficient cleaning materials.

- **Chart table** Instruments, VHF, charts and yachtsman's pilot, basic navigators kit, hand bearing compass, torch and binoculars. Check any instruments work and see if there are manuals for them, particularly for the GPS which may have different operating systems to the instruments you are used to. Check the VHF and if necessary make a test call to another boat or the charter base. Check the charts and pilot book are up-to-date and in good condition. Make sure there is a pencil sharpener and an eraser in the navigator's kit.

- **Cabin lockers** Lifejackets (including child's), safety harnesses, fire exting-uisher(s), tool and spares kit, CD player, flares, and first aid kit. Check the fire extinguishers are in-date. Check the tool kit and the first aid kit to be sure everything is there.

- **Other** Linen, pillows, duvets or blankets and windscoop. Duvets and blankets may need airing but this is something you do for yourself as the salty environment always means that things feel a bit damp.

- **Hull** Check to see that any gouges and scratches are known to the charter base staff and make a note of them on the inventory.

- **Tender** Check it over for condition and in some areas like the Caribbean and Seychelles you will need to have a cable to lock it to something solid when you go ashore.

Checking over the inventory in this sort of pedantic fashion is useful for two reasons. First of all you familiarise yourself with where things are stowed. Secondly it eliminates any problems at the end of the cruise about losses or damage when the boat is checked in. This is especially important if you have lodged a security deposit in cash with the charter base office.

FAMILIARISATION

Nearly all companies have a member of staff from the charter base run a familiarisation check on the boat. On flotillas this is carried out by the skipper who will run through all procedures with the group. Don't be afraid to ask questions later if you are not too sure of something. The familiarisation check should include the following.

- **A quick demo** on the roller reefing genoa and mainsail. Mainsails are usually slab reefing or roller reefing into the mast and it is worthwhile putting a reef in on slab reefing systems just to make sure it is set up properly and winding the main and genoa in and out. This demo also allows you to look at the sails and point out any problems and make a note of any damage. Sails are one of those contentious issues when it comes to recovering security deposits.

• **Engine starting and operation** Find out where the oil dipstick is and enquire about any other checks you need to make before starting the engine. The engine should be started and engaged briefly in forward and astern to check the operation of the gear and throttle lever. Check the instruments and ask about cruising revs. A rough guide to fuel consumption should be given although most modern diesels are now so fuel efficient that you can just about motor everywhere and still come back with fuel in the tanks. Check where the fuel stop lever is as boat manufacturers often hide them away in all sorts of places. Ask what happens should the engine break down en route.

• **Outboard motor** Check where the choke, fuel cock and stop button are, and start it up and run it for 30 seconds or so.

• **Gas procedures** If there is a gas sniffer or similar on board get a run down on how it works. Ensure that everyone on board knows where the gas bottles are and that the regulator must be turned off after the cooker has been used.

• **Water and diesel** Check where the fillers are for water and diesel. Putting diesel in the water tank or vice versa is more common than you think. Cleaning out the diesel tank and flushing the engine fuel system is a messy job that can easily loose you a day. Likewise cleaning out the water tank will take repeated flushing. Ensure everyone knows which is which.

• **Batteries** Find out where the battery switch is to switch between batteries for domestic and engine starting. Get an idea of consumption for the fridge and other power hungry equipment like an electric anchor winch.

• **Have a chat** with the charter base staff member about your itinerary. He or she can help you out with all sorts of local knowledge on good anchorages, lively night life, unsafe harbours, possible lunch stops, dangers to navigation, what the prevailing winds are likely to be, all manner of useful information that can enhance your holiday.

They can also tell you how to get forecasts and some will phone if bad weather is expected.

BOAT PAPERS

In most countries there is a fair amount of paperwork involved in getting a charter party onto a boat and away. The charter base will organise all this paperwork for the charter, but you will be required to sign various agreements and forms and may be required to accompany one of the staff members to the harbourmaster, customs or coastguard to finalise it all. This paperwork is a necessary part of the charter and the papers you carry on board may be asked for at any of the harbours along the way. In places like the Caribbean where you will be going from one country to another, it is up to you to clear yourself in and out with the relevant authorities. While you may find this tedious and a blot on your holiday, do not neglect to do it or you may find the holiday is quickly curtailed for illegal entry into a country. The charter base staff will advise you on all this and on any possible pitfalls or fees to be paid.

It is useful to keep all the boat and charter papers together along with any relevant certificates and the passports of those on board. A plastic zip folder is useful to keep papers and passports dry when going ashore from an anchorage.

PROVISIONING

Most bareboat companies will provision up the boat if requested beforehand. The charter company you book with will usually supply a checklist and many companies give you a suggested list beforehand from basic starter pack to super luxury provisioning. If you want to get off quickly then checking off items on a list is the way to do it. The provisions will be either on board when you arrive or will be delivered the same day.

Most flotilla companies provide a basic starter pack with things like oil, sugar, salt

OK, so the anchor goes there and we go...

and pepper, a few tea bags and a packet of biscuits, just so there is something there as soon as you arrive.

If you are provisioning the boat yourself some of the crew can be detailed to go shopping while the skipper and others are briefed on the boat and the area. On flotilla the hostess will be able to direct you to the best places to go shopping and advise you on what days you will be able to stock up again.

For some of us going shopping in a foreign place is part of the fun of being there. If this is the case order a basic starter pack so you can at least make a hot drink when you arrive or gulp down a can of fizzy something or other and then when the boat has been stowed, some of the crew can go off to do the shopping. In most countries there are all sorts of goodies to try whether you are shopping in a supermarket or wandering around a local market with funny looking dried fish and blobs of white goo called cheese by another name.

WATER AND FUEL

Before you leave top up with water and fuel including any reserve supplies in jerry cans. For anyone new to a boat it is difficult to inculcate the need to be careful with water and not to waste it. Invariably ablutions use the most water so educate any new crew about the dire consequences they will face if they take showers that go on for ages, leave pressure taps running while they wash and clean their teeth, and are generally not conscious of rationing water. In some small harbours you may have to lug water from the shore by jerry can and this can have a sobering effect on dissolute water wasters when they have to carry the water they use.

Fuel is less of a problem as the charter base staff will be able to tell you where you can refuel en route. Most diesels are fairly economical these days and it is unlikely you will need to refuel more than once on a two-week itinerary. Bareboats must be returned with full tanks to the charter base, but this is easily arranged once you get back to the base and you are simply charged for however much was needed to top up the tanks.

BOAT SENSE

- Living on board. The good, the bad and the ugly
- Under power
- Organising the skipper and crew
- Etiquette
- Cardinal sins
- Returning the boat

LIVING ON BOARD

For those not used to being on a boat it all seems small unless you are on a superyacht where the space resembles that of a small apartment anyway. Everyone on board should respect the space of the others and endeavour to stow things away and not to hog all the space in the cockpit or saloon. Noise travels without let or hindrance from one end of the boat to another so keep your singing in the shower to a modest level as well as any other noises you might manufacture.

Those not used to moving around a boat should familiarise themselves with the deck layout when in harbour. Wander around it and get the feel of where things are, especially handholds, before you are beating into a healthy breeze and need to go forward to retrieve a fender someone forgot about. Boats move in a fairly rhythmical fashion when underway and it is just a matter of moving about in sync with that movement.

UNDER POWER

It is essential that apart from the skipper someone else on board knows how to start the engine and get underway under power. This is for the simple reason that if the only person who knows how to start the engine and get underway falls overboard, no one else will know how to get back to the unfortunate soul. It is also useful to be able

to hand over to someone else when the skipper has other things he wants to do.

Before you leave harbour at the beginning of the charter instruct one other member of the crew in the basics of starting and operating the engine. Then when you have left harbour let the chosen one helm under power for a bit to get the feel of the boat and later let them have a bit of a potter around in calm water. Remember that someone may have to manoeuvre the boat back to pick you up out of the sea.

Before you start the engine run through a number of basic checks. The charter base will advise you on these which will be basically to check the oil, check the fresh water coolant level, check you are on the engine starting battery, and check the gear lever is disengaged and on throttle only for starting. Once the engine is started check there is water coming out of the exhaust and check the oil pressure gauge. Always let a diesel warm up for a few minutes before getting underway. At the same time make sure there are no warps trailing in the water which might get wrapped around the propeller.

If there is one thing which irritates charter companies it is charterers who insist on gunning the engine up to maximum revs when under power. Most yachts will get up to cruising speed at around half revs or just over. If there is a rev counter the charter base staff will advise you on cruising revs. Gunning the engine up to maximum revs will increase your speed by only a small amount, will dramatically increase your fuel consumption, and will probably lay a film of unburned diesel on the water from the exhaust.

ORGANISING THE SKIPPER AND CREW

On a new boat and in strange waters it is essential that the crew know what to do when coming into an anchorage or a

Is everybody happy? Bareboating in Croatia

harbour. This does not mean that everyone has to jump to navy fashion, rather that the crew know who is doing what in what order. Before coming into harbour it pays to have things prepared well in advance and to detail specific jobs to those on board. Thus someone ties fenders on, someone coils ropes ready for heaving ashore, someone gets the anchor ready to let go, and someone keeps an eye out for a suitable berth or anchoring spot. There is nothing worse than the chaos seen on some charter yachts where lack of preparation has engendered a last minute panic bordering on hysteria as the skipper screams to his crew to get fenders out, find some damn mooring lines, and get the anchor (what anchor) down, all within 50 feet of the quay. Preparation is all and it dramatically decreases divorces and lovers tiffs caused when berthing or anchoring.

It is also distressing to see yachts coming into anchor or berth where the male stands impassively at the helm directing (usually) his female partner to get the anchor ready and drop it or leap 10 foot to the quay with a couple of mooring lines. Usually it would be more appropriate for the hunky male to be handling the anchor or taking lines ashore. In my experience the female of the species is usually better at helming the boat than the male with a more delicate touch on helm and throttle. This may not go down well with macho skippers, but at least try to let your wife or lover have a go at driving the boat once or twice instead of always struggling with a hefty anchor and chain.

When leaving harbour it is likewise necessary that everyone knows their allotted tasks. The boat will need to be stowed so things don't fall about, towels retrieved from drying on the lifelines, fenders and lines put away, the anchor must be secured, and someone needs to keep an eye out up forward for swimmers in the water and ferries charging into the harbour at speed.

ETIQUETTE

While you are on holiday to relax and have fun it remember that you have a responsibility to be polite to those whose country you are visiting and especially to those on the water. Think about the following:

Boat boy in Dominica in the Caribbean

- When you go into a harbour do not take berths obviously occupied by fishing boats or local boats of any description. After all it is their harbour and they are working on the water for a living.
- Take care of other peoples yachts. Ensure you have sufficient fenders out to avoid damage to other yachts and that your lines do not chafe on theirs or on their boat. And if you befriend them there may well be some interesting salty yarns in return for a drink or two.
- All-night parties are fine if that is what you are after, but to others in an anchorage it may be just plain irritating when they are trying to get some sleep. Sounds carry wonderfully well across a quiet anchorage as I've discovered on not a few occasions when alcohol-inspired conversations have been louder than intended and have been repeated word for word in the morning from yachts a considerable distance away.
- In some anchorages, particularly in the Caribbean, boat boys will row or motor out to yachts to assist when anchoring and taking a line ashore, tout for restaurants or sell you fresh fruit and vegetables and souvenirs. There is a strict protocol to follow in the Caribbean which applies equally well elsewhere. The first boat boy who gets to you should be engaged after ascertaining the price and asked to keep the others clear and wait until you are ready for his services. If you don't do this, mayhem will result with a cluster of boats impeding your way and a lot of arguments over who should be employed. The charter base can give you a pretty exact idea of what the going rates are for services so you will not be out of pocket when engaging the first one to arrive.
- Touts on the land will also offer you an array of goods and services. If you are not interested decline politely and if they persist just walk on by having made a first refusal. Touting in many countries is a way of life and even when touts are persistent, don't get upset with them.
- When double or triple banked outside other yachts on a quay ask permission to walk across the inside boats to the quay. Do not put your shoes on until onto the quay and try to tread gently, especially when returning at night. Anyone trying to sleep will not be amused by you banging across the decks in the wee hours with little regard for the amount of noise you are making. And try to avoid peeking down hatches and through the main hatchway – it's called being a peeping tom in most parts of the world and you can be arrested for it on land.
- Boats with generators should not run them at night or during siesta time when people are trying to get to sleep. In harbour be careful of where the generator exhaust is squirting its cooling water. In an anchorage generators should be run sparingly if at all. If you have toys on board like sailboards and waterbikes, stay clear of anyone swimming in an anchorage. A sailboard or a waterbike can cause severe injury to a swimmer if you hit them and it takes little time for someone who has been knocked out to drown.

Cardinal sins

❖ **Anchoring** Careless anchoring causes a lot of damage to the sea bottom. On sand and mud the damage is not great, although efforts are being made in the Mediterranean to preserve Posidonia seabed grass. Over coral damage is long-lasting and can be catastrophic. There is a global effort underway to establish a code of anchoring in coral reef areas which suggests the following. Never anchor on coral reefs themselves. Reconnoitre an area and drop your anchor in sand. If mooring buoys are available use them. Even if it means anchoring in comparatively deep water to be free of coral, do it. Living coral has a relatively thin and delicate tissue covering the hard skeleton and is easily damaged by anchors and chain which can cause a coral colony which was hundreds of years old to die.

❖ **Consideration for others** Anchoring close to another boat when there is room elsewhere, playing loud music or staging an all-night party in a quiet bay is just not on.

❖ **Garbage** Always dispose of your garbage in proper areas. No inorganic rubbish should be thrown into the sea and even organic rubbish should be sparingly dumped overboard when at least three miles off the coast.

❖ **Holding tanks** Never pump out the holding tank in harbour or in an anchorage. In many places heavy fines will be levied for the smallest infringement. Most authorities recommend you be at least three miles off the coast before pumping out holding tanks although regulations vary and the charter company will be able to inform you on specific regulations in force.

❖ **Sailing at night** Most charter companies have restrictions on sailing at night. These restrictions apply mostly because a lot of charter areas are comparatively poorly lit and buoyed compared to Europe or the USA and sailing in coral at night is a simple NO. Moreover, local boats may not be carrying lights or may have incorrect navigation lights which can cause confusion and a possible accident. Sneaking in at twilight is one thing but sailing back to a charter base at night to make up time will most probably invalidate your own insurance and you may be liable for the cost of replacing the boat should anything happen to it at night. Talk it over with the charter company as conditions vary between companies and charter areas

RETURNING THE BOAT

It all has to come to an end, usually much too quickly after you have settled into the pace of cruising around harbours and anchorages and got used to handling the boat. Still the advantage of chartering is that you can return to exactly the same location next year or extend your horizons and head off somewhere else. For the time being there is the nitty gritty of returning the boat and heading home.

• I know I've already said this, several times, but allow for plenty of time to get the boat back to the charter base. If you are flying out on say a midday or early afternoon flight then you need to be back the night before. Leave an easy leg for the last day so you do not arrive back exhausted and stressed out. After all your holiday is about leaving your normal hectic and cluttered lifestyle behind for two weeks so make the final few days a relaxed affair.

• Once back at the charter base the inventory will have to be checked off (careful checking when you arrived pays off now), fuel tanks filled, and your safety deposit retrieved if it was lodged with the charter base office. It is common practice to donate any left over provisions and booze to the charter base staff.

• In some countries, particularly the Caribbean and USA, it is normal to tip skippers and crew. The usual going rate is 2–5% of the charter fee. For staff at the bareboat base the going rate is less.

WORLD CHARTER AREAS

Introduction

The information in the round-up of charter areas is fairly straightforward to follow. More space is allocated to areas where there is a good deal of charter or which has several popular charter areas. A small section at the end of the book is allocated specifically to the more unusual charter areas.

At the beginning of each charter area there is a brief box with pros and cons and the sort of charter to be found in that area. It also indicates what level of experience you may need. The latter is a bit of a 'cheat' because the level of experience you need is dictated by the type of charter you go on and the specific area within a country that you charter in. So while the Ionian in Greece is suitable for a range of experiences such as flotilla or bareboat charter, the Dodecanese over the other side of the country is not really suited to the novice for, say, a bareboat charter. You need to talk to a charter company and do some of your own reading on an area to make the decision on whether it is suitable for you.

Included for many of the charter areas are climate tables and average wind strengths for the charter season. Most of the data, average maximum and minimum temperatures, highest recorded temperature, and sea temperature give a clue as to how comfortable or inviting an area will be. Other data in the tables needs a bit more interpretation.

Antigua is a stunning charter location

Wind strength is given as a Force on the Beaufort scale. For those not used to the Beaufort scale, I have included the table on p.47 which gives the Beaufort strength in knots and kilometres per hour. So a wind of Force 4 is 11–16 knots or 20–28 km/hr. It must be stressed that the wind strength given is the average for the month along with the prevailing wind direction(s). Over any month, winds from other directions can be expected, but the general direction will be that given. Likewise the average wind force will include days with stronger winds and days of calm all averaged out to the figure given. This has its uses but also limitations as all mean figures do.

The number of days of rain with X amount falling should be interpreted with care. In the tropics there will often be a downpour for an hour or less in the afternoon and that is the rain over and done with. In other areas that rain may be a grey drizzle falling all day.

Sea State	Beaufort No	Description	Velocity in knots	Velocity in km/h	Term	Code	Wave height in metres
Like a mirror	0	Calm, glassy	<1	<1	Calm	0	0
Ripples	1	Light airs	1–3	1–5	Calm	1	0–0.1
Small wavelets	2	Light breeze	4–6	6–11	Smooth	2	0.1–0.5
Large wavelets	3	Gentle breeze	7–10	12–19	Slight	3	0.5–1.25
Small waves, breaking	4	Moderate breeze	11–16	20–28	Moderate	4	1.25–2.5
Moderate waves, foam	5	Fresh breeze	17–21	29–38	Rough	5	2.5–4
Large waves, foam and spray	6	Strong breeze	22–27	39–49			
Sea heads up, foam in streaks	7	Near gale	28–33	50–61	Very rough	6	4–6
Higher long waves, foam in streaks	8	Gale	34–40	62–74			
High waves, dense foam	9	Strong gale	41–47	75–88	High	7	6–9
Very high tumbling waves, surface white with foam, visibility affected	10	Storm	48–55	89–102	Very high	8	9–14
Exceptionally high waves, sea covered in foam, visibility affected	11	Violent storm	56–62	103–117	Phenomenal	9	Over 14
Air filled with spray and foam, visibility severely impaired	12	Hurricane	>63	>118			

The relative humidity of an area needs to be linked to average maximum temperatures and the graph opposite shows a 'comfort index' for maximum temperatures and relative humidity. Basically the maximum temperatures of an area do not tell the whole story and unless linked to the relative humidity will not give you an idea of how comfortable the heat is. With high humidity, clothes do not dry out and body perspiration cannot evaporate easily, leaving you feeling sticky and hot. For example at 30°C (86°F) and 20% humidity a few people will feel uncomfortable, but for most it is quite bearable. At 30°C and 60% humidity everyone feels distinctly uncomfortable. There are some modifying factors of which the

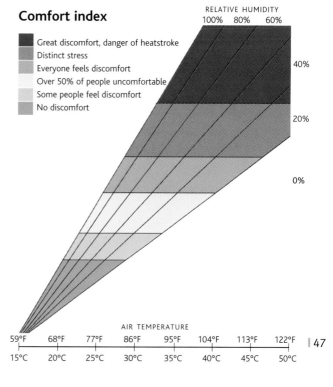

Comfort index

- Great discomfort, danger of heatstroke
- Distinct stress
- Everyone feels discomfort
- Over 50% of people uncomfortable
- Some people feel discomfort
- No discomfort

RELATIVE HUMIDITY
100% 80% 60%
40%
20%
0%

AIR TEMPERATURE

| 59°F | 68°F | 77°F | 86°F | 95°F | 104°F | 113°F | 122°F |
| 15°C | 20°C | 25°C | 30°C | 35°C | 40°C | 45°C | 50°C |

47

most important is wind speed and fortunately on the sea there is usually a bit of breeze. This explains why when you get off a yacht at anchor where there is a bit of breeze across the water it feels quite comfortable, but when you go ashore and walk around it seems less comfortable and somehow hotter.

ANCHORING WITH A LONG LINE ASHORE

In some parts of the Mediterranean, in Scandinavia and a few other countries, where you must anchor in deep water on an upward slope, the practice has evolved of taking a line ashore to a tree or rock. The prevailing winds in summer are constantly from the same direction and you will normally be taking the line ashore to 'anchor' the boat against an offshore wind and also to hold the real anchor in place in the uphill-sloping seabed. If you were to swing around the anchor it would be pulled downhill and into deeper water. This manoeuvre is usually carried out using the main bower anchor and tying ashore from the stern.

When you are anchoring in this fashion, have the dinghy in the water and ready to go with a long line – you will often need 50 or 60 metres – flaked down in the dinghy and the end tied off on the boat. Drop the anchor and go astern until you are where you want to be off the shore. Once the anchor is in you should be able to hold the boat in position with the engine idling astern while the person in the dinghy rows like fury to the shore.

Anchoring with a long line ashore

UNITED KINGDOM

Britain has a long sailing history and much of it has been preserved one way or another around the coast. From Portsmouth harbour where old sailing ships vie for space with modern navy aircraft carriers to Beaulieu River where many of the old sailing ships were built; from Cowes, home to yacht racing in Britain to the Hamble where the fashionable people go; from Plymouth Hoe where Drake played bowls before going out to take on the Spanish Armada to Falmouth where oysters are still dredged under sail; the coastline is so drenched in nautical history you will wind up feeling a bit salty yourself. On the east coast, a long seafaring tradition is encapsulated in the voyages of Captain Cook in his doughty Whitby ship *Endeavour*. Scotland lays claim to some of the most spectacular coastline with deep inlets cutting into a mountainous coast and some of the best seafood in Britain. And of course it was home to the classic Fife's which included two J-class yachts built here for the America's Cup.

The coastline itself is a varied feast for the eyes and you will cruise past cliffs and rolling countryside, marshes and deep-throated estuaries, jagged capes and rocky shores. When you are safely tied up in a harbour or on a mooring there will inevitably be a convivial watering-hole ashore with all sorts of salty tales being swapped at the bar. English pubs are an institution much copied but rarely emulated outside Britain and they have the added bonus these days of serving good food.

There is more yacht charter in Britain than most people realise despite the vagaries of the weather. There are also a lot of variations on the basic yacht chartering you get in many other parts of the world with a strong emphasis on learning sailing skills rather than just sitting back and enjoying a sailing holiday. As well as mini-flotillas, bareboat and skippered charter, there are all sorts of learning to sail programmes including Royal Yachting Association (RYA) courses and short courses for those going on flotilla holidays

BEFORE YOU GO

For

✔ Easy international access and good infrastructure.

✔ Long sailing tradition with lots of interesting boats around and maritime heritage sights ashore.

✔ Wide range of charter options including many sailing schools and specialist skills like racing and learning to sail old timers.

✔ Magnificent scenery and peace and quiet in Scotland.

✔ English pubs.

Against

✘ Unpredictable summer season.

✘ Some areas like the south coast crowded in the summer.

Types of charter

❖ Sailing in company
❖ Bareboat
❖ Skippered charter
❖ Luxury charter
❖ Sailing schools and advanced teaching courses
❖ Corporate charter

Suitable for

❖ Novice to experienced depending on the area and time of year.

ESSENTIAL INFORMATION

Capital London

Time zone UT DST (+1 hr) Apr–Sep

Language English

Telecommunications Automatic dialling. Country code 44. Good public telephone service with phonecards. GSM phones supported throughout the UK. Internet cafés and wifi.

Electricity 230V 50Hz AC

elsewhere, competitive sailing including match racing and entering some of the big races such as the Round the Island Race, sailing older traditional craft, corporate and team sailing, and day charters on large classic yachts and ocean racing yachts. Chartering a yacht in Britain is a bit if a lottery depending on the weather and you can expect to spend a few days weather-bound even in the summer. But there are good hostelries ashore.

WHEN TO GO

The season in Great Britain normally starts around May and runs through to October. In the early and late season in spring and autumn there is a good chance that weather will hold you up for around 25% of the time.

Early season May to June. Day temperatures are typically 15° to 18°C in the south and 14° to 16°C in Scotland, but drop at night to 6° to 11°C at night. Wind patterns are not regular with depressions coming in from the Atlantic, determining much of what happens. The sky is frequently overcast and there are numerous days of rain.

High season June to September. Day temperatures are typically 19°C in the south and 17°C in Scotland in July and August. The sea breeze is well established in the summer blowing onto the coast except

when a depression coming in from the Atlantic disturbs the normal wind pattern.

Late season October. Temperatures and wind patterns are much as for the early season. Sometimes at the end of October there is a period of settled weather and higher temperatures.

GETTING THERE

From overseas there are numerous international flights into many British airports. From Europe there are frequent air, rail and ferry connections.

Getting to a charter base will usually be a simple matter of a rail or coach connection and then a taxi to the base. In Scotland some of the charter bases may be a little more difficult to get to but your charter company will usually advise on the best way. Residents will usually choose to go by car as will many continental visitors. Hire cars are easily arranged in most centres of population and can be booked from outside the UK.

WHEN YOU'RE THERE

Visas and documentation
Members of the EU must carry their passport or identity card. All other visitors must carry a passport but many do not require a visa for a temporary stay but may be asked for evidence of an onward ticket or sufficient funds. Check with your charter company on the current situation.

Proof of competence to handle a yacht will usually be asked for by most companies. For some of the more tricky cruising areas off Scotland and for cruises outside the normal cruising area for a company you will require some sort of certificate of competence. A licence to operate a VHF (short range certificate) is required.

Health
Medical services Generally good. Reciprocal medical care is available for EU nationals. It is advisable to take out medical insurance if you are not from an EU country although

At Plymouth	Av max °C	Av min °C	Highest recorded	Relative humidity	Days 0.25 mm rain	Sea temp °C	Wind direction & force
Apr	12	6	22	69%	12	9	SW/NE F3-4
May	15	8	26	71%	12	11	W-SW F3
Jun	18	11	28	73%	12	13	W-SW F3-4
Jul	19	13	29	74%	14	15.5	W-SW F3-4
Aug	19	13	31	75%	14	16	W-SW F3-4
Sep	18	12	27	75%	15	15.5	SW-NE F3-4
Oct	15	9	23	77%	16	14.5	W-SW F4

At Edinburgh	Av max °C	Av min °C	Highest recorded	Relative humidity	Days 0.25 mm rain	Sea temp °C	Wind direction & force
May	14	6	24	76%	14	8	All dir F4
June	17	9	28	75%	15	11	All dir F3-4
July	18	11	28	78%	17	13	NW-W-SW F3-4
Aug	18	11	28	80%	16	13	W-SW-S F3-4
Sep	16	9	25	89%	16	12.5	W-SW F4
Oct	12	7	20	82%	17	11	W-SW-S F4

care will still be provided by the National Health without insurance but a fee may be incurred. The RNLI provides an extensive rescue service.

Water Everywhere potable.

Money and banks

The unit of currency is the pound sterling. Exchange for other currencies can be obtained at banks or post offices everywhere.

Banks are open 0900–1600 Monday to Friday. All major credit cards and charge cards widely accepted. ATM machines commonplace and work with most credit cards.

Eating and drinking

Once considered to have the worst food in Europe, things have changed radically in the last 20 years and Britain now has a cosmopolitan fare probably unequalled for its diversity. Fish and chips have been replaced in popularity by Indian restaurants, pub food has improved dramatically and a mix of cuisines can be found in all larger towns and cities. In the more out of the way places the fare is often simple but tasty.

Britain offers perhaps the most diverse choice of wines in the world with a mix of old world and new world varieties. For the sheer variety of countries wine is imported from, it can't be bettered. British beer is likewise unequalled in its diversity. If chartering in Scotland you are of course in the home of malt whiskies.

Provisioning

Straightforward in larger centres except that large supermarkets tend to be outside the town centres. Limited choice in some places in Scotland although the charter base can make arrangements for provisioning in advance or will help out in getting supplies.

SAILING GUIDES AND CHARTS

There are a large number of sailing guides to different parts of the country. Have a look in any chandlers or nautical bookshop. The following may be useful.

The Shell Channel Pilot Tom Cunliffe. Imray. Covers all south coast harbours.

South Coast Cruising Mark Fishwick. Yachting Monthly. Good coverage of most of south coast including the Solent.

West Country Cruising Mark Fishwick. Wiley Nautical. Covers Devon and Cornwall.

East Coast Pilot Jarman, Holness, Cooper. Imray. Covers Lowestoft to Ramsgate.

Clyde to Colonsay/ Crinan to Canna/ Castle Bay to Cape Wrath Martin Lawrence. Imray. Covers west coast of Scotland.

Admiralty, Imray and Stanfords charts cover the British coastline in great detail.

Reeds Nautical Almanac Annual publication. Adlard Coles Nautical. Covers whole UK and Ireland.

Cruising Association Almanac (biennial) Imray.

Costs

The overall cost is around the EU average. Typical costs for eating out are £10–£30 a head, wine is around £5–£15 a bottle in the shops, beer around £2.50 a pint in a pub.

Provisioning is around the EU average with a wide range of imported goods available.

Transport varies with taxi fares at or slightly above some other EU countries. Car hire is generally around the EU average at £20–30 per day.

Crime and personal safety

Reports of horrific crimes figure prominently in the tabloid press but in fact statistically the UK is a relatively low risk country. In large cities the risk of mugging and theft is appreciably greater than in the country and since charter bases are far removed from the large centres of population there are few problems. Theft from a yacht can be a problem and the boat should always be locked when you leave it and loose items removed from the deck.

CHARTER AREAS

SOUTH COAST

The south coast of England extending from Brighton to Falmouth. This is the sailing and charter hub of England with charter companies large and small operating from bases along the coast. The largest concentration of yachts in England is around the Solent which also naturally enough has a large concentration of charter yachts.

Wind and sea

Winds are much dependent on the Atlantic and the passage of depressions in from the west. In the summer when a high is stationary over Britain there is some sea breeze effect and along the south coast it can last for a week or more if you are lucky. During these periods in summer there are wonderful sunny days with sufficient sea

RYA training course on the Solent

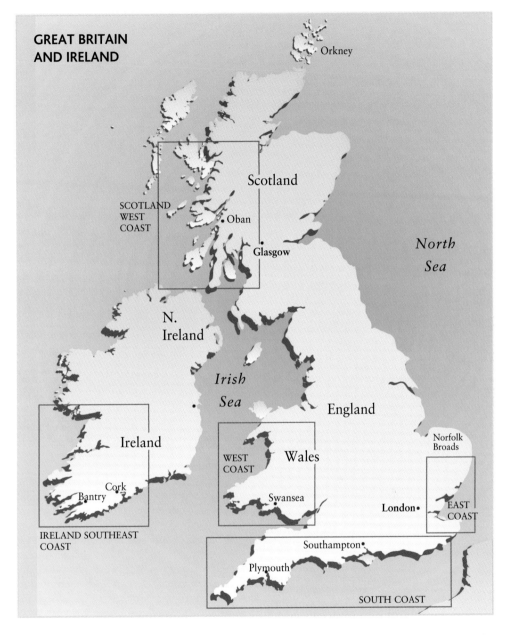

GREAT BRITAIN AND IRELAND

Orkney

Scotland

SCOTLAND WEST COAST

Oban

Glasgow

North Sea

N. Ireland

Irish Sea

England

Ireland

Norfolk Broads

WEST COAST

Wales

Cork
Bantry

Swansea

London

EAST COAST

IRELAND SOUTHEAST COAST

Southampton

Plymouth

SOUTH COAST

breeze for a good sail. Winds in the English Channel are channelled into a westerly or easterly direction when light, but with stronger winds the pressure differences are the major determinant of direction. Weather forecasts are widely available either on VHF in marinas, on the internet, by telephone, or on BBC Radio 4 on the *Shipping Forecast*.

Pilots for the area carry all necessary details.

The seas along the south coast are generally moderate except of course in strong winds generated by depressions passing over. Where there are strong tidal currents there can be dangerous overfalls with wind against tide with the Portland Race and the Needles just two notorious areas.

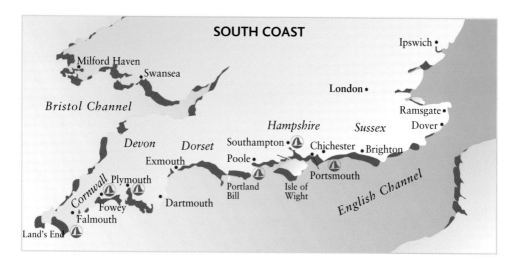

SOUTH COAST

Tides

Tides along the south coast are not extreme but do give rise to problems where there are complex streams and eddies. Around the major headlands there is often a tidal race and when wind is against tide (and sometimes even when it is not) there can be severe overfalls. It is prudent to keep well off the headlands where this happens and which are well known and mentioned in the relevant pilots.

All tidal data is referenced to Dover. The tidal range at springs varies from around 5.3 metres (17ft+) at Falmouth, 4.9 metres (16 ft) at Torquay, 4.7 metres (15ft+) at Portsmouth, to 6.5 metres (21ft+) at Brighton. The tidal streams generated in the Channel and in areas like the Solent are complex and reference must be made to a tidal stream atlas.

Suitable for...

The area is for everyone from the novice to experienced sailors. Those with less experience will find ample opportunity to go on sailing courses or get an RYA qualification. There are sufficient harbours within a close distance along the coast for plans to be changed in the event of deteriorating weather conditions when it may be necessary to seek shelter. For sailing schools and learning to sail charters, the skipper/instructor will of course be on hand although the conditions can at times be trying, especially in early or late season.

Harbours and anchorages

There is a mix of everything from yacht marinas, commercial ports, fishing harbours, river and estuary anchorages and a few sheltered bays. Many harbours and most estuaries and rivers have a bar or shifting sand-banks at the entrance and can only be entered a number of hours either side of high water. Many of these are dangerous to enter with strong onshore winds and the pilot should be consulted or local knowledge sought. Once you have discussed your itinerary with the charter company they will be able to advise on tricky entrances and possible safe alternatives.

Berthing in marinas is generally on finger pontoons. Berthing in commercial and fishing harbours will generally be alongside and in summer there can be as many as ten boats deep, requiring some planning for boats on the inside to get out. Anchorages frequently have moorings and many harbour authorities provide visitor moorings. Some of these will have either a maximum tonnage or LOA on them or be colour coded for the size of boat and this must be adhered to.

Main charter bases

The main charter bases are concentrated around the Solent in the River Hamble,

On the Solent

Southampton, Portsmouth, Chichester and Lymington. Smaller concentrations of yachts will be found at Brighton, Poole, Plymouth and Falmouth and there are small numbers of charter boats dotted in just about all the major yacht harbours in between. Boats can frequently be delivered to a convenient harbour along the coast for a fee depending on the weather. It is essential to get a forecast for each day and when cruise planning ensure there are options and free days built into it so you can get the boat back on time.

To get some ideas go to www.enjoy england.com

Sailing area

The sailing area is basically along the coast from your chosen charter base. Most charterers will want to potter around the coast locally whether it be the West Country or the Solent. Some charter companies will arrange for cross Channel passages with a skipper or for experienced bareboat charterers to France and the Channel Islands. Effectively it all depends on your experience and the vagaries of the weather. A number of the charter companies can arrange for you to pick the boat up at one base and leave it at another for a fee.

SCOTLAND

The west coast of Scotland is dramatic with hundreds of miles of coast sheltered by islands and cut by lochs extending miles inland. The scenery is superlative and for peace and tranquillity there are few places to equal it. It has a few drawbacks including midges in the summer and changeable weather. On a yacht the midges are less of a problem than ashore and the changeable weather at least includes heat-waves as well as Arctic-like winds. Bring both the sun tan cream and your wet weather gear.

Wind and sea

Winds around the Scottish coast are dependent on the Atlantic influence – as for the south coast, except more so. The prevailing winds in the summer are westerlies between NW and SW, but winds are channelled and funnelled locally to give significant variations on the breeze out to sea. Winds can change quickly and one day there may be a balmy westerly and the next a cold Arctic blast funnelling down the mountains and lochs. In the summer you can strike it lucky with a week or more of balmy breezes without interruption, but in the early and late season this is less than likely. It is essential to anticipate how the weather may change in one day and from day to day. Weather forecasts are as for the south coast on VHF, in marinas and on the internet and from the BBC.

Seas around the Scottish coast vary from the large Atlantic swell rolling in on exposed coast to calmer waters behind the islands and in the lochs. However strong breezes funnelled into the lochs and passages between the islands mean it can be wet and bumpy with strong breezes even in these comparatively sheltered waters. The strong tides in the channels and around headlands can give rise to overfalls, even whirlpools, and it is essential to consult the pilot for dangerous areas during the flood and ebb.

Tides

The tides around the west coast are not extreme, ranging from around 1.5–2 metres (4.9–6.5ft) in the outer islands to 5 metres (16ft+) or so along the mainland coast at springs. It is the narrow channels that the water is forced through which give rise to fierce races, overfalls and in places whirlpools.

The whirlpool at Corryveckan between Jura and Scara is reckoned to be the second biggest whirlpool in the northern hemisphere and the tide through Dorus Mor reaches 8 knots at springs. It hardly needs to be said that it is essential to plan passages with tide tables and a tidal atlas to hand.

Suitable for...

The area is for intermediate and experienced sailors. This is no place for the novice to be and even for intermediate

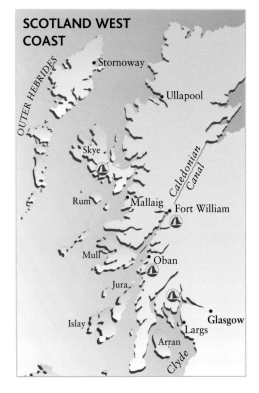

SCOTLAND WEST COAST

sailors some care is necessary to plan a cruise within the capabilities of the crew. The changeable conditions and climate mean that prior cruise planning is essential.

Harbours and anchorages

There are a few purpose-built yacht marinas and yacht pontoons at some harbours, but mostly there are endless anchorages in bays and bights in the lochs or between islands and islets. Some of the anchorages will have visitors moorings laid either by the Highlands and Islands Enterprise Board or by local hotels and restaurants eager to increase trade. In popular spots in the summer there may be more than one yacht on a laid mooring. Anchorages in many of the bays have a weedy bottom which can be difficult for the anchor to get through and dig in on the bottom, so care is needed.

Main charter bases

There are no large concentrations of charter bases along the coast, rather a scattered collection of bases including around the Clyde, Ardfern, Oban and Skye amongst others. The Scottish Tourist Board issues a free brochure on watersports which includes most yacht charter companies large and small. http://sail.visitscotland.com. For those who like a wee dram the Classic Malts Cruise is a 200 mile meander around the Scottish coast sampling malt whiskies from the various distilleries along the way. www.worldcruising.com/classicmaltscruise

Sailing area

Nearly all of the charter companies restrict the sailing area to within the islands and adjacent coast, the exact definition varying somewhat between companies. It is possible to extend this area for experienced charterers and usually an additional fee is payable for this extension.

In truth the best part of the area is within the islands and coast, the offshore area being often rough and uncomfortable with few places to visit anyway.

WALES AND THE WEST COAST OF ENGLAND

Along the west coast of England and Wales there are a number of small charter bases offering bareboat and skippered charter. The cruising area is restricted by the paucity of good harbours within easy reach of one another and an exposed coast with strong tidal races and overfalls. Charter companies operate from Swansea marina and a few other places where owner operators base their boats.

The area is for experienced skipper and crew combinations and some care must be put into planning a cruise. There is the possibility of crossing to Ireland or around Swansea there are sufficient places to the west for a mini-cruise.

EAST COAST

There are few charter companies around the east coast of England with two exceptions. The Norfolk Broads have long been involved with yacht charter and there are numerous charter companies operating in the Broads. The east coast is also home to a number of traditional craft which are available for charter around different parts of the coast, mostly between Ipswich and Burnham-on-Crouch.

Sailing on the Broads is about as English as you can get. It has a pedigree stretching back to the beginning of the last century and it is an experience that should not be missed and which for some is addictive. The skills required for sailing through the channels in the Broads are particular to the area and skill is required to get the best out of the yachts that operate here. However the sheltered waters mean that beginners can get underway after a short period of tuition. Many of the craft are gaff or gunter rigged and masts are counter-balanced for when the mast needs to come down to go under bridges. The sailing is not demanding but the tides do run at an appreciable rate. Fortunately there are lots of places to stop at whether for a night in a convivial hostelry or just parked up by the bank. Motorboats are also available for charter on the Broads.

The shallow muddy waters of the east coast have bred boats adapted to the area and in many circles the east coast is considered the bastion of traditional sail, a mecca for lovers of gaff riggers as well as a few others like the spritsail and lug. Many of these craft are available for charter, including a number of Thames barges, and enthusiasts of traditional boats can find a wide variety of different shapes and sizes and sail plans available for skippered charter.

IRELAND

The Irish will tell you that their sailing history stretches further back than the British – what with St Brendan the navigator setting off for the Blessed Isles in the 6th century AD. The Irish have always been involved with boats and not just fishing boats and coracles. Cork has the oldest yacht club in the world, founded in 1720 and today known as the Royal Cork Yacht Club. Ashore in this green and slightly damp land there is history galore all liberally sprinkled with the craic (crack), the Irish sense of mischievous fun, lubricated by excellent ales in some of the best pubs in the world. Going into an Irish pub is like entering another world and by the time you wobble out you will probably feel a little extra-terrestrial.

Ireland has long been a favourite with cruising yachts, but until recently there have been relatively few charter yachts. There are now charter yachts, bareboat or skippered, available for charter on the west, south and southeast coast of Ireland. The area is not a place for beginners to take a bareboat with considerable tides, challenging navigation and the possibility of depressions coming across the Atlantic and causing delays. There is also the matter of 'soft' weather, the rain that keeps Ireland green and can fall for days. Ireland has a long racing tradition and the oldest yacht club in the world is at Cork. Not far from here is the Fastnet Rock that yachts must round after sailing from the UK in the famous race named after the rock.

WHEN TO GO

Early season May to June. In May there is a good possibility of unsettled weather. June is a better bet when there can be periods of wonderful sunny weather, though it is still chilly at night.

High season July to August. This is the most settled period when depressions from across the Atlantic are least likely to hold

BEFORE YOU GO

For
✔ Outstanding hospitality and the best pubs anywhere.
✔ Wonderful scenery and idyllic anchorages.

Against
✘ Weather unpredictable.
✘ Expensive.

Types of charter
❖ Bareboat
❖ Skippered charter

Suitable for
❖ Intermediate to experienced although less experienced can take skippered charter.

you up. There can be periods when the weather will be hot at times, evenings are balmy and sometimes cool.

Late season September. Can be warm but turns chillier at night.

GETTING THERE

There are daily scheduled flights to Dublin, Cork and Shannon from the UK. Ferry services to Dublin and Rosslare from the UK and France. Internal flights and buses, train and hire car. Taking your own car across on the ferry is also an option.

WHEN YOU'RE THERE

Visas and documentation
Members of the EU must carry their passport or identity card. Most non-EU countries do not require visas.

You will require some certification to show you are competent to handle a yacht.

Health
Medical services are generally good. Reciprocal medical care is available for EU nationals. It is advised you take out private

	Av max °C	Av min °C	Highest recorded	Relative humidity	Days 1 mm rain	Sea temp °C	Wind direction & force
Apr	13	5	22	81%	11	9.5	W-SW-S F4
May	16	7	26	78%	11	11	W-SW-S F4
Jun	19	10	29	79%	10	14	W-SW F4
Jul	20	12	28	80%	11	15.5	W-SW F4
Aug	20	12	29	83%	11	16	W-SW F4
Sep	18	10	26	86%	12	15	W-SW F4
Oct	14	7	21	90%	12	14	W-S-SE F4

medical insurance for the trip as medical costs are medium to high. Travel insurance should also be taken out.

Money and banks
The unit of currency is the Euro. There is no problem changing most European currencies or the US dollar in most places. Banks are open 0900–1700 Mon–Fri. Major credit cards and charge cards accepted in cities, towns and tourist areas. Most ATM machines will take the major credit cards (Visa and Mastercard).

Eating and drinking
Eating out has much improved in Ireland in the last 20 years and the food is now varied and of good quality. Some of the seafood restaurants around the coast are exceptional with excellent fresh fish and crustaceans. Quantity is not something you have to worry about in Ireland where portion sizes are legendary. Many of the Irish pubs around the coast serve good food at good prices.

In Ireland you must of course drink Guinness, or should I say stout – whether it be Guinness, Murphy's or Beamish. It tastes a world away from the brew served in other countries under the same name. Irish pubs have a reputation bar none for their hospitality, joviality or just for a bit of craic, the Irish term for sitting around talking (and drinking). Other alcoholic beverages, wine, Irish whiskey and spirits are available, but it is likely you will be drinking the black brew once introduced to it.

ESSENTIAL INFORMATION

Capital Dublin

Time zone UT DST (+1 hr) Apr–Sep

Language English and Gaelic (W coast)

Telecommunications Automatic dialling. Code 353. Good service. Public telephones with phonecards. Mobile phones with GSM card supported. Wifi and internet cafés.

Electricity 220V 50Hz AC

Provisioning
All provisions are available in the larger towns and tourist centres. In more out of the way places some things can be hard to find, but there will invariably be someone around to help you out.

Costs
The overall cost of living is at the top end of EU averages and is considered by some to be a bit on the expensive side. Typical costs for eating out are €50–60 a head and a pint of Guinness is around €4. Provisioning is about on a par or slightly higher than other EU countries.

Transport varies with taxi fares relatively high and car hire around €20–25 per day.

Crime and personal safety

Ireland has a comparatively low crime rate. The Irish are an honest race and in general you need be less worried here than in other EU countries about theft and muggings. That said it is wise to lock up your boat when you go ashore and take normal precautions with money and valuables.

CHARTER AREAS

Most of the charter companies in Ireland are concentrated around the southwest corner between Cork and the Shannon River. There are a few small companies elsewhere, mostly concentrating on skippered charter.

Wind and sea

The weather around Ireland, especially on the west coast, is variable depending on the general synoptic situation regarding areas of high or low pressure in the vicinity. Depressions travelling across the Atlantic disrupt any prevailing weather caused by a high sitting over Ireland and the UK and the weather forecasts need to be constantly monitored. Most people use the internet for forecasts these days but the shipping forecast on the BBC gives useful long range information. There are VHF forecasts and the Irish Meteorological Service also issues detailed weather reports on RTE Radio 1.

Any seas generated by depressions in the Atlantic travel across to hit fair and square on the west coast. This can make some harbours and bays with a bar dangerous to enter. In the summer there is less swell, but still large watery dales and valleys to sail 'up and down' off the coast. There are a number of sheltered estuaries in which to sail should it be too uncomfortable outside.

Tides

The tidal range varies between 4 metres (13ft) at Dublin, 4.5 metres (14.6ft) at Cork and 3.8 metres (12.3ft) at Dingle. This can give rise to some swift streams over shallow

entrances and to overfalls around prominent headlands. In an estuary like the Shannon it is essential to work the tides which can get up to 6–7 knots. Around headlands it is wise to stay 2–3 miles off to avoid overfalls especially when there is wind against tide.

Suitable for...

Experienced and intermediate sailors. Intermediate sailors should take a skipper for a few days because of the numerous hazards to navigation around the coast and the strong tidal streams. Anyone sailing around this area needs to pay constant attention to their navigation and monitor the weather forecasts assiduously.

Harbours and anchorages

There are a few marinas, but for the most part you will be tying up next to a trawler on the town pier or at anchor along the indented coastline. There are mooring buoys in a few places. When anchoring, care is needed to cope with the thick kelp which makes it difficult for the anchor to get through and dig in.

Main charter bases

Bareboat and skippered charter is largely out of Cork. There are also boats near Dublin and at Dingle. There are a few other companies like the one operating a traditional Galway Hooker out of, naturally enough, Galway.

Sailing area

If starting from Cork, it makes sense to shape a cruise around the southwest corner of Ireland. Between Cork and Galway there are so many places to visit along the indented coast that you would need more than a month to visit half of them. From Cork there are places like Crosshaven, Kinsale, Castlehaven, Baltimore Haven, Bantry Bay, Castletown, Kilmakilloge in the Kenmare, and Portmagee that will leave you with a taste for Ireland and returning here. It is a wild spectacular coast with deserted anchorages and small fishing harbours. There are pubs everywhere as

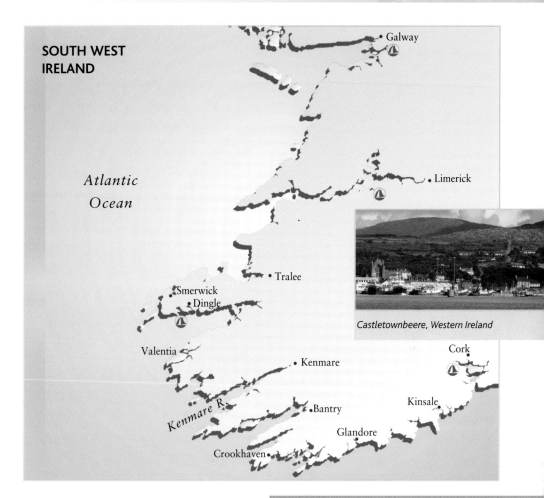

SOUTH WEST
IRELAND

*Atlantic
Ocean*

Galway

Limerick

Tralee

Smerwick
Dingle

Castletownbeere, Western Ireland

Valentia

Kenmare

Cork

Kenmare R.

Bantry

Kinsale

Glandore

Crookhaven

anyone who has been to Ireland knows. From the Shannon, a cruise can be planned north or south depending on inclination. Because the weather can deteriorate quickly cruising plans must remain flexible with a few days earmarked for getting back to the charter base.

In the event of unsettled weather the Cork estuary, Dingle Bay and the Shannon provide fairly sheltered waters.

Land excursions
Some time should be allotted for looking around Cork and if you are transiting through Dublin, around that fair city as well. The pubs (and the music), the dramatic scenery and the people are the best thing

SAILING GUIDES AND CHARTS

Sailing Directions for the South and West Coasts of Ireland Irish Cruising Club Publications.

Cruising Cork & Kerry Graham Swanson. Imray.

Admiralty and Imray charts cover the coast adequately.

Reeds Nautical Almanac. Adlard Coles Nautical. Covers the whole of Ireland.

going, but there are castles and monasteries aplenty if you decide to escape the local pub and do some sightseeing.

Northern France

In northern France there is really only one charter area of consequence and that is Brittany. On both the Channel and Atlantic coasts there are a number of charter bases offering bareboat and skippered charter.

Brittany has one of the most spectacular razor-backed coastlines in Europe. With the Atlantic beating onto its coast and some of the biggest tides in the world it is also fortunately endowed with a much indented coastline with good anchorages, some of the prettiest fishing harbours in the world and a liberal smattering of marinas where you can find good shelter. Add to that the delight of Breton cuisine ashore with excellent seafood including the best oysters, no. 1 fine de clair, in the world and those funny square crêpes.

WHEN TO GO

The season runs from May to September or October at a pinch. At the beginning and end of the season there is some likelihood of depressions crossing the Atlantic and causing periods of unsettled weather, sometimes for 5–7 days.

Early season May to June. Day temperatures are warm at around 15–18°C and when the sun is out it gets pleasantly balmy. Nights are still chilly enough to require a pullover. Wind patterns are irregular in May with the westerly sea breeze becoming more dominant in June. There is a good possibility of depressions passing over and bringing a period of unsettled weather.

High season July to August. Day temperatures are warm or hot at around 19–20°C and on sunny days you may need to retreat into the shade when temperatures can get up to the high 20s and low 30s on occasion. The weather is predominantly settled with a westerly sea breeze, usually force 4, with the chance of a land breeze at night which can sometimes be strong.

Late season September to October. Temperatures are mostly warm at 10–13°C but it can be chilly at times. Care is needed when depressions pass over and bring long periods of unsettled weather.

GETTING THERE

International flights to Paris. There are daily scheduled flights to St Malo, Lorient, Nantes and La Rochelle from Paris. The TGV high speed train takes around three hours to Nantes, Vannes and Auray from Paris. From across the Channel there are car ferries to Cherbourg, St Malo and Roscoff. Driving to Brittany is a feasible option from neighbouring countries as the autoroutes in France are fast and well maintained.

General information – See Mediterranean France section.

At Cherbourg	Av max °C	Av min °C	Highest recorded	Relative humidity	Days 1 mm rain	Sea temp °C	Wind direction & force
Apr	12	7	24	73%	12	8.5	All dir
May	15	9	30	73%	11	10.5	SW/NE F 3-4
Jun	18	12	31	74%	10	13	W-SW F3-4
Jul	19	14	32	74%	12	15	W-SW F3-4
Aug	20	14	33	75%	12	16	W-SW F3-4
Sep	19	13	30	74%	15	15.5	NW-W-SW F4
Oct	15	10	26	73%	16	14.5	W-SW F4
Nov	12	8	19	77%	17	12	NW-W-SW F4-5

CHARTER AREAS

ATLANTIC COAST

The main charter area extends along the western Atlantic coast of Brittany from Brest to La Rochelle. There is some charter on the north coast, but the bulk of it is concentrated on the western coast. This western coast is much indented and there are enough offshore islands to make up an interesting cruising area. It is a rugged rocky coast, supremely beautiful in places, though not somewhere to be trapped on a lee shore. Charter here is mostly bareboat with some skippered charter as well. The Bretons are passionate about their traditional sailing craft and there are a number of typical traditional sailing craft for skippered charter. The area can be crowded in July and August when the French are on holiday so it may pay to go just before or just after high season if possible.

Wind and sea

The prevailing wind is a sea breeze blowing onto the land anywhere between NW and SW. It generally blows around Force 3–5. At night there may be a land breeze from an easterly direction which can at times get up to Force 5 or so, though generally less. The main disruption to the normal sea breeze is from depressions passing across or north or south of the area. These are not infrequent and in early and late season you should listen carefully to weather forecasts. Fortunately weather forecasts in the area are good with radio, VHF, forecasts posted daily in the marinas, and a telephone forecast service.

Seas are generally moderate in the summer except when a disturbance out in the Atlantic sends a large swell in. This will not necessarily be accompanied by wind and by the time the swell has reached the coast the wave period is long and it is pretty much like sailing up a gentle dale and down into a valley. With a depression around heavy seas set onto the coast, it is wise to be

The Bretons are passionate about traditional craft

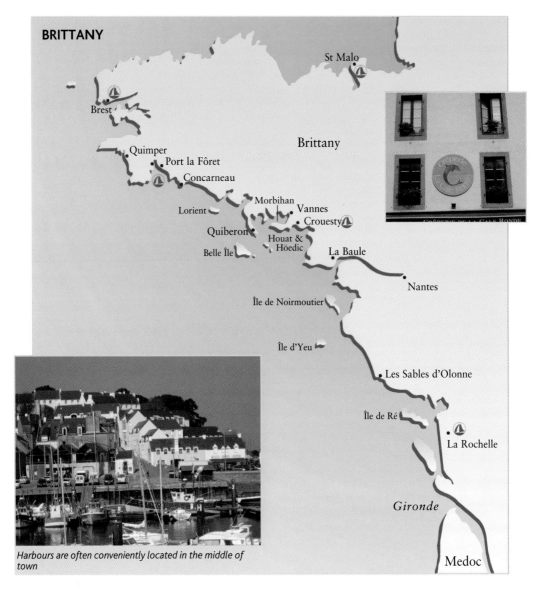

BRITTANY

Brest

St Malo

Brittany

Quimper
Port la Fôret
Concarneau

Lorient
Morbihan
Vannes
Crouesty

Quiberon
Houat &
Höedic
Belle Île
La Baule

Nantes

Île de Noirmoutier

Île d'Yeu

Les Sables d'Olonne

Île de Ré

La Rochelle

Gironde

Harbours are often conveniently located in the middle of town

Medoc

tucked up in harbour or a safe anchorage. With the wind against tide there are severe overfalls and rips in some areas and care is needed.

Tides

The tidal range in the area is high at around 7.5 metres (24ft +) at springs in the Chenal du Four and 6.2 metres (20ft) at La Rochelle. The consequence of these tides over some comparatively shallow parts of the coast are

extremely strong tidal flows with around 9 knots in the entrance to Morbihan at springs. Care and attention to tides is required over the whole area if you are not to spend fruitless hours stemming the strong tidal flows. The strong tides also require you to plan anchorages and visits to drying harbours with due care if you are not to be left high and dry until the next tide. Many of the harbours are either dredged or have a locking in system so care is needed to arrive near high tide to get into some harbours depending on what allowance there is either side of high tide for the lock gates to open.

Suitable for...
The area is for intermediate and experienced sailors. Intermediate sailors can stick around Morbihan and the immediate coast where there are plenty of places to visit and still enough challenges to navigation.

Harbours and anchorages
There is pretty much an even mix of marinas, harbours which yachts use and anchorages. In this respect the area offers a little of everything and you can mix and match marinas with every facility, old harbours in the middle of a small town and peaceful anchorages. In the inland sea of Morbihan it is usually possible to find somewhere to anchor away from it all even in high season. In the high season of July and August you may find that you are rafted out up to five or six deep in popular harbours. In marinas berthing is typically on finger pontoons, but in many of the harbours you will be rafted out from harbour walls. In a number of the outer harbours there are fore and aft moorings for yachts and again in summer there may be up to six or seven yachts rafted up together between just one pair of mooring buoys.

SAILING GUIDES AND CHARTS

North Brittany RCC Pilotage Foundation. N Heath. Imray. Covers St Malo to Ushant in detail.

Secret Anchorages of Brittany Peter Cumberlidge. Imray.

North Biscay RCC Pilotage Foundation. N Heath. Imray. Covers Brest to the Gironde in detail.

Admiralty, SHOM (French Hydrographic Service), Navicarte and Imray charts cover the coast in detail. They are readily available in most places including large centres in Brittany.

Legs on a local boat for drying out

This can cause some problems if the wind blows into the harbour and also from the wash of ferries and fishing boats entering or leaving harbour. In some anchorages there are mooring buoys to pick up, but check whether they belong to a local boat first.

Main charter bases
The main charter bases from north to south are at St Malo, Port La Fôret, Port de Crouesty and La Rochelle. Getting to any of these is relatively easy by air, train within France or probably the easiest option, by car and ferry. There are low cost airline flights within Europe to airports close to most charter areas.

Sailing area
Depending on the charter base, yachts cruise pretty much north or south along the coast. There are sufficient indentations and offshore islands so that you can vary the

Douarnenez on the Brittany coast

itinerary when returning to the charter base. Most charter companies on the west coast will restrict your cruising area to between Brest and La Rochelle. Yachts from St Malo will often go to the Channel Islands or in inclement weather can lock into the Rance estuary.

Land excursions

To some extent, in the Morbihan and the Loire river, you can get some distance inland by boat. Many will have driven to the charter base and it is not a bad idea to allot a couple of days to a leisurely drive back home so that you can dally along the way. On some of the islands, bicycles are available for hire and it is well worthwhile getting off the boat for half a day and exploring the island by bicycle. In much of the area there are peaceful walks to be had, whether to get to the local village bar a few miles away or to explore the rugged coast-line and get some exercise.

Most of the old towns and cities in the area are worth an excursion ashore, as much just to wander around and look in the shops and boutiques as to come to grips with the architecture and 'must see' monuments. On several of the islands there are the remains of fortresses built to defend the coast and at St Nazaire are the remains of the old German U-boat docks.

SCANDINAVIA

Everyone who charters in Scandinavia is an enthusiast on the area. The scenery is often spectacular, especially in the Norwegian fjords. In the Baltic there are islands everywhere and you will only be able to explore a small part of the archipelago off Sweden and Finland. The locals are sailing enthusiasts and it is no surprise that a large boat-building industry exists here, exporting yachts with famous marques like Swan, Baltic Yachts, Najad and Halberg Rassey all over the world.

Despite the long indented coastline of Scandinavia, there are no large charter companies operating here and only pockets of charter by small companies in a few places. The principal reason for this is the short summer season. Nonetheless, sailing in Scandinavia is well developed with large numbers of yachts registered in each country and extensive facilities for yachtsmen. Praise for this area is universal from those who charter there. Indeed its lack of tropical allure should not mean it gets struck off your list of possible destinations.

There is yacht charter in Denmark, Sweden and Finland and more limited opportunities in Norway. In the summer months the weather is reasonably settled and it can be surprisingly hot although evenings are always cool.

BEFORE YOU GO

For
✔ Wonderful cruising areas and friendly locals.
✔ Warmer in the high summer than you might think.
✔ No tides in the Baltic.
✔ In the high latitudes seeing the Aurora Borealis, the Midnight Sun.

Against
✘ All Scandinavian countries are expensive.
✘ Short season.

Types of charter
❖ Bareboat
❖ Skippered charter

Suitable for
❖ Novices to experienced sailors.

WHEN TO GO

The yachting season in Scandinavia lasts from mid-May to mid-September, with June–July being the high season. Effectively the low temperatures in May mean June to August are the best months. The long summer days, especially in the

At Copenhagen	Av max °C	Av min °C	Highest recorded	Relative humidity	Days 0.1 mm rain	Sea temp °C	Wind direction & force
Apr	10	3	22	68%	13	5	All dir F4
May	16	8	28	59%	11	8.5	E/W F3-4
Jun	19	11	33	60%	13	13.5	NW-W-SW F3-4
Jul	22	14	31	62%	14	16.5	NW-W-SW F3-4
Aug	21	14	31	64%	14	14	NW-W-SW F3-4
Sep	18	11	27	69%	15	15	All dir F4
Oct	12	7	20	76%	16	16	W-SW-S F4

At Stockholm	Av max °C	Av min °C	Highest recorded	Relative humidity	Days 0.1 mm rain	Sea temp °C	Wind direction & force
Apr	8	1	20	60%	11	1.5	N/S F3-4
May	14	6	28	53%	11	4.5	All dir F3
Jun	19	11	32	55%	13	8.5	SW-S F3
Jul	22	14	35	59%	13	14	SW-S F3-4
Aug	20	13	31	64%	14	15.5	SW F4
Sep	15	9	26	69%	14	12.5	SW F4
Oct	9	5	17	69%	14	9.5	SW F4-5

At Helsinki	Av max °C	Av min °C	Highest recorded	Relative humidity	Days 0.1 mm rain	Sea temp °C	Wind direction & force
May	14	4	26	58%	12	1	SW-S F3-4
Jun	19	9	31	59%	13	6	SW-S F3-4
Jul	22	13	33	63%	14	12	SW-S F3-4
Aug	20	12	30	67%	15	13	N/S F3-4
Sep	15	8	24	72%	15	10.5	All dir F4

Denmark

north, give you the opportunity to travel easily between anchorages and harbours. Around Denmark and southern Sweden and Norway the season can be longer, but in the north it can get very cold at night. The temperatures in the tables are average temperatures and this far north they mask dramatic swings between high day temperatures and low night temperatures. As the temperature changes can at times be dramatic, take adequate clothing and good wet weather gear.

GETTING THERE

There are regular scheduled flights to the capitals, to Copenhagen, Stockholm, Oslo and Helsinki. There are also scheduled flights by the no-frills airlines like EasyJet and Ryanair to over a dozen destinations in Sweden, Norway and Finland.

From northern Europe it is possible to drive to Scandinavia, but the distances are considerable and the actual size of the countries is disguised by the bunching together of latitude on the Mercator projection as you get towards the north pole. There are also train, coach and ferry connections, but generally it is best to fly to destinations in Sweden, Norway and Finland.

WHEN YOU'RE THERE

Visas and documentation
Members of the EU must carry their passport or identity card. Although access is not restricted there are frequent checks at airports and ports of entry. Most non-EU countries do not require visas.

In some cases proof of competence to handle a yacht may be asked for, but this is rare. The charter company will advise you on documentation and provide the relevant papers for the boat at the charter base.

Health
Medical services are excellent everywhere. Reciprocal medical care is available for EU nationals with the European Health Insurance card in Denmark, Sweden and

ESSENTIAL INFORMATION

Capitals Denmark/Copenhagen; Sweden/ Stockholm; Norway/Oslo; Finland/ Helsinki

Time zone Denmark, Sweden & Norway UT + 1. Finland UT + 2. From late September the time is put back 1 hour for 1 month.

Language Danish/ Swedish/ Norwegian/ Finnish. Swedish widely spoken in southern Finland. English widely spoken.

Telecommunications Automatic dialling. Code Denmark 45/ Sweden 46/ Norway 47/ Finland 358. GSM phones supported throughout Scandinavia. Internet cafés and wifi.

Finland and there is a reciprocal agreement between many countries with Norway. Health insurance is advisable as health care is expensive.

There are few health risks and no inoculations are necessary except standard tetanus. The only pests in the summer are mosquitoes, especially in the north, which are everywhere and ferocious little beasties. Take a good supply of insect repellent.

Money and banks
The unit of currency is the krone in Denmark, the krona in Sweden, the kroner in Norway and the Euro in Finland. Euros are widely accepted everywhere.

Banks are open around 0900–1500/1630 Mon–Fri. In Norway banks are open 0800–1530 Mon–Fri. Major credit cards and charge cards can be used in most centres of population to get goods and services. ATM machines are common and work with most foreign credit cards for cash advances.

Eating and drinking
Food in Scandinavia is good. The buffet style meal, which features hot and cold dishes plus bread, butter and cheese, is 69

SAILING GUIDES AND CHARTS

Cruising Guide to Germany and Denmark Brian Navin. Imray. Covers North Sea and Baltic coasts.

Arholma – Landsort and Gotland Lars Hassler and Lars Granath. Covers the Stockholm archipelago.

The Baltic Sea Anne Hammick. RCC Pilotage Foundation. Imray.

Norway Judy Lomax. RCC Pilotage Foundation. Imray.

commonly known as the Smörgåsbord and is a very Scandinavian affair. It is fresh, often features seafood, and for those who like clean uncluttered flavours, is a delight. It is also very expensive although lunches are less so compared to the evening meal. Fish, including the ubiquitous herring, salmon, whitefish and crustaceans, are prepared in all sorts of scrumptious ways. Meat includes interesting things like reindeer and elk meat. Usually vegetables and salads accompany these dishes. There are ethnic restaurants, Chinese, Lebanese, Turkish etc. where prices are cheaper and also local eating houses where there may be set menus. Vegetarians will have a hard time in Scandinavia where restaurants are not really geared up for them.

Alcohol has long been a state monopoly in the Scandinavian countries and it is quite simply costly. Beer is mostly of the lager type and wine is imported from southern Europe. Aquavit is worth trying once or twice.

Provisioning

There are supermarkets in the major centres of population and smaller shops elsewhere. There will be no problem finding what you want although it is expensive. Some of the pressed and processed meats are worth sampling as are fishy things like rollmops and gravad lax. If you are sailing off the beaten route in Norway or Finland remember that the population is scattered thinly in places and provision accordingly.

Costs

The overall cost of living is high and for eating out and provisioning it can be 2–3 times the EU average. Denmark is the least expensive followed by Sweden, then Norway and finally Finland where eating out is particularly expensive. On a boat you at least have the advantage of being able to cook on board and unless you intend to splash out very large amounts of money every evening, this gives you the chance to trim costs. Prices in supermarkets are likewise high and you need to shop carefully if you are on a budget.

Typical costs for eating out range from around €50 a head in Denmark and €60–100 in Sweden, Norway and Finland. This is for a restaurant meal with a bottle of wine and maybe a small beer. Ethnic restaurants and local eating houses are cheaper. The cost of wine with a meal can send the bill sky high with the cheapest house wine costing around €30 in Denmark and €50 in Norway.

Buying beer or wine in a supermarket or state controlled shop is a lot cheaper, but still 2–3 times above the EU average. When you arrive in any of these countries be sure to take full advantage of your duty free allowance. Even if you don't drink it, any alcohol will be a prized gift for anyone here.

Car hire and taxis throughout Scandinavia are uniformly much higher than the EU average. Taxi fares commonly have a minimum charge of around €5–7 when you step inside and rates per kilometre are high. There are also a lot of unlicensed taxis that can empty your holiday funds with one trip – take an official cab. Car hire is typically €200 a week in Sweden for the cheapest car with unlimited mileage, but you may be able to arrange special deals before you leave.

Crime and personal safety

Scandinavia is one of the safest places to visit in Europe with very low rates of violent crime and theft and most of these concentrated in the cities. Invariably the people are helpful and polite and with a few normal precautions it is unlikely you will be troubled by anything anywhere.

CHARTER AREAS

DENMARK

Denmark forms a natural land bridge across the western end of the Baltic Sea and the best sailing here is in the Baltic. All charter is within the Kattegat around the islands of Fyen (Funen) and Sjoelland off the eastern side of Denmark proper. Yachts potter around the indented coast and between the smaller islands with a good choice of

marinas, yacht harbours and anchorages available. Actual charter bases tend to shift but are usually around Fyen and Copenhagen.

Tides in this area, a sort of halfway house between the Baltic and the North Sea, are not great, but in confined channels can reach appreciable rates – up to 5 knots in the channel between Helsinger and Helsingbord has been recorded. Most of the currents are north-going with the water from the Baltic escaping into the North Sea, but there can be curious reversals of currents depending on

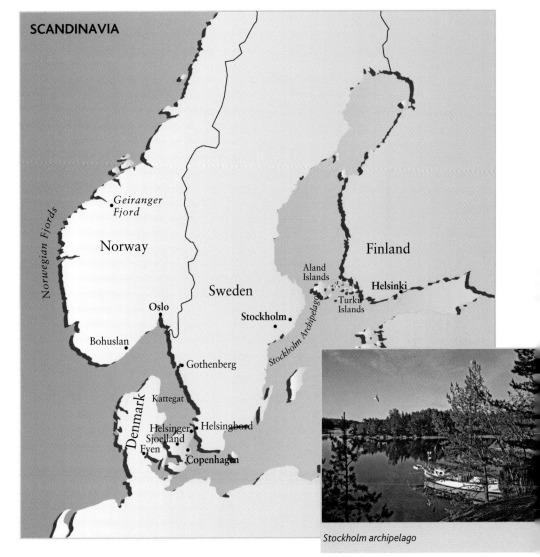

SCANDINAVIA

Norwegian Fjords

Geiranger Fjord

Norway

Oslo

Bohuslan

Gothenberg

Kattegat

Denmark

Helsinger Helsingbord
Sjoelland
Fyen
Copenhagen

Sweden

Stockholm

Stockholm Archipelago

Aland Islands

Turku Islands

Finland

Helsinki

Stockholm archipelago

the conditions, particularly if there is a depression around.

Winds are variable depending on the passage of pressure zones across the area. In the summer there will often be westerlies influenced by the continental land mass.

The area is suitable for those with a little experience up to more experienced crews.

SWEDEN

Most charter here is out of Stockholm in the Baltic where the much indented natural harbour allows for plenty of exploration along with an indented coastline to the north and south. The Stockholm archipelago in the approaches to Stockholm proper provides a myriad choice of anchorages and routes amongst the many islands and islets. There are also yachts in Gothenburg on the western coast of Sweden. There are yacht marinas and yacht harbours here and numerous anchorages everywhere. The coastline is so indented that you can easily find your own little patch. Many of the small islands have

holiday homes on them with a private jetty and if you enquire, you may be able to use a jetty to tie up alongside overnight. You may even get invited ashore, but do not ramble ashore without permission as many of the islands/islets are privately owned.

Winds here are mostly sea and land breezes with the predominant sea breeze blowing from the SE. Tides in the Baltic are of course next to non-existent although there may be surface drift currents set up by the wind blowing constantly from one direction.

NORWAY

Most charter is out of the capital Oslo with some adventure charter operating further north. There are a few yacht marinas and numerous harbours which a yacht can use. There are enough anchorages to satisfy anyone for a long, long time in surroundings that the word magnificent doesn't do justice to.

Most bareboat or small skippered yachts will cruise around the coast near Oslo. However some adventure cruises now go

Bohuslan, Sweden

much further north past the Arctic Circle and here the sailing, while hard, takes you to areas that are well off traditional cruising routes and where the surroundings are spectacular. The Gulf Stream running up the side of Norway keeps things warmer than you might think although temperatures can suddenly plummet at times. The midnight sun (late May to late July) throws body clocks out of sync but is a phenomenon well worth experiencing and the Norwegians just seem to forget about sleeping altogether.

FINLAND

Most charter is out of Turku near the Aland Islands although there is some charter from Helsinki. There are also some charter bases through the islands themselves. The Aland Islands are a huge archipelago of islands and islets lying off the SW corner of Finland and indeed stretching pretty well right across to Sweden.

The area is well charted but navigation amongst the islands and islets needs constant attention to rocks and reefs in the channels which thankfully are well marked. There are a number of marinas, yacht harbours and the possibility of mooring at private jetties on some of the islands. As far as the latter goes it is always necessary to get permission although having done so you

Geiranger Fjord, Norway

may find the owner of the jetty provides additional hospitality for nothing more than a bit of conversation. Most of the islands are part or wholly privately owned and are used just during the summer although there are permanent settlements as well.

The most popular sailing period is July and August although the months either side are warm enough. The prevailing wind is a sea breeze blowing from the NE on the eastern side going to east and SE on the Swedish side. As elsewhere in the Baltic tides are virtually non-existent.

ANCHORING SCANDINAVIAN STYLE

Around much of Scandinavia the depths drop off quickly and when anchoring it is common practice to drop the anchor and then take a line ashore. It is also necessary to do this in tight inlets where there is insufficient room to swing to an anchor. In many places you can get the yacht nearly right up to the shore. It takes a bit of practice and co-ordination between the helmsman, the person on the anchor and whoever is delegated to row the line ashore, but after the first or second time it becomes a relatively easy process.

Other Northern European Destinations

NETHERLANDS

A number of charter companies operate in the Netherlands offering bareboat and skippered charter. There are numerous opportunities to charter traditional Dutch sailing yachts such as the botter, complete with leeboards and lots of bits of string to pull on the gaff rig. The Dutch are passionate about their sailing and spend a lot of time on the water in both traditional craft and more high-tech yachts.

Nearly all of the sailing in the Netherlands goes on in the protected inland stretches of water, especially the Ijsselmeer. The outer 'sea' coast of the Netherlands is beset by shifting sandbanks and has few harbours that are not actually in the inner enclosed areas. It is also one long lee shore to the prevailing winds. It should not be assumed that the inner areas are tame bits of water as in strong winds they get very rough and are not at all pleasant places to be out and about on.

The authorities in the Netherlands are very strict about certification and you will need to have a certificate of competence such as the RYA Helmsmans certificate and a VHF licence.

GERMANY AND POLAND

The German and Polish coasts are interesting areas, but demanding on navigation and seamanship. There are numerous shifting sandbanks, strong currents in places, and few harbours with all-weather access. It is also a comparatively flat and uninspiring coast although ashore there is much of interest to do and see.

Germany's yachting history is well known, but its neighbour Poland also has a long yachting tradition. For both countries there is little charter around apart from local skippered charter which is the recommended way to go along this coast.

BALTIC STATES

All the Baltic states and neighbouring Russia have a long seafaring tradition. In recent years the interest in yachting has increased dramatically since it is no longer seen as an elitist occupation of the West. Not surprisingly many of the inhabitants of this area sail south to the sun and longer seasons.

There is little in the way of yacht charter in the old Baltic states of Latvia, Lithuania and Estonia, but some skippered charter is available and it may be possible to get a bareboat here with some research. Neighbouring Russia also has skippered charter and again it may be possible to organise a bareboat.

MEDITERRANEAN

On a map of the world the Mediterranean looks like a big lake at the bottom of Europe. Compared to the Atlantic, it looks like a backwater creek running inland from the sea. But it exerts a pull way beyond its geographical scale on all of us. For some, it is a place where the sun shines from an azure sky, over an anchorage with a few white fishermen's houses ashore. For others, the virtual absence of tides removes at a stroke a complication of sailing that has bedevilled them for years. It is warm spray over the bows, from a blue sea. It is a sea stretching from the Occident to the Orient, a sea surrounded by a variety of countries and cultures that have played a significant part in shaping our own history. Whatever the images are, they wield a powerful lure on us to visit this sea and sail around it: although you'll have to find out for yourself whether they reflect the reality.

There are problems particular to the Mediterranean, and variations on problems encountered in sailing elsewhere. The weather is an example. In many parts of the world weather patterns can be reliably predicted by observing cloud, pressure and wind changes. In the Mediterranean the track and speed of a depression can vary so much that weather forecasts give little indication of what is going to happen locally, or worse give you yesterday's weather. Thermal effects in the summer can change the weather with frightening rapidity from a flat calm to a gale in half an hour.

SAILING GUIDES AND CHARTS

Adlard Coles Book of Mediterranean Cruising Rod Heikell. Adlard Coles Nautical.

Mediterranean Cruising Handbook Rod Heikell. Imray.

Berthing stern or bows-to is standard practice in the Mediterranean and you are going to have to sort out how to do it one way or another

There are also new techniques to learn and old ones to be refined. Berthing Mediterranean style, either stern or bows-to the quay with an anchor holding you off, is the accepted practice in nine out of ten harbours, and you are going to have to learn to do it without fuss or bother – even when the space looks impossibly small and it's blowing half a gale. Anchoring techniques need to be carefully examined as you will often be anchoring in deep water on a weedy bottom that will apparently defy your best attempts at getting the anchor to bite. You will need to learn to anchor with a long line ashore, a common practice in many anchorages in the Mediterranean.

GIBRALTAR

Once seen, the Rock of Gibraltar is never forgotten. It stands sentinel at the entrance to the Straits of Gibraltar between Europe and North Africa a short distance away and has always been of strategic importance for the flow of maritime traffic in and out of the straits it gives its name to. Gibraltar town sits on a narrow strip of land around the

BEFORE YOU GO

For

✔ Access to Costa del Sol and Morocco

Against

✗ Often strong winds and significant tides in the Strait of Gibraltar.

ESSENTIAL INFORMATION

Time zone UT + 1 DST Apr–Sep

Language English

Telecommunications Automatic dialling. Code 350. GSM phones work here. Internet and wifi available

Electricity 240V 50Hz AC

SAILING GUIDES AND CHARTS

Imray Mediterranean Almanac editor Rod Heikell. Imray. Covers Gibraltar and the Strait of Gibraltar.

Costa del Sol and Blanca Robin Brandon. Imray. Covers Gibraltar.

Reeds Western Mediterranean Almanac. Adlard Coles Nautical.

Admiralty charts cover Gibraltar and approaches.

The Mediterranean

1 Gibraltar
2 Balearics
3 South of France
4 Corsica & Sardinia
5 Italian Riviera & Tuscan Islands
6 Naples to Sicily
7 Malta
8 Slovenia & Croatia
9 Ionian
10 Saronic
11 Cyclades
12 Northern Sporades
13 Khalkidiki
14 Dodecanese
15 Bodrum to Marmaris
16 Marmaris to Antalya
17 Cyprus
18 Tunisia

THE MEDITERRANEAN

western side of the protected anchorage under the 'rock'.

There are a number of small charter companies and sailing schools based here. Sailing schools based in Gibraltar benefit from the fact that you get tidal experience here whereas in the rest of the Mediterranean you do not. Yachts usually head off for either Atlantic or Mediterranean Spain or Morocco.

WHEN TO GO

The season runs from around mid-May to mid-September although the sailing schools operate throughout the year.

GETTING THERE

There are scheduled flights from Britain and some charter flights in the summer to Gibraltar or you can get budget flights to Malaga.

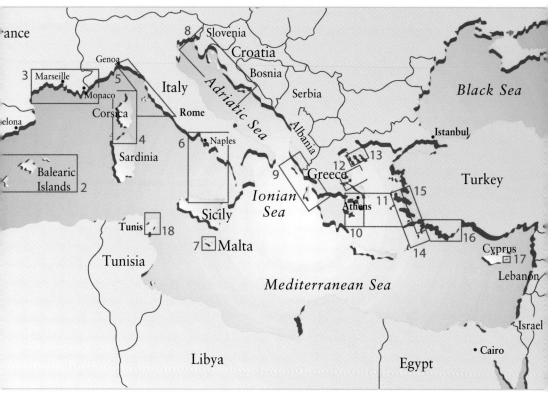

WHEN YOU'RE THERE

Visas and documentation
Members of the EU must carry their passports. Gibraltar is not a full EU member but most EU nationals and most non-EU nationals do not require visas.

Sailing area
Charter yachts based in Gibraltar usually cruise along the Spanish Mediterranean coast or along the Atlantic coast once through the Strait Of Gibraltar. They also often cross to Morocco and the Spanish enclave of Ceuta. The Strait of Gibraltar is a windy area and one of the few areas in the Mediterranean subject to significant tides. The sailing schools all operate skippered boats and any charters here will usually be skippered or for bareboat the skipper must be experienced. It is not an area for beginners.

Gibraltar, looking up at the 'Rock'

SPAIN

Spain has been identified with huge hotels and cheap resorts along its coast for decades and there is some truth in that along the Costa del Sol and nearby costas. Around the Costa Brava and the Balearics you come across a wilder coast, though in truth there is still a lot of development. At least in a sailing boat you can escape much of it.

Ashore there is still all that hustle and bustle of Mediterranean life on the go. When the sun goes down the locals take their leisurely evening stroll, the paseo, in the cool of the evening and the bars and cafés come alive with people drinking, eating and exchanging all the latest gossip. Spanish food has all those wonderful tapas where you can pick and mix flavours and textures to your heart's content.

Inland in the Balearics is wilder and less crowded than you might imagine. It's worth taking a hire car to explore the interior away from life on the coast where small villages are perched on hilltops and in valleys looking down to the coast and the Mediterranean beyond.

Spain, despite its long coastline, has little charter except around the Balearics. Probably 90% plus of yacht charter in Spain is based around Majorca, Ibiza and Minorca.

ESSENTIAL INFORMATION

Capital Madrid

Time zone UT + 1 DST Apr–Sep.

Language Castillian Spanish. Catalan. Some English and French.

Telecommunications Automatic dialling. Code 34. GSM phones supported throughout Spain. Internet cafés and wifi.

Electricity 220/125V 50Hz AC.

BEFORE YOU GO

For
- ✔ Good mix of marinas, harbours and anchorages around the coast.
- ✔ Picturesque rocky coastline.
- ✔ Good food and bars ashore.
- ✔ Settled summer weather patterns.
- ✔ Cruising programme can be extended from Majorca to Ibiza or Menorca to get more sailing in.

Against
- ✘ Possibility of strong winds in spring and autumn.
- ✘ Many of the calas have been turned into marinas restricting the number of anchorages.

Types of charter
- ❖ Sailing in company
- ❖ Bareboat
- ❖ Skippered charter
- ❖ Luxury charter

Suitable for
- ❖ Novices to experienced.

Between these islands there is a good mix of marinas, harbours and anchorages within convenient sailing distances. Much of the mainland charter is from the coast adjacent to the Balearics.

WHEN TO GO

The season in Spain runs from around mid-May to mid-September although weather patterns do not settle down properly until June.

Early season Mid-May to June. Day temperatures are warm, 22–30°C in the day and evenings are balmy. Sea temperatures have not warmed up at this time of year at

At Palma (Majorca)	Av max °C	Av min °C	Highest recorded	Relative humidity	Days 0.1 mm rain	Sea temp °C	Wind direction & force
Apr	19	10	26	66%	6	14	NE/SW F3-4
May	22	13	31	67%	5	17	NE-E/SW F3
Jun	26	17	37	65%	3	20	NE-E/SW-S F3
Jul	29	20	39	65%	1	23.5	NE-E/SW-S F3
Aug	29	20	37	65%	3	24.5	S-NE F3
Sep	27	18	35	69%	5	23.5	SW-NE F3
Oct	23	14	31	71%	9	20.5	N-NE F3-4
Nov	18	10	26	47%	8	17	W-NE F4

around 15–17°C. The sea breeze, the *brisa de mar*, blows intermittently. There is a good chance of a *tramontana* or *mestrale* blowing up to Force 7–8 (28–40 knots) from the NW-N-NE. There is on average 3–5 days of rain per month.

High season June to mid-September. Day temperatures are hot, often around 29–32°C, and evenings are pleasantly warm. Sea temperatures are around 23–24°C. Wind patterns have settled down and the *brisa de mar*, blowing from the NE-SE along the coast and the east-SE over the Balearics, is the prevailing wind. There is still a chance of a *tramontana* blowing, though usually at less than gale force.

Late season To the end of September. Air temperatures are around 27–29°C and sea temperatures remain as for the high season. There is a likelihood of a *tramontana* blowing at gale force.

GETTING THERE

There are daily scheduled flights, both from national and budget airlines from many European destinations, charter flights to most of the Mediterranean coast, and internal flights between the airports. Budget flights run all through the year to the Balearics (to Mallorca, Ibiza and Menorca)

and charter flights run for most of the year. The Spanish Mediterranean coast and the Balearics are probably the easiest places to fly to from northern Europe and competition is fierce so prices are keen.

There are regular ferry services from Barcelona to Palma and Menorca and also ferries and hydrofoils from Alicante and Valencia. It is possible to drive from nearby European countries and put the car on the ferry from Barcelona to Palma, but this is not a cheap option and you are better off flying. Barcelona is connected by good rail services.

Getting to the charter base will usually involve a taxi or bus. If the charter company offers a transfer service use it as it is much the easiest way of getting from the airport to the charter base.

WHEN YOU'RE THERE

Visas and documentation

Members of the EU must carry their passport or identity card although there are no real controls on internal EU borders. Most non-EU countries do not require visas.

In some cases proof of competence to handle a boat will be asked for and you should carry a recognised qualification, although this is rare. If you are worried consult the charter company. All other boat documentation will be provided by the company although it will rarely be asked for.

Andraitx on Mallorca

Health

Medical services range from good to excellent. Reciprocal medical care for EU nationals. It is advised you take out private medical insurance for the trip as medical costs are high. Most charter operators will be able to organise something and flotilla operators and some bareboat operators make travel insurance mandatory.

The water is potable everywhere. Those with delicate stomachs and babies should drink bottled water.

Money and banks

The unit of currency is the Euro.

Banks are open 0900–1400 Mon–Fri and 0900–1300 Sat. Exchange offices and travel agents operate outside these hours. All major credit cards and charge cards commonly accepted. ATM machines are common and work with most major credit cards.

Eating and drinking

Spanish food is varied fare which unfortunately has been swamped in some of the more popular resorts by the ubiquitous steak and chips, so loved by the English. My advice is to stay away from these places and seek out local restaurants which will have an interesting variety of stews, grilled meat and fish, and tapas. The latter are small dishes of anything from roast meats, vegetables in a vinaigrette, salads, olives of all types, and fried seafood, which you order individually and gives you the chance to sample all sorts of things you might not otherwise have tried as a plateful. *Paella* is of course everywhere, but remember a good paella takes time to cook and if you see it arriving instantly at another table as soon as it is ordered, try it elsewhere.

Most restaurants offer a *menu del dia* or set menu which will usually have three courses for a set price. These are generally good value. Don't be afraid to investigate dishes and stay away from 'English pubs' and anyone offering 'English food' (how do they have the gall?) and you will find interesting and tasty food.

Spanish wine is good, relatively cheap and has some excellent varieties which are little known outside Spain. Local wine can often be bought by the carafe in restaurants and this is a good way to get going. Spanish beer is of the lager type and eminently thirst quenching. Spirits are cheap and Spanish brandy is not at all bad.

Provisioning

All provisions are easily found in the larger towns and resorts and most supermarkets will have some recognisable names on the shelves and clearly priced goods. At Palma there are several supermarkets which supply yachts and will deliver to the yacht. In the larger towns there are good fish markets, bakeries and groceries cum delicatessens which have good cured meats, salamis and a mind-boggling range of olives.

Costs

The overall cost of living is medium plus on EU averages. Typical costs for eating out are €20–30 a head and up depending on the class of restaurant. Local wine is around €10 a bottle in a restaurant and beer is around €2–3 in a bar. Provisioning is on a par with other EU countries and wine and beer is cheap in the supermarkets.

Public transport is relatively cheap and bus and rail services are good. Taxis are moderate and hire cars average at around €30–40 a day. Motorbikes can be rented in a number of places.

Crime and personal safety

Mugging and petty theft occur with increasing frequency in Spain, but for those cruising in the Balearics the chances of anything happening are very low. Afloat you are unlikely to have any problems but the yacht should always be locked when you leave it to go ashore and loose items on deck should be locked to the boat or removed. When wandering around ashore, few precautions are necessary except perhaps in the larger resorts and cities. If you do not ostentatiously display items like cameras and camcorders or expensive jewellery, you are unlikely to be troubled.

CHARTER AREAS

BALEARICS

The Balearics account for more than 90% of charter in Spain with most charter bases in Mallorca. The three major islands provide a large cruising area with numerous marinas, harbours and anchorages in the calas around their coasts. All charter here is either skippered or bareboat although at times there are 'cruises in company' with between three and five boats. The climate is hot in the summer with temperatures frequently around 30–32°C, although there is frequently a cooling breeze.

Wind and sea

The prevailing summer wind is the *brisa del mar* blowing from the east-SE over the islands. It typically gets up at midday, blows at Force 3–6 (7–27 knots) and dies in the evening. At times the *tramontana* will blow down from the Gulf of Lions and this can blow up to Force 8 (40 knots) at times, especially in the spring and autumn. In the summer the *tramontana* is rare and does not blow as strongly.

Seas around the Balearics are generally higher than in more enclosed areas of the

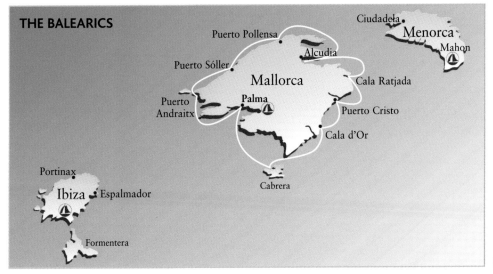

THE BALEARICS

Ciudadela
Puerto Pollensa
Menorca
Mahon
Alcudia
Puerto Sóller
Mallorca
Cala Ratjada
Puerto Andraitx
Palma
Puerto Cristo
Cala d'Or
Portinax
Cabrera
Ibiza · Espalmador
Formentera

SAILING GUIDES AND CHARTS

There are several useful guides to Mediterranean Spain. British produced guides are best purchased before you go or you may have difficulty tracking them down. The following may be useful:

East Spain Pilot (in 3 volumes: *Costa del Sol and Blanca, Islas Baleares, Costa del Azahar, Dorada and Brava*) RCC. Imray. Covers the Mediterranean Spanish coast and Balearics in detail.

The Yachtsman's Directory ed. Richard Ashton. PubliNautic. Annual publication in English and Spanish covering marinas around the Spanish coast. Available in Palma.

Admiralty charts cover all areas adequately. Imray produce a set of small scale charts. Spanish charts give excellent coverage.

Mediterranean. Even when it is calm there may be a ground swell from wind blowing elsewhere in the sea area around the Balearics. With the *tramontana* a steep high sea is set up from the north-NE and care is needed. Some harbours can be difficult to enter with a heavy *tramontana* blowing.

Suitable for...
The Balearics are suitable for intermediate to experienced sailors. A number of companies have tried to run flotillas around Mallorca but for various reasons these have failed, but there is no reason why a group of beginners cannot get together with some more experienced crews and arrange a cruise in company.

Harbours and anchorages
Around the islands there are now numerous marinas, as well as fishing harbours and calas, the latter being the name for rocky inlets. Mallorca is the most developed of the three major islands with numerous marinas all the way around the coast. Palma is one of the hubs of yachting in the western Mediterranean and is a cosmopolitan place. Out of Palma you will be surprised at some of the wonderfully isolated and beautiful places that can be found, something belied by the huge numbers of tourists which arrive here in the summer. In some of the anchorages you will be anchoring with a long line ashore as there is not room to swing. Berthing in the harbours is stern or bow-to using laid moorings in the marinas and your own anchor in a few other harbours.

Main charter bases
Mallorca/Palma and nearby harbours The main charter base for most companies. Scheduled, charter and internal flights. Transfer time is around 30 minutes.
Menorca/Mahon Small charter base. Transfer time around 20 minutes.
Ibiza/Ibiza Small charter base.

Sailing area
Most yachts will content themselves with sailing around Mallorca. Some will venture across to Ibiza or Menorca before returning to Mallorca unless on a one-way charter.

Onward routes
Some charter companies arrange one-way routes between the Balearics and the mainland coast around Barcelona, but you will need to have experience of night sailing to do the overnight trip. It is around 125 miles from Barcelona to Palma. One-way trips can sometimes be arranged between Palma and Ibiza and Palma and Menorca.

Other charter bases
Around Barcelona and Valencia there are small charter bases where yachts can be hired to explore the adjacent coast.

A typical two-week intermediate itinerary is as follows.

Palma – circumnavigation of Majorca – Palma

Total 180 miles

Starts at Palma

Day 1	**Puerto Andraitx**	Large steep-sided bay with a yacht harbour at the NE end. Berth stern or bow-to or anchor off. Restaurants.
Day 2	**Puerto Soller**	Enclosed bay with a fishing harbour tucked into the NE corner. Stern or bow-to if room or anchor off. Restaurants.
Day 3	**Puerto de Pollensa**	Yacht harbour in the NW corner of the magnificent Bay of Pollensa. Restaurants.
Day 4	**Puerto de Alcudia**	Marina in the NW corner of the magnificent Bay of Alcudia. Stern or bow-to. Restaurants.
Day 5	Lay day	Sail around the bay or just relax.
Day 6	**Cala Ratjada**	Short hop around the eastern corner of Mallorca. Berth stern or bow-to in the yacht section of the harbour. Restaurants.
Day 7	**Puerto Cristo**	A dog-leg cala where the marina is hidden from view until you are right up to the entrance. Stern or bow-to. Restaurants.
Day 8	Lay day	Visit the Caves of Drach.
Day 9	**Cala d'Or**	Another dog-leg cala with a marina tucked into the west creek. Stern or bow-to. Restaurants.
Day 10	**Cabrera Island**	You will need a permit to visit here. Moorings. A maritime reserve. Alternatively go to Puerto de la Rapita.
Day 11/12	Two lay days	There are bays and harbours around the south coast.
Day 13	**Palma**	

The itinerary can be significantly extended by including Ibiza. It is around 65 miles from Palma to Puerto Ibiza. Remember to allow for getting back in the event of unsettled weather.

Land excursions

Palma	This large city has much to do and see in it including the huge cathedral, various churches, good markets, shopping galore, Bellver castle and an outdoor reconstructed Spanish village/museum.
Cuevas del Drach	A labyrinth of caves that can be explored by boat. Near Puerto Cristo.
La Cartuja	Chopin lovers will want to visit this monastery in the highlands where Chopin and his lover George Sands spent the winter of 1838, described in Sands's, *A Winter in Majorca*.

FRANCE

In the 18th century sun-starved northerners started migrating to the French Côte d'Azur and the Riviera to escape the cold winters. It started a fashion that continues to this day and the south of France is still a fashionable resort and one of the oldest in the modern world. For this reason it has less of the awful high-rise that blights so many other coasts and more gentle 18th- and 19th century architecture along the coast. This gives it a stability and vaguely genteel veneer that anyone sailing along the coast will soon come to appreciate. There are good restaurants, chic boutiques, elegant squares with cafés for a mid-morning coffee or post prandial drink.

Neighbouring Corsica by contrast is a rough diamond with granite mountains rising sheer from the sea. It is a more savage place where the seas beat onto rocky coasts and the roads wind precariously around the cliffs and mountains. Fortunately the French influence means you will still find good food and drink in the populated areas.

Along the Mediterranean coast of France there are probably more marinas per mile than anywhere else in the Mediterranean or the world for that matter. However the large

ESSENTIAL INFORMATION

Capital Paris

Time zone UT + 1 DST Apr–Sep

Language French. Italian and English spoken in some areas.

Telecommunications Automatic dialling. Country code 33. GSM phones supported throughout France and Corsica. A few internet cafés and wifi.

Electricity 220V 50Hz AC.

BEFORE YOU GO

FRANCE
For
- ✔ Sympathetic marinas and harbours in chic resorts.
- ✔ Cuisine ashore that is superb, often superlative, and excellent value for money.
- ✔ Good wines at good prices.
- ✔ Easy sailing along a coast dotted with marinas.
- ✔ Festivals and exhibitions.
- ✔ Settled summer weather patterns.

Against
- ✘ Marinas and harbours often crowded and expensive in the summer.
- ✘ Few anchorages' all of which will be hideously crowded in the summer.
- ✘ Gulf of Lions area can be windy in the summer and very windy in spring and autumn.

CORSICA
For
- ✔ Settled summer weather patterns and consistent winds.
- ✔ Lots of wonderful anchorages and clear turquoise water.
- ✔ Breathtaking mountain backdrop.
- ✔ A cruise can easily encompass Corsica and Sardinia from one of the more southerly charter bases.
- ✔ A good mix of marinas and harbours in between anchorages.
- ✔ Good food and convivial bars ashore.

Against
- ✘ Chance of strong winds and heavy seas in spring and autumn.
- ✘ Some navigation is tricky in the rock-strewn Strait of Bonifacio.
- ✘ Costs in Sardinia can be high for eating out and harbour charges.

Types of charter
- ❖ Flotilla
- ❖ Bareboat
- ❖ Skippered charter
- ❖ Luxury charter

Suitable for
- ❖ Intermediate to experienced although less experienced can take skippered charter.

Marseille	Av max °C	Av min °C	Highest recorded	Relative humidity	Days 0.1 mm rain	Sea temp °C	Wind direction & force
Apr	18	8	29	54%	7	13.5	NW F4-5
May	22	11	31	54%	8	16	NW F4
Jun	26	15	37	50%	4	18.5	NW F3-4
Jul	29	17	39	45%	2	20.5	NW F3-4
Aug	28	17	37	49%	5	21.5	NW F3-4
Sep	25	15	34	54%	6	20.5	SW/SE F3-4
Oct	20	10	29	61%	8	18	NW F4
Nov	15	6	23	66%	9	16	NW F4

Ajaccio (Corsica)	Av max °C	Av min °C	Highest recorded	Relative humidity	Days 0.1 mm rain	Sea temp °C	Wind direction & force
Apr	18	7	29	66%	9	14	NW-W F3-4
May	21	10	33	69%	8	17	NW-W-SW F 3-4
Jun	25	11	37	65%	4	20	NW-W F3-4
Jul	27	13	37	65%	1	22.5	NW-W F3
Aug	28	13	39	64%	2	23.5	NW-W F3-4
Sep	26	12	36	64%	6	22	NW-W F3-4
Oct	22	11	31	63%	10	19.5	NW-W/SE F3-4

offshore island of Corsica with a good mix of harbours and anchorages extends the cruising area with almost as much coastline again and significantly adds to the attractions of cruising in Mediterranean France. Charter mostly tends to be concentrated around a number of marinas along the Cote d'Azur and Riviera and in Corsica.

WHEN TO GO

The season in France runs from around mid-May to mid-September although really settled weather can only be expected from June to early September.

Early season Mid–May to mid-June. Day temperatures are warm, around 22–29°C in the day, but drop at night. Sea temperatures have not yet warmed up at around 13–17°C.

Wind patterns are irregular and there is the likelihood of gale force winds from the north (the *mistral*) or south. There are on average 4–8 days of rain per month.

High season June to mid-September. Day temperatures are hot, often around 26–30°C, and the evenings are balmy. On windless days it can feel very hot. Sea temperatures are around 21–23°C. Wind patterns have settled down and there is usually an onshore sea breeze. Along the Gulf of Lyon and around Marseille the *tramontane* or *mistral* may blow, occasionally up to Force 6–7 (22–33 knots), making it feel a lot cooler.

Late season To the end of September. Air temperatures are around 25–28°C and sea temperatures remain as for the high season. 85

The *mistral* and *tramontane* is more likely to blow and a depression may pass through bringing strong southerlies.

GETTING THERE

In France proper there are daily scheduled flights, national and budget to Perpignan, Marignane (Marseille), and Nice from many European airports. In the summer there are some charter flights to Marignane and Nice. Good and comfortable Eurostar and TGV connections from the UK and other European countries. It is also an easy enough drive to the south of France from many European countries.

There are national and budget flights to Ajaccio, Bastia and Figari in Corsica. In the summer there are charter flights as well. There are also internal flights from France to Calvi, Ajaccio, Figari and Bastia. You can also get a ferry to Calvi, Ajaccio or Bastia from the south of France or Italy.

Getting to the charter base will usually involve a bus or taxi trip if you do not drive. If the charter company offers a transfer service this should be taken as it is much the easiest way of getting from the airport to the charter base, especially on Corsica.

WHEN YOU'RE THERE

Visas and documentation

Members of the EU must carry their passport or identity card although there are no real controls on internal EU borders. Most non-EU countries do not require visas.

In some cases proof of competence to handle a yacht will be asked for. All other boat documentation will be provided by the company, but it will rarely be asked for. Occasionally the customs (Douane) make spot checks on boats and in this case all documents should be presented.

Health

Medical services are excellent. Reciprocal medical care for EU nationals. It is advised you take out private medical insurance for the trip although medical costs are reasonable. Most charter operators will be able to organise something and flotilla operators and some bareboat operators make travel insurance mandatory.

The water is potable everywhere. Those with delicate stomachs, and babies, should drink bottled water.

Money and banks

The unit of currency is the Euro. Banks are open 0830–1200 and 1400–1700 Mon–Fri although hours may vary in the summer. All major credit cards and charge cards are commonly accepted. ATM machines are common and work with most major credit cards.

Eating and drinking

I hardly need to recommend French cuisine although I do believe its reputation out-shines the reality in many restaurants. That said most French food is of superior quality and exceptional value. Even Corsican food which once had a bad reputation has improved significantly. The French are serious about food, sometimes to the point of pomposity, and you should indulge yourself and immerse your palate in the national hobby of eating good food and drinking good wine. This is a country for gourmets and gourmands alike.

A French meal usually has a *hors d'oeuvre* which can range from a salad to finely prepared seafood or patés, the main course which is nearly always meat or fish accompanied by a garnish or vegetables, and a dessert. As you go up the scale of restaurant, more dishes can be jammed between these. Many restaurants offer a tourist menu, usually with a choice of dishes for each course on it, and these can be exceptional value.

Seafood should be sampled somewhere along the way, preferably several times over. The French know about seafood and if nothing else, you should try a few oysters, a *moule marinière*, fish soup or a *bouillabaise*, and a freshly caught fish or crustacean of some description.

French wine is a bargain although restaurants add a substantial percentage of profit on top of the base price. Local wine by the carafe is usually good value after which you can start by price, region, variety or just at random to begin sampling the massive choice available. Most of it is good, all of it is relatively cheap for the quality, and some of it is just exquisite. Although new-world single variety wines are good, they cannot touch the subtlety of blended varietal wines. French beer is of the lager type, light and fizzy, and eminently palatable. Spirits are relatively cheap. The coffee is good and an institution.

Provisioning

All provisions are easily found in the larger towns and resorts and most supermarkets will have recognisable brands all clearly priced. Unfortunately the large super-markets are often in out-of-town sites and can be difficult to get to from a harbour without a car. At a number of harbours there are supermarkets who will supply yachts and deliver goods to you on the boat. In somewhere like Antibes you can order everything from groceries to handmade chocolates from the boat. If possible go to the local *Les Halles* for fresh fruit and

SAILING GUIDES AND CHARTS

There are numerous guides to Mediterranean France. Obtaining English guides in France can be difficult except in places like Antibes and Beaulieu, so they are best purchased before going on charter. The following may be useful.

Mediterranean France and Corsica Rod Heikell. Imray. Covers Mediterranean France and Corsica in detail.

Reeds Western Mediterranean Almanac Adlard Coles Nautical.

Admiralty charts cover all areas only just adequately. French hydrographic (SHOM) charts give more detailed coverage. Navicarte yachtsmen's charts are available in many areas.

vegetables, cheeses of which there are many regional varieties, and good fresh fish and shellfish. And of course there are all the local *boulangeries*, *patisseries*, *charcuteries* and *poisonneries*.

Costs

The overall cost of living is medium on EU averages and for food France is particularly good value. Typical costs for eating out range from €20 a head for a half reasonable *Menu Turistique* and upwards depending on how high you want to go. Local wine is around €5 for a pichet and €10–25 a bottle in a restaurant and beer is around €2 a *demi* in a bar. Provisioning is on a par with other EU countries except for wine and beer which is cheap in supermarkets. Cured meats and cheeses are excellent and good value and seafood is reasonably priced and invariably fresh.

Public transport is reasonably priced, comfortable and efficient – this after all is the land of the TGV (*Train à Grande Vitesse*). Taxis are expensive and hire cars are also expensive at around €30–40 a day. Mountain bikes can be rented in a few places.

Ashore in La Ciotat

Crime and personal safety

Muggings and petty theft exist in France (foreign cars seem to be a speciality for break-ins) but on the whole the charterer afloat is unlikely to encounter much in the way of local crime. Care should be taken to lock the boat and remove all expensive items from the deck. Alternatively lock items like outboard motors and dinghies to the boat as any loss will probably come off your safety deposit. When wandering around larger cities like Marseille and Cannes care should be taken not to ostentatiously display valuables such as cameras, camcorders and expensive watches and jewellery.

CHARTER AREAS

SOUTH OF FRANCE

There are no obvious clusters of charter boats with bases being distributed all along the coast. Most bases are smallish affairs with half a dozen boats at most. Some of the more important charter bases are at Argelès, Marseille, Bandol, Bormes-les-Mimosas (larger base), Le Lavandou, Hyères, Toulon, Saint Mandrier, Cogolin, Cannes, Antibes, and Nice. This list is not exhaustive and new

bases come and go every year. There are major airports handling European flights at Marignane (Marseille) and Nice and smaller airports at Perpignan and Hyères. There are good road and rail connections all along the south of France.

Wind and sea

Along the Côte d'Azur and Riviera from Toulon to the Italian border, the prevailing wind is a sea breeze, the *vent du midi*, blowing onto the land from the S-SE-E. From Toulon to the Spanish border the prevailing wind is from the N-NW although a SE sea breeze blows when the NW wind is not blowing. The sea breeze typically gets up around midday, blows at Force 3–5 (7–21 knots) and dies at night. The NW wind blows at Force 4–6 (11–27 knots) although at times when the *tramontane* and *mistral* blow (from the N-NW) the wind often gets up to Force 6–8 (22–40 knots). The latter are more frequent in spring and autumn and blow infrequently in the summer.

Seas are moderate with the sea breeze although some of the harbours with entrances in comparatively shallow water in the Gulf of Lions will have a confused swell heaping up at the entrance. With a strong *tramontane* and *mistral* there are heavy confused seas along the coast.

Suitable for...

The area east of Toulon is suitable for intermediate and experienced sailors. The Gulf of Lions is really only for experienced sailors because the weather can change so quickly and the wind can get up very quickly to strong to gale force winds and heavy seas.

Harbours and anchorages

There are few anchorages around the coast (except for the *calanques* east of Marseille and a few other anchorages such as around Iles des Lerins) and you will invariably be in a marina for the night. Marinas are reasonably priced and provide all facilities. Berthing is stern or bow-to using laid moorings tailed to the quay or a buoy and in some cases posts.

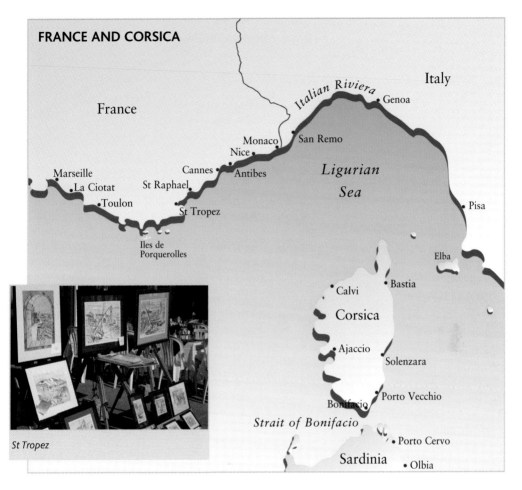

FRANCE AND CORSICA

St Tropez

Sailing area

Effectively you will be sailing either east or west along the coast and then back again unless you are doing a one-way charter. The south of France is typically thought of as being all Nice and Cannes and St Tropez, elegant old resorts with elegant people and lifestyles to match. In fact, the coast varies considerably depending on where you are. Around the low sandy shores of the Gulf of Lions are the new resorts built in the 1960s and 70s to bring employment to the area. They are not elegant but do provide a useful string of harbours around the coast. From Marseille to Toulon there are a mix of marinas, old resorts and commercial harbours. The area has a number of spectacular anchorages in the calanques

east of Marseille and some gems of harbours. Both the Gulf of Lions and the area around Marseille are subject to the *tramontane* or *mistral* and it can get very windy at times.

The area from Toulon to the Italian border, encompassing the Côte d'Azur and the Riviera, is the most popular area with all the well-known names. It can get crowded in the summer but there is much to do and see ashore and it is this area I would recommend.

Onward routes

One-way routes can usually be organised along the south of France so you do not have to retrace your steps. A charge may be made for the service.

Land excursions

For the most part visitors will just want to wander around the old resorts, sit in a café and watch the sun go down, and enjoy a slow evening meal with a good bottle of wine while people-spotting. This is the best part. Apart from that think about the following:

Aigues-Morte	13th century walled town built for Louis IX as a base to set off from during the crusades. Preserved more or less intact although now prettied up for tourists. Taxi from La Grande Motte or Port Camargue. Recommended.
Sainte-Marie de La Mer	Site of gypsy church and annual gypsy festival deep in the Camargue. From Port Gardian.
Grasse	Centre of the perfume industry in the hills behind Cannes. Tours of the perfume houses can be arranged. By bus or taxi from Cannes or nearby ports.
Fort Royal and Monastery of St Honorat /Îles de Lerins	Anchor off Îles de Lerins or take a boat from Cannes. Fort Royal was where the 'Man in the Iron Mask' was imprisoned and the monastery was founded in the 4th century by St Honorat. Recommended.
Chapel of St Peter	Decorated by Jean Cocteau. Near Villefranche.
Villa Kerylos	Facsimile of an ancient Greek villa built by the eccentric Theodore Reinach. Furnished as per ancient times. Near Beaulieu.
Monaco	The old town, casino, palace and Oceanographic Museum are all worth a visit. Recommended.
Coastal corniche	Wonderful drive or rail ride along the coast into Italy.

CORSICA

Corsica has been described as a mountain surrounded by sea and there is not a better description. It is everywhere rugged and steep-to and few islands rival it for spectacular coastline. Yachts based in Corsica frequently cruise the south of Corsica and north end of Sardinia so I have included the latter in this section. The area around the Strait of Bonifacio has been described as the best cruising area in the western Mediterranean and it is difficult to disagree with this. There are numerous bareboat companies and some sailing in company in the area. The climate is generally warmer than the south of France and temperatures frequently reach 30–32°C in the summer.

Wind and sea

The prevailing summer wind is a sea breeze blowing from the west onto the west coast although it is channelled to the SW in the north and the NW in the south of the island. It is generally from the west through the Straits of Bonifacio. It usually gets up at midday and blows anything from Force 3–6 (7–27 knots) before dying at night. On the east coast there is generally a light SE sea breeze unless the stronger breezes on the west coast climb over the mountains and fall down onto the east coast. The sea breeze is often augmented in the summer by the *libeccio*, a strong west-SW wind which can blow up to Force 7–8 (28–40 knots) and usually blows for several days. Occasionally a strong *mistral* may reach Corsica although it has usually lost a good deal of its strength by this time.

Seas can be substantial along the west coast when westerlies have been blowing for some time and there is frequently a large swell running. Around Cap Corse, care is needed of large and confused seas in strong winds.

Anchorage in Îles Lavezzi on the bottom of Corsica

Suitable for...

Corsica is for intermediate to experienced sailors who will usually find enough wind to satisfy them and some interesting navigation in the rock-strewn Strait of Bonifacio.

Harbours and anchorages

Corsica and Sardinia have a good mix of marinas, harbours and anchorages around the coast and it is not too difficult to arrange an interesting itinerary. Many of the anchorages are fringed by above and below water rocks requiring care with your navigation and some expertise in rock-hopping. In some of the anchorages you will be taking a long line ashore as there is not room to swing. Berthing in the harbours is stern or bow-to using laid moorings which are usually tailed to the quay or a small buoy. In a few harbours you will have to use your own anchor.

Main charter bases

There are numerous charter bases around the island.

Calvi Internal flights to Calvi from France. Transfer time around 20 minutes.

Ajaccio Major base. Some European and internal flights from France. Transfer time around 20 minutes.

Macinaggio Internal flights to Bastia. Transfer time around 1$^1/_2$ hours.

Bastia European and internal flights including flights from Paris. Transfer time around 20 minutes.

Solenzara Bareboats. Some European and internal flights to Bastia or Figari. Transfer time around 2 hours from either.

Land excursions

Calvi	A wander up to the citadel, now a base for the Foreign Legion, is undemanding and interesting.
Bonifacio	A wander around the citadel and old town above the harbour is fascinating, with wonderful views from the cliff-top (not for sufferers of vertigo).
Porto Cervo	The jewel of the Costa Smeralda and a fascinating look at the habitat of the rich. You can anchor free of charge on the north side of the bay.

A typical two-week intermediate itinerary is as follows:

Solenzara – Sardinia – Solenzara

Total 130 miles

Starts at Solenzara

Golfe de San Ciprianu	Large bay with a sheltered anchorage in the north or south. Clear turquoise water. Restaurant. You may have to go around into Baie de Stagnolo in the Gulf of Porto Vecchio if there are strong easterlies.
Port de Rondinara	Well sheltered bay. Care needed of rock in the middle. Restaurant.
Bonifacio	Difficult to see the entrance. Magnificent fjord-like bay and harbour. Berth stern or bow-to. Restaurants.
Two lay days	Explore anchorages along the coast. Climb up to the old town above the harbour.
Lavezzi	Leave early to find a place in one of the anchorages. Care needed of above and below water rocks everywhere.
Saint Teresa Gallura	Long inlet with a harbour at the end. Berth stern or bow-to. Restaurants.
Porto Pollo	Anchorage behind an islet. Bad holding.
Cannigione	Anchor or stern or bow-to if there is room. Restaurants.
Porto Cervo	Playground of the very rich. Anchor off on the north side inside the buoys or go into the marina if you are feeling excessively wealthy. Restaurants.
La Maddalena	Stern or bow-to in the harbour. Restaurants.
Porto Vecchio	Difficult approach. Stern or bow-to in the cramped marina. Restaurants.
Solenzara	

The itinerary can be easily shortened by cutting out some of the places on Sardinia.

Porto Vecchio Some European and internal flights to Figari. Transfer time around 1 hour.
Bonifacio Some European and internal flights to Figari. Transfer time around 20 minutes.

Sardinia
Cannigione Bareboat base. Some European and internal flights to Olbia. Transfer time around 30 minutes.
Porto Rotondo Bareboat base. Some European and internal flights to Olbia. Transfer time around 15 minutes.
Marina di Portisco Bareboat base. Flights to Olbia.

Sailing area
Most yachts based near the south end of Corsica (on either the west or east coast)

will cruise south to the Strait of Bonifacio and will usually cross to the northern coast of Sardinia as well. This way you get a bit of Corsica (nominally French) and a bit of Sardinia (nominally Italian) in the one cruise. Despite their proximity, both islands are a totally different mix of culture and cuisine. There are sufficient harbours and anchorages along the way so that you hardly ever have to revisit a place on the return leg.

Onward routes
Some companies arrange one-way routes between bases on Corsica. Occasionally yachts can do one-way routes from Corsica to the Tuscan islands or adjacent coast of Italy.

ITALY

Italy conjures up images of Rome and the Vatican City, Venetian Canals and maybe Vesuvius brooding over Naples. Sailing around the coast away from the big cities you will still get your share of Baroque architecture and the spin-off from the Renaissance, but on a lesser scale and imbued with the everyday life of Italians going about their business. Somehow it seems more manageable. Italy also has a passion for food and in most places you go there will be a little trattoria or ristorante serving everything from pasta in all its varieties to wonderful fish and meat dishes with sauces that rival French cuisine. And a cappuccino in a small bar in Italy is an experience to linger over.

Beyond the Baroque architecture the coastline is magnificent and in many places the mountains rise sheer from the sea and the rocky coastline has been sculpted by sea and wind into fantastic shapes. Ashore the towns and villages have their own mix of architecture and culture often far removed from the familiar Italy we normally conjure up. In Sicily the North African influence is readily apparent and the buildings are a subtle merging of European and African architecture. The food too has strong influences from the Maghreb. In Sardinia the locals are Sards first and Italians second and this mysterious island comes as a gentle surprise with its startling turquoise water and its own culture and cuisine ashore.

For the length of coastline Italy has few established charter areas. Skippered yachts will often visit areas like the Italian Riviera or the Bay of Naples, but not in numbers. There are bareboat and skippered charter fleets around the Bay of Naples, Sardinia, Sicily and in a few of the other mainland harbours. Small charter companies come and go and if you miss one in an area, the odds are another will have started up nearby.

BEFORE YOU GO

For

✔ Fine old resorts and enchanting villages and towns around the coast and islands.
✔ Wonderful cuisine every bit as good as France.
✔ Good restaurants and bars with the best coffee in the world.
✔ Settled weather patterns in the summer.

Against

✘ Inconsistent winds except around Sardinia.
✘ Costs are high for eating out and in marinas and harbours.
✘ Marinas and harbours can be very crowded in the summer.

Types of charter

❖ Bareboat
❖ Skippered charter
❖ Luxury charter

Suitable for

❖ Intermediate to experienced sailors.

WHEN TO GO

The season in Italy runs from around mid-May to the middle of October in the south. At the beginning and end of the season the weather is not as settled as in the eastern Mediterranean and you can expect periods of stronger winds and rain.

Early season Mid-May to mid-June. Day temperatures are warm, around 18–24°C in the day, but drop at night. Sea temperatures have not yet warmed up and are around 16–18°C. Wind patterns are irregular although westerlies predominate. There is a good possibility of a depression passing nearby and bringing gale force winds. There are on average 4–6 days of rain per month.

High season June to mid-September. Day temperatures are hot, often around 25–32°C,

At Naples	Av max °C	Av min °C	Highest recorded	Relative humidity	Days 1 mm rain	Sea temp °C	Wind direction & force
Apr	18	9	27	61%	8	15.5	SW/NE
May	22	12	32	63%	7	17.5	SW/NE F3
Jun	26	16	35	58%	4	21	SW/NE F3
Jul	29	18	36	53%	2	23.5	SW/NE F3
Aug	29	18	37	53%	3	25	SW/NE F3
Sep	26	16	34	59%	5	24	SW/NE F3
Oct	22	12	29	63%	9	22	N-NE F3
Nov	17	9	26	68%	11	19	N-NE F3

and evenings are balmy. It can feel very hot on windless days. Sea temperatures have warmed up to around 23–25°C. Wind patterns have settled down with a prevalence of westerlies. The sea breeze is common along much of the coast although the local topography can significantly alter the direction of the wind.

Late season To the end of September. Usually much as for the high season with slightly lower air temperatures but similar sea temperatures.

GETTING THERE

There are daily scheduled national and budget flights to numerous destinations on mainland Italy and in Sardinia and Sicily. There are also some charter flights in the summer.

Getting to the charter base will usually be by bus or taxi. If a charter company offers a transfer service this is well worth taking as buses are irregular in some places such as Sardinia and taxis are not cheap.

It is of course possible to drive from neighbouring European countries and this is not unduly arduous if you have the time, inclination and if you make the journey part of the holiday by budgeting a number of days for it.

WHEN YOU'RE THERE

Visas and documentation

Members of the EU must carry their passports or identity cards although there are usually no real controls on internal EU borders. Most non-EU countries do not require visas.

In some cases proof of competence to handle a yacht will be asked for although this

Scario on the Calabrian coast

is rare. The yacht charter company can usually provide something suitable once it is convinced of your ability to handle a yacht. All other boat documentation will be provided by the company. Charter documentation and clearance does not usually take very long and once cleared you are unlikely to be checked for paperwork in subsequent harbours.

Health
Medical services are generally good. Reciprocal medical care is available for EU nationals. It is advised you take out private medical insurance for the trip as medical costs are high and most charter operators can arrange insurance quickly. Travel insurance (including medical cover) is mandatory with many bareboat companies.

The water is potable nearly everywhere except for the area around Naples which has had water shortages and problems with water quality for a number of years. Those with delicate stomachs, and babies, should drink bottled water.

Money and banks
The unit of currency is the Euro. Banks are open 0830–1330 Mon–Fri. Major credit cards and charge cards can be used in some places, but are not as widely accepted as in most other European countries. Most ATM machines will work with foreign credit cards.

Eating and drinking
Italy offers the gastronome a cuisine on a par with – and, according to some, superior to – French cuisine. Italian food is certainly an experience not to be missed with many regional variations on the rich cuisine. Part of the art of Italian cuisine lies in blending what often appear to be diverse ingredients, pasta and seafood for example, to produce wonderfully subtle dishes.

An Italian meal usually starts with an *antipasto* or pasta dish, then the main dish of meat or fish, followed by dessert. The prices shown on a menu do not include the *coperto* (cover charge) or the service charge, both of which will be added at the end of the bill. Many restaurants offer a *menu turistico*:

ESSENTIAL INFORMATION

Capital Rome

Time zone UT + 1 DST Apr–Sep

Language Italian. French, German and English spoken in some areas.

Telecommunications Automatic dialling. Code 39. GSM phones supported throughout Italy. Internet cafés are scarce and wifi only in the larger centres.

Electricity 220V 50Hz AC.

usually three courses from a limited choice at a fixed price. These are good value and often you will be offered a limited choice of the *à la carte* menu for less than the total it would otherwise cost. In any restaurant enquire if there is a pasta made in the restaurant as some of these are just mouth-watering.

Categories of restaurant vary and the old titles do not carry the indication of quality or price that they used to. *Pizzerias* are still around the bottom rung and usually have a selection of other dishes apart from pizzas and pasta. Traditionally a *trattoria* meant a middle-priced place that focused on home cooking without pretensions, but many restaurants now call themselves a *trattoria* to impart a homely atmosphere.

Italian wine is always drinkable and often excellent. Many restaurants will have a local wine by the carafe and this is usually good. Otherwise equip yourself with a guide to the wines of Italy and pick your way through the wine list. Italian beer is of the light lager type, usually *Peroni* or *San Miguel*, and eminently drinkable. Spirits are relatively cheap and measures are generous. The coffee is the best in the world.

Provisioning
All provisions are easily found in the larger towns and villages and most supermarkets will have recognisable brand names as well

SAILING GUIDES AND CHARTS

There are several sailing guides to Italy although most are in Italian only. Obtaining these guides in Italy can be difficult outside of large yachting centres so it is best to obtain them before you go on a charter. The following may be useful.

Italian Waters Pilot Rod Heikell. Imray. Covers all Italian waters, including Sardinia and Sicily, but not the eastern Adriatic coast.

Pagine Azzure An annual almanac with harbour plans. In Italian only.

Admiralty charts cover all areas and are available from Admiralty agents. Imray charts cover some areas.

Italian charts, which are beautifully produced although expensive, are available in the larger yachting centres.

thieves on scooters, in Naples who snatch jewellery and valuables from people that you must constantly be vigilant, but the Mafia are not concerned with tourists and in only a few places, notably Genoa, Rome and Naples, do you need to be on your guard against purse-snatchers and pick-pockets. If you take normal precautions and do not wear jewellery ostentatiously, keep a firm hold on your camera and camcorder, and put your wallet and credit cards in an inside pocket then you are unlikely to be troubled.

One thing you should do is make sure you lock the dinghy up when you go ashore and to the boat when you come back. Dinghies seem to attract local thieves like bees to the honey pot.

CHARTER AREAS

as all those wonderful Italian cured hams, salamis and cheeses. Prices will all be clearly marked and in general shopping is as much a delight as a chore.

Costs

The overall cost of living is around the middle of EU averages although costs have remained static in recent years and so in real terms have come down somewhat. Typical costs for eating out are €20–50 a head, local wine is around €15–25 a bottle in a restaurant and beer is around €2–3 for the local brew. Provisioning is about on a par or slightly higher than other EU countries, but the quality of many goods such as cured hams and cheeses is higher than many.

Transport varies with taxi fares being on the high side. Car hire is expensive at around €40–50 per day. Hire motorbikes and bicycles are not common.

Crime and personal safety

Italy has a crime problem in the shape of muggings and petty theft in urban centres, but these do not usually affect the visitor afloat. You might get the impression with the recent Mafia trials and the *scippatori*,

SARDINIA

This area is covered under the itinerary from Corsica in the section on France. Many of the charter yachts based in Corsica normally cruise between the bottom end of Corsica and top end of Sardinia. There are also charter bases in northern Sardinia, which is the most popular destination for chartering on the island. Bases are principally at Portisco, Olbia and Cannigione.

ITALIAN RIVIERA AND TUSCAN ISLANDS

Situated between the border with France and down around the coast to the island of Elba. Charter here is mostly skippered charter and a few bareboats. Some bareboats from Corsica also head over this way. The season gets going fairly late in May and finishes around October. The climate is significantly cooler than further south and not as settled as that south of Rome.

Wind and sea

The prevailing wind in the summer is a sea breeze blowing onto the coast from the

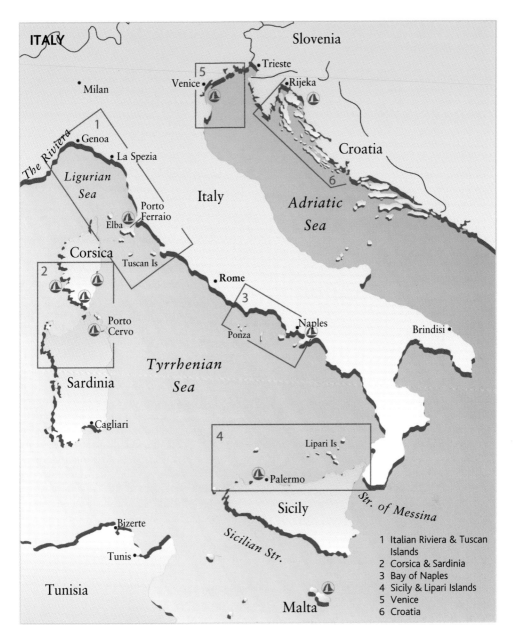

1 Italian Riviera & Tuscan Islands
2 Corsica & Sardinia
3 Bay of Naples
4 Sicily & Lipari Islands
5 Venice
6 Croatia

SW-SE. It is not consistent or developed at all times although in July and August it will usually blow at Force 4–5 (11–21 knots) in the afternoon. There are often days of calm. In the early and late season no one direction prevails although there can frequently be a *libeccio* blowing strongly from the SW.

Seas are often confused when the wind blows and even with calms there can be some ground swell. Strong southerlies heap up dangerous seas along the coast and can make entrance to some harbours difficult.

Suitable for...
The area is suitable for intermediate and experienced sailors.

Land excursions

Around the coast and islands the old Ligurian villages and towns are often wonders in themselves, all pastel washed buildings and brightly tiled entrances. Most have attractive waterfronts with lots going on where you can sit and watch the locals going about their daily business. Outside of the villages and towns there are a few well-known sites to look at.

Loano/Caves of Toirano	Labyrinth of caves with traces of Neanderthal occupation. Close inland from Loano.
Pisa	Leaning Tower of Pisa and associated buildings. Easily visited from Viareggio.
Portoferraio/Villa dei Mulini	Napoleon's House when he was exiled on Elba.

Harbours and anchorages

There are only a few anchorages around the coast and islands and for the most part you will spend the night in a marina or yacht harbour for which an equivalent charge is made. In July and August during the high season, charges can be high and harbours and marinas are busy. Berthing is stern or bow-to normally with a laid mooring tailed to the quay except in a few places where you will use your own anchor.

Main charter bases

Bareboat charter is based around Genoa, Viareggio, Elba, Salivoli, Marina di Scarlino, Marina Cala di Medici, Cala Galera and Punta Ala. There are no real clusters of charter boats and all bases are fairly small scale affairs that will often migrate to another harbour or marina in subsequent years. There are major airports handling European flights, both national and budget flights, at Genoa, Firenze (Florence), Pisa, Elba and Rome. International flights go to Genoa and Rome.

Sailing area

The area cruised depends to an extent on where the base is situated. Genoa based yachts go either west along the Italian Riviera or south to Portofino and La Spezia. Viareggio based yachts generally go south to the Tuscan islands and Elba based boats likewise cruise the islands and adjacent mainland coast. Cala Galera based yachts also usually head north for the Tuscan islands and adjacent coast.

If you had to pick an area, the Tuscan islands and adjacent coast is the best cruising area with numerous attractive harbours and some anchorages within easy sailing distances. For the more ambitious the east coast of Corsica is not that far away.

One way routes are sometimes arranged between bases in the Tuscan islands and Naples depending on the charter company. They are generally less common than elsewhere.

BAY OF NAPLES

The bay of Naples and offshore islands of Capri and Ischia are well known and all sorts of images and historical footnotes immediately come to mind. The area in the Bay of Naples and the coast to the south makes up a useful cruising area and some one-way trips are organised to Sicily. The climate is warmer than further north and temperatures often reach 30–33°C in July and August. Out of the wind it feels very hot.

Wind and sea

The prevailing summer wind is again a sea breeze blowing from the SW-SE depending on the local topography. It generally gets up around midday and blows at Force 3–4 (7–16 knots). In the early and late season weather patterns are less settled and there may be stronger winds, particularly from the north, when a depression passes nearby. The *sirocco* also blows at times from the south and can blow up to Force 7 (33 knots) and set up a considerable sea.

Savona. Right in the heart of the city on the Italian Riviera

Seas on the whole are small except when the *sirocco* blows as indicated.

Suitable for...

The area is suitable for intermediate to experienced although some frustration may be expressed by experienced sailors over the calms encountered in July and August. Experienced sailors can also do one way trips to Sicily where distances are greater and there is commonly more wind.

Harbours and anchorages

The area has a mix of marinas and fishing or commercial harbours around the coast and islands. There are only a few well sheltered anchorages. Many of the fishing harbours and commercial harbours have a section of quay devoted to yachts and prices equivalent to marina prices will be charged here. Berthing is stern or bow-to using laid moorings if provided or otherwise your own anchor.

Main charter bases

Procida A small bareboat charter base on the island of Procida. Charterers normally fly into Naples and transfer by ferry to the

Land excursions

There is really only one must-see in the area.

Pompeii/Herculaneum	It is worth the effort. The ancient city preserved under lava and volcanic ash when nearby Vesuvius erupted in AD79 is fascinating to walk around, even for those who do not like old bits of Roman rock. It is probably easiest to reach from the charter base at Procida where you can safely leave your boat and get a ferry and train to the site. Alternatively leave your boat at Marina di Stabia.
Ventotene	The old harbour is the old Roman harbour excavated from the rock.
Paestum	The ruins of ancient Greek Paestum are said to be the finest Greek architecture in Italy. Can be visited from Agropoli.

island. Transfer time around 1 hour. There are also other small charter bases in harbours close to Naples including Marina di Stabia.

Nettuno A marina south of Rome. Yachts usually cruise south through the Pontine islands to the Bay of Naples. Charterers fly into Rome. Transfer time 1½ hours.

Salerno Small charter base with easy access to Naples Airport.

Tropea Small charter base just above the Strait of Messina and handy for the adjacent Calabrian coast, the Lipari Islands and Sicily.

Sailing area

From Nettuno yachts normally head down south through the wonderful (and popular) islands of Ponza and Ventotene to the Bay of Naples. From Naples yachts will want to visit Ischia and Capri and can then head off north or south. South of the Bay of Naples there is a wonderful cruising area along the coast to Amalfi, Salerno, Agropoli, Acciaroli, Camerota, Scario and Sapri. Some yachts will want to head for the Lipari islands. Some companies can arrange one-way charters between Naples and bases in Sicily.

In the season, harbours near major cities like Naples and Rome can get very busy, but south of Naples the concentration of yachts thins out dramatically.

Onward routes

Nettuno One way charters are sometimes arranged between Nettuno and the Bay of Naples or vice versa. Easily accomplished within two weeks with a total of around 150 miles.

Sicily One way charters are sometimes arranged between the Bay of Naples and Sicily via the Lipari islands. Yachts normally go to Portorosa or Palermo on Sicily. Total of around 240 miles with a long overnight passage to the Lipari islands and some other longish day passages.

SICILY

At Portorosa and Palermo there are small bareboat operations. The charter base at Tropea is also handy for Sicily and the Lipari Islands. The cruising area is usually along the northern coast of Sicily and around the Lipari islands. Intrepid sailors can also sail around Sicily although you need to plan carefully as Sicily is the largest island in the Mediterranean and it is a considerable distance to get around in two weeks.

Charterers normally fly into Palermo. Transfer time to Palermo is around 30 minutes and to Portorosa around 3 hours.

Cefalu on the north coast of Sicily

CROATIA

When Yugoslavia split asunder after the death of Tito, the lion's share of the coast fell to Croatia. This includes over 1,000 islands and a much indented mainland coast that makes up a vast cruising area. It also includes a substantial chunk of Dalmatian history with any amount of beautiful Baroque architecture that has been sympathetically restored since the civil war. For most people this coastline and its people and culture comes as something of a pleasant surprise; in many ways a variation on the culture across the water with a vibrant café life and a love affair with the siesta, meaning everything slowly winds down in the afternoon until early evening when the inhabitants re-emerge to promenade around town.

There are charter bases all up and down the coast and you need to do some prior research to work out where you want to go and what you want to see. Basically the coast can be split up into north, middle and south. In the north, bases are clustered around Zadar; in the middle charter bases are clustered around Split Airport, and in the south around Dubrovnik.

WHEN TO GO

The season in Croatia runs from around mid-May to mid-October. At the beginning and end of the season the weather is not as settled as in the eastern Mediterranean and you can expect periods of stronger winds and rain. Temperatures vary from the north to the south. It is definitely cooler in the north, especially at the beginning and end of the season.

Early season Mid-May to mid-June. Day temperatures are warm, around 18–22°C in the day, but drop at night. Sea temperatures have not yet warmed up and are around 16–18°C. Wind patterns have not yet settled down and care needs to be taken when a depression passing north brings the dreaded

bora whistling down from the northeast into the Adriatic.

High season June to mid-September. Day temperatures are hot, often around 25–30°C, and evenings are balmy. Sea temperatures are around 20–25°C. Wind patterns are predominantly a sea breeze, the *maestrale*, which gets up in the late morning and dies in the evening. It will usually blow from the northwest at anything from Force 3–6 depending on temperatures, although the local topography can significantly alter the direction of the wind. It is also possible to get humid southerlies (the *jugo*) which can blow quite strongly for a period of days.

Late season To the end of October with weather conditions similar to early season

At Sibenik	Av max °C	Av min °C	Highest recorded	Relative humidity	Days 1 mm rain	Sea temp °C	Wind direction & force
Apr	17	11	22	66%	9	14	NW/SE F3-4
May	21	14	27	69%	8	17	NW/SE F3-4
Jun	25	14	30	65%	4	20	NW/SE F3
Jul	29	21	33	60%	3	24	NW/SE F3
Aug	28	21	32	59%	3	24	NW/SE F3
Sep	25	18	29	63%	6	22	N/SE F3-4
Oct	21	14	25	63%	9	20	NW/SE F3-4
Nov	17	10	21	66%	14	16	N/SE F3-4

ESSENTIAL INFORMATION

Capital Zagreb

Time zone UT + 1 DST Apr–Sep

Language Croatian. Many locals speak Italian or German rather than English.

Telecommunications Automatic dialling. Code 385. GSM phones supported throughout Croatia. Internet cafés are common in tourist centres with wifi only in the larger centres.

Electricity 220V 50Hz AC.

although sea temperatures will be higher. Again care is needed of the *bora*.

GETTING THERE

There are daily scheduled national and budget flights to Zagreb, Pula, Zadar, Split and Dubrovnik. There are also numerous charter flights in the summer. It is also possible to fly to nearby airports in Italy and cross to Croatia, though there is really nothing to be gained by this except for a Trieste to Pula connection.

Getting to the charter base will usually be by bus or taxi. If a charter company offers a transfer service this is well worth taking as buses are irregular and taxis are not cheap.

WHEN YOU'RE THERE

Visas and documentation
Members of the EU, USA and most other countries must carry their passport or identity card although no visa is required.

The skipper of the yacht must have a qualification like the International Certificate of Competence or at least a Day Skipper ticket. The yacht charter company will be able to advise on what is necessary. All other boat documentation will be provided by the company. Charter documentation and clearance does not usually take very long although it is likely to be checked in other major harbours.

Health
Medical services are generally good. It is advised you take out private medical insurance for the trip as medical costs are high and most charter operators can arrange insurance quickly. Travel insurance (including medical cover) is mandatory with many bareboat companies.

The water is potable nearly everywhere. Those with delicate stomachs, and babies, should drink bottled water.

Money and banks
The unit of currency is the kuna (HRK) although euros are widely accepted. Banks are open 0830–1330 Mon–Sat. Major credit cards can be used in most places including

bars and restaurants. ATMs are common and work with most credit cards.

Eating and drinking

Croatian cuisine has moved on from the monochrome stodge which was served up in the socialist era. The food is still basically peasant cuisine, but it has been refined and the cooking is now an interesting blend of mainland Slavic cuisine which focuses on meat blended with Mediterranean coastal cuisine. The food is basically good solid fare in the tourist areas, although only in a few restaurants is it outstanding in French or Italian terms.

Commonly you will get kebabs, roast lamb and pork and stews which often combine meat and beans in interesting ways. Dalmatian hams are excellent. Along the coast fish are an important part of the diet and there are numerous fish restaurants which will grill fish over charcoal or more interestingly roast it.

Dalmatia has long established vineyards and the wines are generally good, if a little variable. Local beers (*pivo*) are all palatable and relatively cheap. And neighbouring Italy ensures that the coffee is excellent.

Provisioning

All provisions are easily found in the larger towns and villages. The supermarkets will not always have recognisable brand names

SAILING GUIDES AND CHARTS

Adriatic Pilot T & D Thompson. Imray. Covers all of Croatia.

Croatia, Slovenia & Montenegro 777 Harbours & Anchorages Rod & Anna Bailey. TBC.

Croatian and Imray charts cover all areas.

but there are good local alternatives. Prices will all be clearly marked and in general shopping is not too confusing for the newcomer.

Costs

The overall cost of living is around the middle of EU averages although costs have remained static in recent years and so in real terms have come down somewhat. Typical costs for eating out are €20–30 a head, local wine is around €10 a bottle in a restaurant and beer is around €2 for the local brew. Provisioning is about on a par or slightly higher than other EU countries, but the quality of many goods such as cured hams and cheeses is higher than many. There is a definite difference between mainland costs and island costs with the latter being anything from 15–20% higher than the mainland.

Suggested itinerary from Sibenik

Approx 100 miles

7 day charter from Skradin (near Sibenik) around the Kornati Islands

Day 1	Sibenik to Primosten. Wonderful village built on an island joined by a causeway to the mainland.
Day 2	Sail across to the fishing village of Zirje Luka on the island of Zirje.
Day 3	Sail to Marina Piskera on the island of Piskera in the Kornati National Park.
Day 4	Sail to Luka Zut on the island of Zut. Go into the marina or anchor off.
Day 5	Lay day.
Day 6	Sail back to Skradin. Take a water taxi to the Krka Falls upriver from Skradin.

On a two week charter yachts will often go south to Primosten, Milna on Brac Island, the Pakleni Islands, Maslinica on Solta Island before going north to the Kornati Islands as above.

Crime and personal safety

Croatia has a low incidence of theft and muggings and apart from a bit of pick-pocketing in urban areas, it is generally safe. Sailing around the coast you are unlikely to encounter crime of any sort.

CHARTER AREAS

Croatia can be roughly divided into north centred around Zadar, middle centred around Split and south centred around Dubrovnik.

DUBROVNIK

Yachts will usually circumnavigate Korcula Island with stops on the inside passage of Mljet Island. You should spend some time exploring the old walled city of Dubrovnik and ashore on Mljet and Korcula. You can do a short one week flotilla taking in Mljet or a two weeker circumnavigating Korcula and perhaps visiting as far north as Hvar Island.

Winds around this area are usually a bit stronger than further north around Sibenik and the Kornati Islands with either north-west or south to southeast winds blowing around Force 5. Temperatures are a little warmer in early and late season than further north.

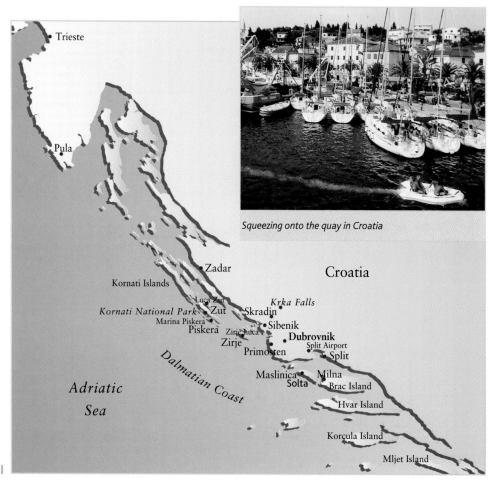

Squeezing onto the quay in Croatia

Trieste

Pula

Zadar

Kornati Islands

Croatia

Luca Zut

Kornati National Park Zut Skradin

Krka Falls

Marina Piskera

Piskera Zirje Luca Sibenik

Zirje Dubrovnik

Primosten Split Airport

Split

Maslinica Milna

Solta Brac Island

Dalmatian Coast

Adriatic

Sea

Hvar Island

Korcula Island

Mljet Island

GREECE

If you think of Greece you probably have an idea of sun-baked islands with white cube houses moulded into the landscape under an eternally blue sky. This is just one part of Greece and in fact the coast and islands encompass a huge variety of landscapes from green wooded mountains, coastline dotted with the remains of ancient Greece and huge Venetian castles, natural stone houses with tiled roofs, white chapels perched on mountain tops and the jagged end of a cape, and everywhere a wonderful aquamarine sea that shallows to turquoise near the shore.

One of the joys of sailing around Greece is coming across a little harbour or hamlet where you tie up to the quay outside a taverna and go ashore for a leisurely meal with your yacht often just metres away from your table. Greek waters are the quintessence of day sailing, a 10 or 30 mile sail and you are in another small harbour or a bay that wriggles inland to give perfect shelter. Whatever the Greek gods are doing now, they are surely smiling over the yachts exploring their old playground and why not, it is a huge natural sailing area for those of us who want to potter and enjoy the simple things in life.

Greece is a long established charter area with all types of charter and numerous different bases amongst the islands and mainland. Large skippered yachts have toured Greece since the 19th century, often incorporating a shooting trip for wild fowl on the itinerary. In the 1960s, small skippered yachts appeared and in the late 1970s, bareboats and flotillas started to operate here. Greece has more coastline than any other Mediterranean country, nearly 7,400 miles if you unravel the coastline of all those islands, and importantly a much indented coastline providing an abundance of natural harbours and anchorages around the mainland coast and islands. Add to this a settled summer climate and constant prevailing winds and you wind up with a wonderful sailing area.

BEFORE YOU GO

For
- ✔ Settled summer weather patterns and a long season.
- ✔ Range of winds across the different areas suitable for beginners to experienced sailors.
- ✔ Longest coastline in the Mediterranean with harbours and anchorages everywhere.
- ✔ Magnificent scenery and lots of anchorages with clear blue water and the possibility of getting away from the crowds.
- ✔ Informal and enjoyable life ashore.
- ✔ Numerous packages available with all types of charter catered for from flotilla to skippered luxury yachts.

Against
- ✘ Some areas crowded in the summer.
- ✘ Cyclades and Dodecanese can be very windy in July and August.
- ✘ Cuisine ashore is simple fare and you need to search for good Greek food.

Types of charter
- ❖ Flotilla
- ❖ Shore-based clubs
- ❖ Bareboat
- ❖ Skippered charter
- ❖ Luxury charter
- ❖ Learning to sail and sailing schools

Suitable for
- ❖ Novices to experienced sailors depending on the area

There are few people who do not return to Greece having once chartered there.

WHEN TO GO

The season in Greece normally starts around mid-April and runs through to the middle of October. In general it is more settled and warmer in the Dodecanese in

At Levkas	Av max °C	Av min °C	Highest recorded	Relative humidity	Days 0.1 mm rain	Sea temp °C	Wind direction & force
Apr	20	11	32	48%	9	16	NW/SE F4
May	25	16	36	47%	8	18	N-NW F4
Jun	30	20	42	39%	4	21.5	NW F3-4
Jul	33	23	42	34%	2	23	NW F3-4
Aug	33	23	43	34%	3	25	NW F3-4
Sep	29	19	38	42%	4	24.5	N-NW F3-4
Oct	24	15	37	52%	8	22.5	NW/SE F3-4
Nov	19	12	28	56%	12	19	NW/SE F4

the east than in the Ionian in the west and Northern Sporades.

Early season April to May. Day temperatures are warm, around 19–24°C in the day, but drop at night when a sweater will be needed. Sea temperatures have not yet warmed up and are generally around 18–19°C. Wind

Milos in the Cyclades

patterns will not yet have settled down and there is the possibility of a depression coming through bringing strong winds and rain.

High season June to September. Day temperatures are hot, around 26–32°C, and evenings are warm. Some nights will be hot and it takes a while to get used to sleeping in these temperatures. Sea temperatures have warmed up to around 21–26°C and can be as much as 28°C in the SE Aegean. Wind patterns are dependable and the prevailing winds constant in direction and strength. There are few days of rain.

Late season October. Day temperatures are still hot, around 21°C in the west and 23–24°C in the east. Sea temperatures remain warm, around 22–24°C. Wind patterns are relatively settled although there is the possibility of a depression passing through bringing strong winds and rain.

GETTING THERE

There are daily national and budget scheduled flights to Athens, Corfu and Thessaloniki. In the summer there are frequent charter flights from many European airports and these can be substantially cheaper than scheduled flights. Charter flights connect not only with Athens, but with many smaller airports including Corfu, Preveza, Kalamata, Thessaloniki, Crete, Kos, and Rhodes.

Getting to the charter base will usually be by bus, taxi, ferry, or a combination of these. If a charter company offers a transfer service this is well worth taking to cut the hassle out of arranging your own transport to and from the airport and will usually cost less than arranging your own transfers.

WHEN YOU'RE THERE

Visas and documentation
Members of the EU must carry their passport or identity card. Non-EU nationals must have a valid passport. Most non-EU countries including America, Canada, Australia, New Zealand, Norway, Austria and Switzerland do not require visas.

In some cases proof of competence to handle a yacht will be asked for and you need to ask the charter company about requirements. Most charter companies will require some sort of qualification for more difficult areas. All other boat documentation will be provided by the company. It can take several hours for clearance of the charter documentation before you leave. It is normal for the representative of the charter company to arrange this and to advise on procedures at subsequent harbours.

Health
Medical services range from good in the cities to adequate in the smaller towns. Reciprocal medical care is available for EU nationals with the European Health Insurance Card. It is advised you take out private medical insurance for the trip and most charter operators can arrange this. Travel insurance (including medical cover) is mandatory with all flotilla operators and many bareboat companies.

Water In most places the water is potable, but it is likely that delicate stomachs will react to local micro-organisms in the water and for a few days some people will have a mild case of the runs. Those with delicate stomachs and babies should drink bottled water.

ESSENTIAL INFORMATION

Capital Athens

Time zone UT + 2 DST Apr–Sep

Language Demotic Greek. English and German also spoken.

Telecommunications Automatic dialling. Country code 30. GSM phones supported throughout Greece. Internet cafés and wifi.

Electricity 220V 50Hz AC.

Money and banks
The unit of currency is the Euro.

Banks are open 0800–1300 Monday to Friday. Exchange offices and travel agents operate outside these hours. All major credit cards are widely accepted. ATM machines can be found in the towns and tourist resorts and work with most credit cards.

Eating and drinking
Greece is not a gourmet destination, but eating out is an essential part of the Greek experience and tavernas are often sited in the most wonderful places. You will frequently be able to eat out a step or two from the harbour or trek a bit further and find shaded courtyards or wonderful views. Greek food majors on charcoal grilled meat and fish, pre-cooked dishes such as *moussaka*, *pastitsio*, lamb and beef stews, and stuffed peppers, all of which will be served with the ubiquitous chips and Greek salad. Food presentation is not high on the list of taverna protocol, but Greek food should be considered part of the overall experience of sitting in a wonderful location on a balmy night and gently mellowing amidst the chaos of waiters rushing hither and thither.

Most Greek wine is now good and some of it is very good. Greek wine has changed radically in recent years and even bulk wine is much better than it used to be. Greek beer is of the lager type, often with a recognisable

SAILING GUIDES AND CHARTS

Greek Waters Pilot Rod Heikell. Imray. Covers all Greek waters in detail.

Ionian Rod Heikell. Imray. Covers the Ionian from Corfu to Finakounda on the western Peloponnese in detail.

West Aegean Rod Heikell. Imray. Covers the Saronic Gulf (around Athens), eastern Peloponnese, western Cyclades and up to the Northern Sporades in detail.

East Aegean Covers the Dodecanese and adjacent Turkish coast in detail.

Admiralty charts cover all areas and are available from Admiralty agents.

Imray-Tetra charts cover all the charter areas on a scale suitable for yachtsmen and are available from Imray or chandlers.

German or Scandinavian name but usually brewed in Greece, and eminently thirst quenching when cold. *Ouzo*, the aniseed flavoured aperitif common throughout the Mediterranean, is the national drink and is usually mixed with a little water. If you can find an old fashioned *ouzerie* that serves little *mezes* with the *ouzo* then so much the better.

Provisioning

Most provisions are easily found in the larger towns and resorts in Greece and gone the days when you needed to arrive stocked up with coffee and tea and your favourite brand of baked beans. There is not the choice of items you might find in your local supermarket, but most major brands of goods are commonly found and probably a few interesting substitute brands as well.

Stocking up the boat can usually be accomplished in just one nearby supermarket and close to the major yacht charter bases you will generally find one or two supermarkets which will deliver once you have made your purchases. Some of the yacht charter companies will provide an order list which you tick in the appropriate

places and the goods are bought and delivered to the boat before you arrive.

Costs

The overall cost of living is somewhat below EU averages although not as low as it used to be. Typical costs for eating out are €20–40 a head, local wine is around €4–5 a carafe and €10–20 a bottle in a restaurant, and beer is around €1.50–2.50 for the local brew.

Provisioning is about on a par with other EU countries and many imported items are now available for little more than you would expect to pay at home. Some locally produced items, yoghurt, dried fruits and nuts, and spirits like *ouzo* are good value.

Transport varies with taxi fares being somewhat below other EU countries, but car hire being relatively more expensive at around €40–60 per day. Hire motorbikes are fairly cheap, around €20 per day, but the price usually reflects the poor condition of the steed in question. Hire bicycles, including mountain bikes, can be hired in many places.

Crime and personal safety

Greece is a safe and relatively crime-free country to visit. There are few instances of mugging, rape and petty theft and those that occur are unlikely to touch the visitor afloat. In the cities and larger tourist resorts, namely Athens, Thessaloniki, Corfu, Mykonos, some north coast resorts on Crete, and Rhodes, take normal precautions and do not ostentatiously carry valuables with you. Thefts from boats are few and far between and it is extremely unlikely you will have anything stolen from your boat.

CHARTER AREAS

IONIAN

Situated on the west of Greece the Ionian has long been a popular charter area for flotilla, Club holidays, and bareboat charter. The climate is cooler than the areas to the

GREECE

Sea of Marmara

Thessaloniki
Khalkidiki 5
Thasos

Dardanelles

NORTHERN SPORADES
Lesvos

Greece
Volos
Aegean

Corfu
EASTERN SPORADES

IONIAN IS.
Is.
Levkas
1
Skiros
Sea
Khios

Turkey

Samos
6

Cephalonia
Corinth
Athens

Zakinthos
PELOPONNESE
Saronic Gulf
Mikonos
Patmos

Ionian Sea
2
Siros Paros
Naxos
Kos

DODECANESE

Argolic Gulf
Kalamata

Rhodes

3 CYCLADES Thira

Chania
Iraklion
Crete

1 Ionian
2 Saronic
3 Cyclades
4 Northern Sporades
5 Khalkidiki
6 Dodecanese

east although temperatures are still high in July and August with averages of around 30–31°C. The area does not correspond to stereotypical images of Greece with a significantly greener aspect to it and an Italianate aspect to older buildings. Newer buildings are of the pour-and-fill variety common throughout Greece although most must have a red tile roof – eventually.

Wind and sea

The prevailing wind in this area, the *maistro*, is less boisterous than the prevailing *meltemi* in the Aegean. Between June and September the wind blows from the NW-W down throughout the whole area. It usually gets up about midday and blows hardest at around Force 4–6 (11–27 knots) in the afternoon. It dies down around sunset. In the morning there is invariably a calm that is useful if you have to motor north. In early and late season the *maistro* is less developed and some days

barely blows at all. At this time a depression may pass over the area and will often bring strong to gale force southerlies which can abruptly swing around to strong northerlies. There may also be thunderstorms with gale force squalls although they rarely last longer than a couple of hours.

Seas in the area are the typical short Mediterranean chop with longer and higher waves in the sea areas not protected by the outer islands.

Suitable for…

The combination of predictable winds providing a good sailing breeze, a calm at night and in the morning, and a cruising ground protected from large seas by the string of islands running down the coast, makes this an ideal flotilla area for beginners and families and for flotilla or bareboat charterers who like to enjoy a good sail with a calm anchorage at night. This is

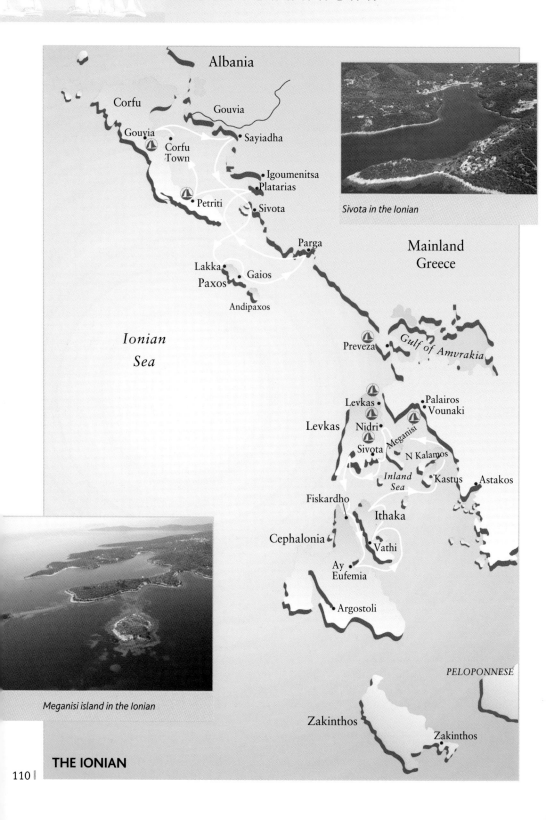

Albania

Corfu

Gouvia

Gouyia

Corfu Town

Sayiadha

Igoumenitsa

Platarias

Petriti

Sivota

Sivota in the Ionian

Parga

Mainland Greece

Lakka

Gaios

Paxos

Andipaxos

Ionian Sea

Preveza

Gulf of Amvrakia

Levkas

Levkas

Nidri

Sivota

Meganisi

Palairos
Vounaki

N Kalamos

Inland Sea

Kastus

Astakos

Fiskardho

Ithaka

Cephalonia

Vathi

Ay Eufemia

Argostoli

Meganisi island in the Ionian

PELOPONNESE

Zakinthos

Zakinthos

THE IONIAN

110

proper gentleman's sailing with the calm in the mornings making it easy to motor back to the north if you don't want to bash to windward. Don't get the impression it is purely a nursery area for would-be sailors though, as the sailing can be exhilarating under the lee of the islands when the afternoon breeze is fully developed.

Harbours and anchorages

There are several marinas and an abundance of harbours with yacht berths and well-protected anchorages on both the islands and the adjacent mainland coast. The whole area is literally peppered with bays and coves and despite the numbers of yachts operating in the area it is still possible to get away and find less crowded spots. Berthing in the harbours is every-where stern or bows-to using your own anchor although a few places have laid moorings tailed to the quay.

Main charter bases

There are two major charter bases and several other smaller bases.

Corfu The principal charter base on Corfu is Gouvia Marina close to Corfu town. It is a short distance from Corfu airport with around a 15 minute transfer time.

Platarias A small harbour on the mainland opposite Corfu is used by a flotilla company as a base. It is around 1 hour 15 minutes transfer time from Aktion Airport near Preveza.

Preveza A small charter base close to Aktion Airport. Around 15 minutes transfer time.

Levkas The other main charter base in the Ionian. There are charter fleets based at Levkas town, Nidri, and Sivota. From Aktion Airport it is around 30 minutes to Levkas town, 45 minutes to Nidri and 1 hour to Sivota.

A typical two-week intermediate itinerary is as follows:

Corfu – Corfu

Total 100 miles

A cruise in the sea area between Corfu and Paxos and the adjacent mainland coast.
Starts at Gouvia marina.

Ay Stefanos	A small wooded bay on the NE end of Corfu. Anchor off. Tavernas ashore.
Lay day	Anchor off in one of the bays south of Ay Stefanos for lunch or overnight.
Platarias	Large harbour with tavernas and bars ashore.
Mourtos/Sivota	Anchorage inside the Sivota islands or on the quay at Mourtos village. A 2 metre bar obstructs the inside channel. Tavernas ashore.
Lakka	Large bay on the N of Paxos island. Clear turquoise water. Tavernas ashore.
Gaios	Small capital of the island. Busy in the season so get here early.
Two lay days	Sail around Paxos to look at the deep caves on the west side of the island or across to unspoiled Andipaxos for lunch and a swim. Return to Gaios or Mongonisi for the night.
Ligia or **Preveza**	Ligia is closer and smaller, just a couple of tavernas. Preveza is a large harbour and all singing and dancing ashore.
Parga	On the mainland opposite Paxos. Small harbour in the west bay or anchor off. Bustling watersports centre. Several tavernas nearby or walk into the village for supper.
Petriti	On Corfu opposite Platarias. Anchor off in the attractive bay or there may be room in the harbour. Tavernas ashore.
Gouvia marina	

The private island of the Onassis family in the Ionian

Inland Sea

Total 120 miles

A cruise in the area called the inland sea bounded by Levkas, Cephalonia, Zakinthos and the adjacent mainland coast. Starts at Nidri on Levkas.

Sivota	A dog-leg bay hidden from seawards on the SE of Levkas. Go on the quay or anchor off. Tavernas ashore.
Vassiliki	Small fishing harbour on the SW of Levkas. A green well-watered spot. Tavernas ashore. World ranked sailboard centre.
Fiskardho	Sheltered bay and harbour on the north end of Cephalonia. Gets busy so get here early. Anchor with a long line ashore if there are no berths on the quay. Tavernas and bars.
Lay day	Walk around to good swimming bays or sail around to Assos.
Ay Eufemia	Ferry and fishing harbour on the east side of Cephalonia. Tavernas.
Vathi	Main harbour on the E side of Ithaca inside a massive land-locked bay. Lunch stop at Perapigadi. Boisterous sail later into Vathi. Tavernas.
Kioni	Small fishing harbour surrounded by steep slopes on the north end of Ithaca. Tavernas.
Kastos	A small island with a small harbour and bay on the SE side. Tavernas.
2 lay days	Cruise around Kastos and nearby Kalamos and return for the night to Kastos, Kalamos, or Port Leone.
Atheni	A large bay on the NE tip of Meganisi. Anchor off with a long line ashore. Tavernas.
Sivota	
Nidri	

Land excursions

There are comparatively few land excursions in the area.

Corfu	Parts of the old town deserve a wander around and tours can be arranged to the over-the-top kitsch casino.
Preveza/Nikopolis	Visit the ruins of Nikopolis, the huge city built by Augustus Caesar after his victory over Antony and Cleopatra in the sea area off Aktion.
Katakolon/Olympus	The port on the NW side of the Peloponnese opposite the bottom of Zakinthos. From here it is possible to arrange a tour of this ancient city remembered in our modern day Olympics. Recommended if you do not mind a lot of sailing getting down to Katakolon and back to the charter base.

Palairos (Zaverda) A small charter base on the mainland opposite Levkas. It is around 1 hour transfer from Aktion Airport.

Vounaki Charter and club base adjacent to Palairos.

Cephalonia A small charter base at Fiskardho.

Zakinthos A small charter base at Zakinthos town. It is around 45 minutes transfer from Zakinthos Airport.

Sailing area

The area is fairly neatly divided up into the north and south. Yachts based in Corfu do a northern itinerary around Corfu, Paxos and the adjacent coast. Yachts based in Levkas and nearby do a southern itinerary around the inland sea bordered by Levkas and Zakinthos. Inevitably there is some crossover with yachts cruising part of the northern and southern areas.

Onward routes

One-way routes are often arranged between Levkas or Zakinthos to Athens. Yachts will either go through the Gulf of Patras, Gulf of Corinth and the Corinth Canal into the Aegean or sail around the Peloponnese and up the eastern side of the Peloponnese to Athens. On either route there is a lot of sailing involved for a two-week trip with a total of around 180 miles through the Corinth Canal and around 270 miles around the Peloponnese.

SARONIC

Situated in the gulf south of Athens and generally extended as an area down the east coast of the Peloponnese. Its proximity to Athens and Athens Airport has meant it has always been a popular area. Despite being close to Athens the area has many small relatively untouched harbours and anchorages as well as more sophisticated resorts. The geography of the area is rugged and rocky with the mountains of the eastern Peloponnese rising abruptly from the sea and providing a magnificent backdrop. The climate is hotter than the Ionian and in July and August temperatures can reach a sizzling 33–36°C.

Wind and sea

There is a mix of prevailing winds over the area. In the Saronic Gulf down to Poros the *meltemi* will often blow although this area is at the limit of the area the wind blows over. The *meltemi* blows from the NE at around Force 4–6 (11–27 knots). It will frequently blow day and night although it generally dies off at night towards Methana and Poros. If the *meltemi* does not blow there will often be a S–SE sea breeze. In the area between Poros, Hydra and the Argolic Gulf the prevailing wind is a sea breeze blowing from the SE. It usually gets up about midday, blows at Force 4–6 (11–27 knots) and dies down at sunset. Down the eastern Peloponnese from Kiparissia to Monemvasia the prevailing wind is a NE morning breeze around Force 4

(11–16 knots) turning around to a SE sea breeze around Force 4 in the afternoon (the Bouka Doura). In July and August the *meltemi* will sometimes blow onto this coast at anything up to Force 6–7 (22–33 knots).

Seas in this area vary according to the area. Behind the islands and in the Argolic Gulf the seas are typically short and sharp but of no great height. Seas in the Saronic Gulf are a little fiercer when the *meltemi* is blowing. Along the eastern Peloponnese the seas are higher and can become confused when the *meltemi* blows onto the coast.

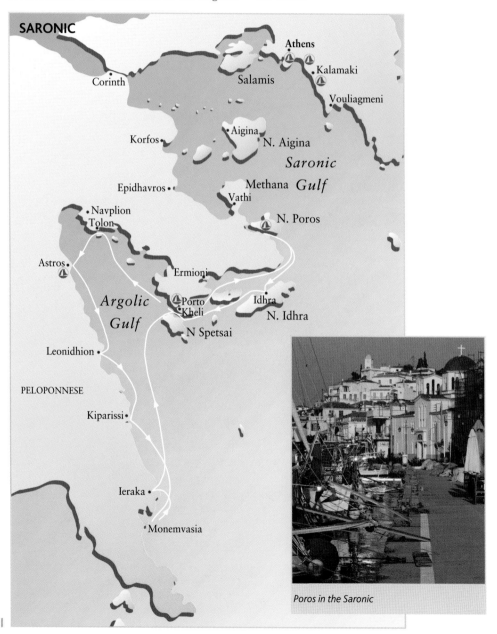

Poros in the Saronic

Suitable for...

The area with a mix of winds and numerous well sheltered harbours and anchorages is suitable for beginners and families. In the area encompassed by Poros, Hydra, Spetsai and the Argolic Gulf, the predictable afternoon breeze and morning calm makes it an ideal flotilla area with longer excursions down the Peloponnese or up to Aegina for the more adventurous. Like the Ionian there is plenty of exhilarating sailing to be had in the area with the morning calm providing the opportunity to motor to windward if desired.

Harbours and anchorages

The area has a mix of yacht harbours, fishing harbours and anchorages amongst the islands and the adjacent coast. Around the coast near Athens are numerous marinas, although most charterers will only use these as the base from which they leave and return to. Some of the harbours close to Athens, notably Aegina, Poros, Hydra and Spetsai, are overcrowded in the summer and especially at weekends when Athens based boats pour out of the capital for the unpolluted air of the islands. Berthing in the harbours is everywhere stern or bows-to using your own anchor except for the marinas where laid moorings are installed.

Main charter bases

The main bareboat and skippered charter bases are in the marinas near Athens, in Poros and Porto Kheli. Flotilla bases are in Epidhavros, Paros and Porto Kheli.

A typical two-week intermediate itinerary is as follows:

Poros – Monemvasia – Poros

Total 125 miles

Starts at Poros

Hydra	An exquisite gem preserved much as it was in the 19th century and where no cars are allowed on the island. A popular destination and you need to get here before 1500 to get a berth (although after that boats stack out from the quay up to three deep). Tavernas.
Spetsai	Anchor with a long line ashore in Baltiza Creek as the inner harbour is usually crowded. Attractive 19th century merchants houses. Tavernas and night life.
Khaidhari	Enclosed inlet with tavernas.
Astrous	A short sail across the gulf. Attractive harbour with good swimming beach nearby. Tavernas.
Lay day	
Leonidhion	A small fishing harbour. A bit uncomfortable but delightful. Tavernas.
Kiparissi	A huge bay with a pier. Anchor or go stern or bows-to according to the wind and sea. Tavernas.
Monemvasia	A Gibraltar-like headland jutting out from the coast. A small marina on the south side or anchor off. Visit the old town on the peninsula for an evening meal.
Lay day	Explore the old fort and old town on the peninsula or anchorages in the bays to the north.
Ieraka	A fjord-like inlet between Monemvasia and Kiparissi. Tavernas.
Porto Kheli	An enclosed bay opposite Spetsai. Watersports centre. Tavernas.
Poros	

Land excursions

Athens	The ancient capital of Greece and birthplace of democracy although it is difficult to discern the ancient bits amongst the high-rise buildings. A visit to the Parthenon and surrounding buildings is a must.
Epidavros	A taxi can be arranged from the harbour of Palaia Epidavros to visit the theatre, an acoustically perfect piece of ancient engineering. Also buildings of the Askeplion and a little museum. Recommended.
Mycenae	An excursion can be arranged from Navplion. An impressive and important site, the centre of the Mycenean civilisation. Navplion itself is a smelly harbour, but the old town and the impressive Venetian citadel of Palamidhi above it merits a visit. Recommended.
Leonidhion	From here you can arrange a taxi to visit the Monastery of Elona tucked into the cliffs in the mountains behind the port.
Monemvasia	The old town on the headland, now a protected site, and the citadel on the summit are a marvellously preserved piece of Byzantine architecture with later Turkish and Venetian additions. Recommended.

Athens In the marinas around Athens there are numerous bareboat and skippered charter companies based at Zea Marina, Flisvos (Faliron), and Alimos (Kalamaki) Marina. The attraction of these charter bases is not the surroundings which are noisy, dirty and subject to noise pollution, but the convenience of a short transfer to your yacht. Transfer times are around 45 minutes from Spata Airport.

Epidhavros Used off and on as a charter base. Transfer time around 2½ hours from Spata Airport.

Poros A flotilla and bareboat base in the harbour sandwiched between Poros Island and the Peloponnese. Around 2–2½ hours transfer time on the hydrofoil or fast ferry from Piraeus.

Porto Kheli A flotilla base in the natural harbour opposite the island of Spetsai. Around 4 hour transfer time.

Sailing area

The area has a fairly standard run from Athens following the coast of the eastern Peloponnese and off-lying islands until turning around and heading back. There are sufficient harbours and anchorages along the way so that you do not have to revisit places on the return leg of the route.

Depending on how much sailing is desired a yacht can cruise up into the Argolic Gulf and/or south down to Monemvasia.

Onward routes

Athens is the centre of yachting in Greece and one-way trips are common to several other areas.

Ionian One-way routes are often arranged between Athens to Levkas or Zakinthos. Yachts will either go through the Corinth Canal to the Gulf of Corinth, Gulf of Patras and into the Ionian or sail around the Peloponnese and up the western side of the Peloponnese. On either route there is a lot of sailing involved for a two week trip with a total of around 180 miles through the Corinth Canal and around 270 miles around the Peloponnese.

Dodecanese One-way routes are common through the Cyclades to either Kos or Rhodes. This route is fairly windy although heading SE to the Dodecanese the wind is mostly aft of the beam when the *meltemi* is blowing. Around 250 miles.

Northern Sporades Not a common route. It involves a lot of uphill work against the *meltemi* in the summer. Yachts usually take the inshore route inside Evia where there are more harbours and anchorages to visit.

Around 170 miles on a straight run which you will emphatically not want to do in the summer against the *meltemi*.

CYCLADES

The scattered archipelago of islands in the central Aegean. These are the islands that correspond most to our picture of Greece with white cube houses sprouting from a rocky landscape and lapped by the blue Mediterranean. Everyone has probably heard of Mikonos and possibly of Thira (Santorini), Paros, Naxos and Milos. But there are many many more islands in this group that are just as wonderful as these and which are less popular (read less crowded) and more suited to exploration by yacht. The two names that roll off everyone's tongue, Mikonos and Thira, are paradoxically least suited for a visit by yacht. Mikonos 'marina' is some way out of town and yachts are no longer permitted in the old harbour. Thira has no good comfortable anchorage and is best visited briefly before going to spend the night in a safe harbour nearby.

The area is hot in the summer with temperatures averaging 33–36°C in July and August although the cooling *meltemi* blowing over the islands makes it appear less.

Wind and sea

Between mid-June and the end of September the Aegean is subject to the full force of the *meltemi*. This is a constant wind formed by the pressure difference between the Azores high and the low over Pakistan when the SW monsoon is established and not a typical thermal sea breeze. It regularly blows at Force 6–7 (22–33 knots) and gusts off the lee side of high islands can be considerably more. It is not to be underestimated. It blows in an arc through the Cyclades and is from the NE in the north, turning to N and then NW in the south and west. It does have some thermal component and may die off to Force 4–5 (11–21 knots) at night although you cannot count on it. The *meltemi* is less well developed at the beginning and end of the season and for this reason, this is the best time to visit the Cyclades. There will be some days of calm.

The *meltemi* causes a steep breaking sea that can be difficult to beat against to windward. Around headlands and through channels there can be exceptionally confused seas where the direction of a local wave train is different to the main swell further out.

Suitable for ...

In the summer the Cyclades should be attempted by experienced sailors only. I used to make a living bringing bareboats back from the islands where desperate charterers had abandoned the yacht and with it their deposit. If you set out for the Cyclades and decide it is just too uncomfortable to continue enjoying it then remember you should be able to head west to the Saronic and eastern Peloponnese where winds are lighter and it is generally calm at night.

Harbours and anchorages

Nearly all of the islands have at least one main harbour and many have numerous harbours and/or protected anchorages. Communication by boat was once the only means of communication for these islands and the harbour was the life-line to the outer world. Berthing in the harbours is everywhere stern or bow-to using your own anchor.

Main charter bases

Athens is the main charter base although yachts may sometimes do one-way trips from Rhodes or Kos back to Athens. Getting back from the Dodecanese against the *meltemi* is a long hard bash to windward and for experienced and hardy sailors only. There are also charter bases in Siros, Paros and Poros in the Saronic is not far away.

Sailing area

There are no obvious routes through the Cyclades for a two week cruise and charterers can pick-and-mix according to their preferences. What is important is to leave enough lay-days and a suitable period of time to get back against the *meltemi* to the charter base, usually Athens. There is nothing more calculated to ruin a relaxed holiday than several days of beating to windward against a Force 7 and early on the skipper should take stock of how his crew or guests are reacting to the wind and sea. If there are muttered threats about mutiny and catching the ferry back, then it is always possible to shorten the trip and do shorter legs back against the wind to Athens.

NORTHERN SPORADES

A string of islands in the NW Aegean off the top of Evia. This group is a popular charter area because the *meltemi* blows with less force here and there are numerous harbours and anchorages along the chain of islands. The islands are also greener than the parched rock of the Cyclades with pine covering large parts of the islands and a number of fine sandy beaches. The architecture, typically red-tiled houses with pitched roofs instead of the square cubes of the Cyclades, lends an individual character to the area. Temperatures in the summer are moderate with an average of 30°C in July and August. In the spring and autumn temperatures are considerably cooler than further south and you will need a pullover in the evenings.

Wind and sea

The prevailing wind in the summer is the *meltemi* blowing from the N-NE over the islands. It blows more fitfully here, usually Force 4–5 (11–21 knots), with numerous days of calm or light southerly breezes. At the beginning and end of the season there may be unsettled weather and strong northerly or southerly winds when a depression passes over.

The seas here are typically a low short chop in the lee of the islands with no great force or height to them. In the passages between the islands or out of their lee the seas can be higher, but usually of no consequence in the summer.

Suitable for ...

The settled wind patterns and moderate winds mean this is a popular area for flotilla and bareboat charter for beginners and intermediate sailors. If venturing out of the area, say down to Skiros and the east coast of Evia, then the *meltemi* is considerably stronger and the seas proportionately higher, so more sailing experience is necessary.

Harbours and anchorages

There are numerous well-protected harbours and anchorages along the chain of islands that make up the Northern Sporades and in and around the northern Evia channel on the mainland opposite. The harbours and anchorages on the main islands of Skiathos, Skopelos and Alonnisos can get crowded in the summer while the harbours on the mainland and Evia are never crowded. Berthing in the harbours is nearly everywhere stern or bow-to using your own anchor.

Main charter bases

The main charter base is Skiathos where there is an airport with direct European flights. Transfer time is around 15 minutes. There are also charter bases in Volos and Vathoudhi in the Gulf of Volos.

Sailing area

The sailing area is under the lee of the chain of islands with a trip south to Skiros for the more experienced or west into the northern Evia channel and Gulf of Volos for those who want to venture further. From Skiathos most yachts head for Glossa or one of the anchorages on the SW side of Skopelos, around to Skopelos depending on the strength of the *meltemi*, to Patitiri on Alonnisos, and then to Pelagos. After that it is a matter of deciding whether you will stay under the lee of the islands and potter, or head off to the northern Evia channel and Gulf of Volos or south to windy Skiros and the east side of Evia.

Ay Yeoryios on Agathonisi in the Dodecanese

Onward routes

Not common. It is possible to do a one-way route to Athens, usually down the inside of Evia.

DODECANESE

The string of islands lying down the eastern side of the Aegean close to the Turkish coast. The islands have had a chequered history and were occupied by the Italians up until the Second World War when they reverted to Greece. In recent years the area has become increasingly popular for yacht charter and because mild weather can be expected later in the season it can be as busy here in late September as it is in August in other areas. The climate here can be very hot in summer and is still warm in late September and October. Temperatures in July and August typically reach 34–36°C although like the Cyclades it feels less because of the cooling *meltemi* blowing over the islands.

Wind and sea

The prevailing wind in the summer is our old friend the *meltemi*. In the SE corner of the Aegean it has curved around to blow from the NW-W. It usually blows at Force 5–7 (17–33 knots) in the summer with stronger gusts off the lee side of the high islands. As in the Cyclades, it blows with less force and frequency at the beginning and end of the season.

Seas around the Dodecanese are the short sharp seas similar to the Cyclades and difficult to beat against to windward. In the summer a fairly constant current flows northwards up the Turkish coast and the prevailing winds blowing against this current can create confused seas, especially around headlands and capes.

Suitable for ...

Like the Cyclades the Dodecanese is for experienced sailors. The strong summer winds and short seas create conditions that can make it difficult to go north. Most yacht charter here is bareboat or skippered charter although there is sometimes sailing in company.

Harbours and anchorages

Like the Cyclades, communication by sea was essential in the past, and all the islands

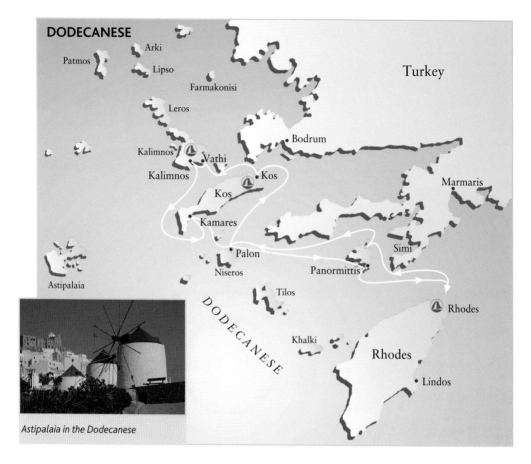

Astipalaia in the Dodecanese

have at least one harbour and frequently more. There are also numerous well sheltered anchorages and the charterer will have no problem arranging an itinerary around the islands. Berthing in all harbours is stern or bow-to using your own anchor.

Main charter bases
The main charter base is at Rhodes. There are frequent European flights to Rhodes airport with a transfer time of around 45 minutes to Rhodes harbour. Charter yachts are also based at Kos where there is around a 25 minute transfer from Kos airport to Kos harbour and in Pithagorion on Samos.

Sailing area
The sailing area extends north from Rhodes to Samos for hardy sailors who want to keep on beating to windward to get this far. There

is a wide choice of harbours and anchorages all along the chain of islands and starting at Rhodes has the advantage that you get the windward leg of the cruise out of the way first and can then coast back south to Rhodes with the wind aft of the beam. From Kos you can go either north or south depending on your inclination and how far you want to sail.

Onward routes
It is possible to charter a yacht in Rhodes and sail up through the Cyclades to Athens. In the summer when the *meltemi* is blowing this is a long hard slog against the prevailing wind and can only be recommended for experienced sailors. Less experienced sailors can contemplate it in early or late season. Around 250 miles.

A typical two-week itinerary is as follows:

Rhodes – Kalimnos – Rhodes

Total 180 miles

Starts at Rhodes

Simi	Until you get up to the entrance you will not see the building block town around the sides of the steep-to inlet that forms the natural harbour. Tavernas.
Lay day	Potter around to any of the bays on the east or south of the island or just relax at Simi town.
Nisiros/Palon	A small fishing harbour on the north side of Nisiros. Several tavernas.
Lay day	Visit the crater at the summit of the island.
Kos	The main harbour of the island. Crowded and chaotic. Tavernas and night life.
Kalimnos/Vathi	A fjord-like inlet on the SE corner of the island. If there is no room on the small quayed area anchor fore and aft further into the inlet. Several tavernas.
Kalimnos	Main harbour of the island. Tavernas and night life.
Two lay days	Potter around the island or go further north to Leros.
Kos/Kamares	Small harbour and bay tucked under the SW corner of Kos. Berth in the harbour or anchor in the bay. Several tavernas.
Palon on Nisiros or **Tilos**	Tilos is not a good harbour with a strong *meltemi* so make your choice depending on the wind.
Simi/Panormittis	An enclosed anchorage on the SW corner of Simi. Monastery ashore. Taverna.
Rhodes	

Land excursions

Rhodes	The old walled town and castle of the Knights of St John is one of the finest surviving pieces of Medieval military architecture. Just wander around and try to avoid the touts.
Nisiros	A visit to the crater is well worth the effort and you get magnificent views over the sea and islands as well. An occasional bus from Mandraki or arrange a taxi from Palon. Do not leave your yacht unattended in Mandraki harbour which is exposed to the *meltemi*. Recommended.
Kos	Around Kos town are bits and pieces of the ancient city and the castle built by the Knights of St John. A visit to the famous Askeplion made famous by Hippocrates is easiest by taxi.
Patmos	The fortified monastery of St John is easily reached by bus or taxi from Skala, the main port on the east side of the island. Recommended.

TURKEY

When you wake up in the morning one of the first things you will hear is the wail of the muezzin from a nearby minaret to remind you that you have ventured east of Christendom. Turkey is a gentle introduction to Islam and while the slender minarets pierce the skyline, ashore you will be surprised at how familiar everything is from the boutiques selling Levi jeans and Prada handbags to marina facilities that are as good or better than any in the Mediterranean. Turkish food has long been considered the eastern equivalent of French food in the west and you will eat well in restaurants large and small. Add to this the flavours, sights and sounds of the east and few fail to be entranced with the country.

Afloat the coast offers a wonderful mix of those all singing and dancing marinas to anchorages tucked away from the razzamatazz of the towns and tourist resorts. In many of the little coves you will find a restaurant with a rickety jetty where you can tie up and eat simply but well. In the smaller places you will likely be introduced to the whole family and these friendly little spots add much to the charm of the coastline.

Like the coasts and waters to the west, Turkey is all mountains dropping sheer into a turquoise sea, although the coast is generally more wooded than in the Greek islands to the west. There are ancient Greek and Roman sites everywhere attesting to the fact that the ancients valued this coastline as well. Even if you are not a lover of things ancient, you will likely be impressed with the situation and completeness of the sites and there are few who would deny the romance of anchoring under the ruins of Knidos or the Crusader castle at Bodrum.

Turkey is now a well established charter destination in the Mediterranean. It supports all types of charter from flotilla, through bareboat to skippered charter with a number of charter bases around the coast. One of the features of chartering here are the local boats, the *gulets*, which are still built in wood and have been adapted for skippered charter. The *gulets* come in all sizes from 15 metres up to 25 metres and all will have a skipper and crew on board who will not only sail you around the coast but also cook and entertain.

Although Turkey has few islands it does have a much indented coastline with deep gulfs making up for the lack of islands. A few skippered yachts cruised Turkey in the 1960s and 70s but it was not until the 1980s that yacht charter expanded in Turkey and flotilla and bareboat fleets were introduced. The area is well suited to yacht charter with a settled summer climate, the prevailing winds tailing off into the gulfs and a magnificent mountainous coastline covered

BEFORE YOU GO

For
- ✔ Settled summer weather patterns and a long season.
- ✔ Numerous packages available with all types of charter catered for from flotilla to skippered luxury yachts.
- ✔ Good and interesting food with a flavour of the east and exceptionally good value.
- ✔ Magnificent mountainous scenery with numerous attractive anchorages.
- ✔ Lots of things to do and see ashore.

Against
- ✘ Some areas crowded in the summer.
- ✘ Long transfers to some charter bases.

Types of charter
- ❖ Flotilla
- ❖ Bareboat
- ❖ Skippered charter
- ❖ Luxury charter

Suitable for
- ❖ Novices through to experienced sailors.

in pine in many places. For most people it is a gentle introduction to Asia Minor and most people come away surprised at the subtle blend of east and west. In recent years a number of marinas have been built around the coast and these rank with any in the Mediterranean for services and facilities.

WHEN TO GO

The season in Turkey starts around mid-April and runs through until the end of October. The weather is warmer and more settled here later in the season than it is further west in the Aegean.

Early season April to May. Day temperatures are warm, around 22–27°C in the day, but drop at night when a sweater will be needed. Sea temperatures have not yet warmed up and are generally around 19–20°C. Wind patterns have not yet become fully established although there is still a preponderance of northerlies. There is a possibility of a depression passing nearby bringing gale force winds, often southerlies, for a few days accompanied by rain and frequently thunderstorms.

High season June to September. Day temperatures are hot, around 33–36°C in July and August, and evenings are warm. On days when there is no wind or in harbours which shut out the wind it can feel very hot. Along the eastern Turkish coast

ESSENTIAL INFORMATION

Capital Ankara

Time zone UT + 2 DST Apr–Sep

Language Turkish (using Roman alphabet since 1928). Kurdish and Arabic. English, German and some French in tourist resorts.

Telecommunications Automatic dialling to most areas. Code 90. Public telephone system with phonecards. GSM phones supported throughout Turkey. Internet cafés and wifi.

Electricity 220V 50Hz AC.

temperatures are higher, often 35–36°C in the day, and a higher humidity saps the energy and can make sleeping at night difficult until you get used to it. Sea temperatures have warmed up to around 22–25°C and shallow water that gets the sun all day is positively tepid. Wind patterns are dependable and the prevailing winds are constant in direction and strength. There are few days of rain.

Late season October. Day temperatures are still hot, around 25–27°C, although the evenings are cooler. Sea temperatures remain warm around 24°C. Wind patterns are still constant although there is the

At Bodrum	Av max °C	Av min °C	Highest recorded	Relative humidity	Days 1 mm rain	Sea temp °C	Wind direction & force
Apr	21	9	33	48%	5	16.5	NW/SE F4
May	26	13	41	45%	4	19	W-NW F4
Jun	31	17	41	40%	2	21.5	W-NW F4-5
Jul	33	21	42	31%	0	23.5	W-NW F4-5
Aug	33	21	42	37%	1	25.5	W-NW F4-5
Sep	29	17	39	42%	1	24.5	W-NW F4-5
Oct	24	13	37	49%	4	22.5	W-NW F4
Nov	19	9	32	58%	6	20	NW/SE F4

Gulets ready for charter

WHEN YOU'RE THERE

Visas and documentation

All visitors to Turkey must have a valid passport. EU members may carry an identity card. Most visitors do not need a visa except for UK nationals. This visa can be obtained when you go through immigration and at the time of writing costs £10.00 in sterling.

In some cases proof of competence to handle a yacht will be asked for. Ask your yacht charter company for advice and if they believe documentation is necessary they will advise you. All other boat documentation will be provided by the company. It can take several hours for clearance of the charter documentation before you leave and as your passports will be required, this cannot be done beforehand. At subsequent harbours you will be responsible for clearing in and out as required if not on flotilla. It is not unusual for the coastguard, the *Sahil Guvenlik*, to check your papers in anchorages and while the process is thorough it is always polite.

possibility of a depression passing through bringing gale force winds, rain, and frequently thunderstorms.

GETTING THERE

Although Istanbul is the main international airport for Turkey, it is too far from the popular charter areas to be useful for most people on a two-week holiday.

Most charterers arrive through one of the smaller airports that have European flights, principally Izmir, Bodrum, Dalaman or Antalya. There are frequent charter flights to these destinations in the summer. Internal flights from Istanbul connect with these airports on a regular basis.

Getting to the charter base will usually be by bus, mini-bus or taxi. If a charter company offers a transfer service this should be taken as it removes the hassles of arranging your transport to and from the airport and will usually cost less than arranging your own transfers.

Health

Medical services in the cities and tourist resorts range from average to very good, depending on whether you go to one of the private clinics. It is advised you have private medical insurance for the trip and most charter travel operators can arrange this quickly. Travel insurance (including medical cover) is mandatory with all flotilla operators and many bareboat companies.

In most places the water is potable, but it is likely that delicate stomachs will react to local and perfectly normal micro-organisms, and for a few days some people will have a mild case of the runs. Those with delicate stomachs, and babies, should drink bottled water.

Money and banks

The unit of currency is the Yeni Turkish Lira (YTL). The currency has been relatively stable for some years now although in the past Turkey has had a

Bozburun between Bodrum and Marmaris

problem with raging inflation (often 40–50% per annum). Euros are now more commonly accepted than US dollars and prices will often be in Euros as well as Yeni Lira.

Banks are open 0830–1200 and 1330–1700 Mon–Fri. Exchange offices, marina offices, and travel agents operate outside these hours. All major credit cards and charge cards are accepted. ATM machines can be found in the larger towns and tourist resorts and work with most credit cards.

Eating and drinking

Eating in Turkey is a delight. The cuisine is as celebrated in the east as French cuisine is in the west. The food is varied, and inexpensive and the service invariably good. Turks are natural entrepreneurs and if half a dozen yachts visit an anchorage, a makeshift restaurant will spring up there in no time. In the villages and towns there is usually a good choice of restaurants of all types. *Lokantas* are the traditional eating place, usually serving an interesting variety of pre-cooked soups, stews and oven dishes as well as grilled dishes. Restaurants are more up-market and usually have fewer pre-cooked and more grilled dishes. Pizza

places may serve the traditional Turkish *pide* and/or adaptations of the Italian pizza. Between these are many shades of grey.

Starters in Turkey are many and varied. There will often be different vegetables in a vinaigrette, salads of all descriptions including seafood and chicken salads, small hot dishes like *borek* (cheese wrapped in a *filo* pastry and deep fried), cooked vegetables like aubergine which are chopped and combined into dips – the list is long and satisfying.

Cooked dishes often revolve around stewed dishes or *pilaf* combinations. Lamb, beef and chicken are used, but not pork as this, at least nominally, is a Muslim country. Grilled meat can be beef, spicy meatballs, kebabs, lamb, chicken or liver. Fish is invariably grilled. Many restaurants will have special dishes they prepare and these can be very good. Most people are impressed by the variety and finesse of Turkish cuisine and a cruise along the Turkish coast can become as much a gastronomy tour as a sailing holiday.

Turkish wine is just acceptable, but it is not a cheap tipple as it is for most of the rest of the Mediterranean. It is neither fine nor consistent and you will often find that one

SAILING GUIDES AND CHARTS

There are several guides to Turkey and charts cover all areas. Obtaining these guides and charts in Turkey can be all but impossible and if you do find them they will cost you a good deal more than in your own country. The following may be useful:

Turkish Waters and Cyprus Pilot Rod Heikell. Imray. Covers all Turkish waters in detail.

East Aegean Rod Heikell. Imray. A guide on things afloat and ashore for the Dodecanese and adjacent Turkish coast from Bodrum to Kekova.

Admiralty charts cover all areas and are available from Admiralty agents.

Imray-Tetra charts cover all the charter areas on a scale suitable for yachtsmen and are available from Imrays or chandlers.

bottle is different to another, sometimes dramatically so. Turkish beer, mostly *Efes* or *Tuborg*, is of the lager type and eminently thirst quenching. *Raki*, the aniseed flavoured aperitif similar to *ouzo*, is potent and drunk in surprisingly large quantities by Turkish males. Turkish gin and vodka is adequate, but Turkish brandy is only really palatable if you like something that tastes like cough mixture.

Provisioning

Most provisions can be found except in some out-of-the-way places. Local produce, especially fruit and vegetables, is excellent. Imported goods can be found in the larger towns and resorts, but naturally prices are substantially higher than you might pay in Europe. In the towns there is a market day once a week (usually Friday) where local produce – fruit and vegetables, dried fruit and nuts, local cheeses, herbs and spices, and local handicrafts as well as the ubiquitous range of plastic goods and knickknacks found all over the world – is on sale. It is worth going to just for the colour and odd interesting stalls even if you don't intend buying anything.

Stocking up the boat can usually be accomplished at a few nearby shops and many will deliver to the boat. Some of the yacht charter companies will provide an order list so that the boat is provisioned when you arrive.

Costs

The overall cost of living is below EU averages although prices have been rising, particularly in some of the restaurants in the larger resorts or where there is a captive market. With a little time you can inspect a number of restaurants and make your choice at leisure. Typical costs for eating out range from around €5 a head in a small lokanta or restaurant to €20–40 a head in a restaurant. Wine can easily push up the cost as it is frequently €15–25 a bottle for a pretty ordinary bottle. Beer is €1.50–2.50 a glass. Spirits are cheap although you may find the label on the bottle does not reflect what is in it. In general wine is expensive and variable while local beer and spirits are reasonably priced.

Provisioning is cheap if you stick to local produce and locally produced staples, but any imported items are expensive. Few spend a lot of time on board cooking because the food ashore is relatively cheap and good, so most provisioning only needs to be for breakfast and lunch.

Transport in Turkey is cheap. Taxi fares are low now that most taxis have meters. Buses run to many destinations and *dolmus* (a shared mini-bus running on a more or less fixed route, *dolmus* literally means 'stuffed') run the locals and tourists alike everywhere else. The low level of car ownership means you can get just about anywhere by bus or *dolmus*. Hire cars are relatively expensive at €40–60 per day.

Crime and personal safety

Turkey is a safe country to visit with few instances of mugging, rape and petty theft. In recent years there has been a rise in the incidence of sexual assaults on lone women in the larger resorts and normal precautions should be taken – do not stay alone in out-of-the-way night-clubs and bars until the wee hours and do not walk home unaccompanied late at night. Taxis run all through the night in most resorts and are cheap. Theft from boats is rare and you are unlikely to have anything stolen from your boat.

CHARTER AREAS

BODRUM

Bodrum sits at the entrance to the Gulf of Gökkova opposite the Greek island of Kos. A number of charter fleets are based at and around Bodrum from where they can explore the Gulf of Güllük to the north, the Gulf of Gökkova, or further south to the Gulf of Hisarönü. The climate can be very hot in the summer and the season lasts well into September and October. Temperatures in July often reach 34–36°C and out of any cooling breeze it does feel hot. Bodrum sits protected by a semi-circle of high land and is a dusty breathless place in July and August.

Wind and sea

The prevailing wind in the summer is the *meltemi*. It blows down the coast from the NW to west, tending to curve and blow down into the gulfs. It usually blows at Force 5–7 (17–33 knots) in the summer with stronger gusts off the high land on the north side of the gulfs. At the head of the gulfs it tends to run out of steam. At the beginning and end of the season when the *meltemi* does not blow winds still tend to be northerly although there may also be a south–SW sea breeze. Also at the beginning and end of the season a depression may

TURKEY'S MAIN CHARTER AREAS

Black Sea

Turkey

Istanbul

Sea of Marmara

Dardanelles

Eski Foca

Turkey

1 Around Bodrum & Marmaris
2 Marmaris to Antalya

Izmir

Cesme

Kusadasi

Güllük

Bodrum

Marmaris

Kemer

Fethiye

Antalya

Kas

Syria

Aegean Sea

Rhodes

Cyprus

GULF OF GÜLLÜK AND GÖKKÖVA

Gulf of Güllük

Asin Limani

Turk Buku
Yalikavak
Gümüslük   Torba
Bitez   Bodrum   BODRUM PENINSULA

Restaurant jetty in Paradise Bay

Cökertme

Sehir Adalari
Söğüt
Degirmen
Marmaris

Gulf of Gökköva

Keçi Buku

DATÇA PENINSULA

Datça   *Gulf of Hisarönü*   Bozburun

Knidus

Simi

---

pass through bringing gale force winds, frequently from the south.

Seas around the coast are the typical short chop of the Mediterranean which can be difficult to beat to windward against. In the summer a fairly constant current flows northwards up the Turkish coast and around headlands and capes and in narrow channels the prevailing wind blowing against the current can kick up a confused sea.

Suitable for ...

The area is suitable for everyone from novice to intermediate and experienced sailors depending on the distances you intend to sail. On a skippered *gulet* charter you need have no experience at all and can do as much or as little on board as you want.

In the *meltemi* season the wind can at times be strong and off the capes considerable confused seas can be raised. Yacht charter here is a mix of flotilla,

bareboat and skippered charter with the local boats, the *gulets*, running what amounts to a mixture of yacht charter and a mini-cruise.

Harbours and anchorages

There are a number of harbours around the gulfs, but for the most part there are a large number of sheltered anchorages. In most of the anchorages yachts anchor and take a long line ashore. Berthing in harbours is stern or bow-to using your own anchor except where laid moorings have been installed.

Main charter bases

The main charter base is Bodrum Marina. Close to Bodrum at Gumbet and Bitez there are also flotilla and bareboat bases. There are also charter boats at the other two marinas on the Bodrum peninsula at Turgutreis and Yalikavak. All three marinas are under one hour from Bodrum Airport.

A typical two-week intermediate itinerary is as follows:

Bodrum – Bodrum

Total 170 miles

A cruise in the Gulf of Güllük and Gulf of Gökköva. Starts at Bodrum.

Bitez	A bay just a few miles along the coast from Bodrum. Gives you a chance to get used to the yacht. Watersports centre. Restaurants.
Gümüslük	An enclosed bay on the western end of Bodrum peninsula. Care needed of the submerged breakwater in the entrance. Anchor with a long line ashore or in calm weather go bow-to the wooden jetty. Restaurants.
Turk Buku	Large bay on the south side of the Gulf of Güllük. Restaurants and bars.
Asin Limani	Narrow inlet in the NE of Gulf of Güllük. Restaurants. Visit ancient Myndos atop the hill.
Lay day	Visit the ruins of ancient Iassus above the harbour or sail to nearby bays.
Yalikavak	Stay in the new marina for some pampering and good restaurants ashore. Visit the village and local market.
Bitez/Bodrum/ bays nearby	Stock up on provisions. A good alternative is Turgutreis Marina.
Cökertme	Anchor with a long line ashore or stern-to on one of the restaurant jetties. Restaurants. Carpets made ashore.
Sögüt	Stern or bow-to one of the jetties. Pine clad bay. Restaurants.
Lay day	Visit Snake and Castle Islands. Return to Sögüt for the night.
Değirmen Buku	Anchor in one of the bays. Restaurants with jetties in the east bay.
Cökertme	
Bodrum	

Land excursions

Bodrum	Visit St Peters Castle by the harbour. Excellent museum of underwater archaeology within. Recommended. Also the site of the Mausoleum.
Ephesus	Excursions can be arranged from Bodrum. It is a full day excursion usually visiting other sites such as the Church of the Virgin Mary. Ephesus is crowded, but recommended.
Iassus	Can be visited from Asin harbour. The setting is exquisite.
Didyma	Can be visited by taxi from Altinkum on the northern side of the Gulf of Güllük. Largest Ionic temple.
Snake and Castle Islands (Sehir Adalari)	Ruins of ancient city and necropolis in an idyllic site. Cleopatra's beach. Islands recommended.
Knidos	Site of the ancient city is immediately above the ancient harbour on the end of the Datça peninsula. Recommended.

Sailing area

The sailing area tends to revolve around the two gulfs of Güllük and Gökkova. The gulfs are deep (the Gulf of Gökkova is over 40 miles long and mostly over 10 miles wide) and much indented, providing numerous sheltered anchorages. The coast is mostly mountainous and much of it is extensively wooded in pine. Although there are relatively few harbours, there are numerous restaurants dotted around the various bays. Provisions are more hard to come by except in the few settlements.

Onward routes

One-way routes are often arranged between Bodrum and Marmaris. This is easily within the compass of a two-week cruise and is not a taxing trip. From Bodrum you have the wind aft of the beam for most of the trip. Around a 110-mile trip without excursions into the gulfs. The total mileage is easily extended by sailing into the gulfs.

MARMARIS

Marmaris sits tucked up in a large bay opposite the island of Rhodes. A number of charter fleets are based at the marina or around the large bay. From here yachts can explore either west towards the Gulf of Hisarönü or SE towards the Gulf of Fethiye. The climate here is very hot in the summer

and is still warm in September and October. Temperatures can reach 34–36°C and it feels hot and sticky out of any breeze.

Wind and sea

The prevailing wind in the summer is the *meltemi* although here it often has a distinct diurnal component and dies off to some extent at night and in the early morning. Often the wind will not penetrate all the way to Ekinçik until the afternoon. On the more exposed coast, especially along the coast running down to Bozburun, the *meltemi* will blow from the NW-west at around Force 4–6 (11–27 knots) in July to September. When the *meltemi* does not blow there will often be a sea breeze from the south–SE. In early and late season a depression may pass through, bringing gale force winds, frequently from the south.

Seas in the area are short and sharp and can become confused around capes and through narrow channels where the prevailing wind blows against the north-going current. Where there is no wind around the coast between Marmaris and south of Ekinçik there will often be a confused sea, the result of wind further out to sea.

Suitable for...

The area is suitable for novices and intermediate to experienced sailors. *Gulet* trips also operate from here. Yacht charter

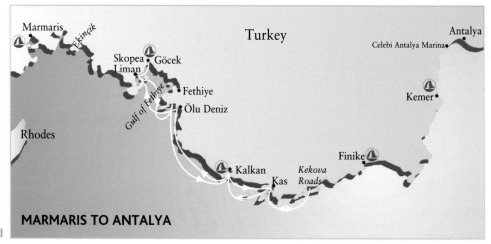

MARMARIS TO ANTALYA

here is a mix of flotilla, bareboat and skippered charter as well as *gulet* mini-cruises.

Harbours and anchorages

There are few harbours around the area and for the most part you will be visiting anchorages. As at Bodrum you will frequently have to anchor with a long line ashore. Berthing in the harbours is stern or bow-to using your own anchor except where laid moorings are supplied as at Marmaris Marina.

Main charter bases

The main charter base is Marmaris Marina with a few other bases scattered around the large bay. There is also a charter base in Keçi Buku. Flights are normally to Dalaman Airport with around a 3-hour transfer from the airport to Marmaris.

Sailing area

Yachts tend to head for either the Gulf of Hisarönü to the west or go SE down to the Gulf of Fethiye. The adventurous in search of sea miles can combine the two. As for Bodrum the deep and much indented coast provides a large cruising area despite the lack of islands to cruise around. Most of the coast is steep-to and wooded in pine. Although there are few harbours, there are typically numerous restaurants in the bays.

Onward routes

Bodrum One-way routes to Bodrum. The one way trip to Bodrum is against the prevailing wind but is not overly arduous at around 110 miles without detours into the gulfs.
Fethiye/Göçek The one way trip to Fethiye or Göçek is around 70–80 miles which can easily be extended.

Land excursions

Caunos From Ekinçik local boats take you up a reed lined river to the ancient site of Caunos. En route you will see Lycian rock tombs in the cliffs above the river. Recommended.

FETHIYE/GÖÇEK

The Gulf of Fethiye is tucked into the coast approximately 40 miles east of Rhodes. A number of charter fleets are based here with access to the cruising area to the NW and south and, importantly, close to Dalaman Airport. The climate here is very hot in the summer with temperatures often reaching 34–38°C. As with further north and west, the season extends well into October.

Wind and sea

The prevailing wind here is the *meltemi* blowing from the west–SW. It has a distinct diurnal component in many parts of the area and often will not reach some areas at all. The *meltemi* blows strongest through August and September at around Force 4–6 (11–27 knots) although there will be days when it is lighter or does not blow at all. Effectively you are on the limit of the *meltemi* area here. In early and late season winds are commonly from the north or south with a light sea breeze from a southerly direction often blowing. In early and late season a depression may pass through, often bring gale force winds, frequently from the south.

Seas along the coast are short and sharp, but moderate with one exception. When the *meltemi* is blowing strongly there can be heavy seas running along the coast between the Gulf of Fethiye and Kekova, especially off Yedi Burunlar, the Seven Capes.

Suitable for...

The area is suitable for beginners and experienced sailors. Beginners in the area should stay clear of the Seven Capes and destinations SE of the Gulf of Fethiye in the *meltemi* season. Yacht charter here is a mixture of flotilla, bareboat and skippered charter as well as *gulet* mini-cruises.

Harbours and anchorages

There are a few harbours along the coast, but for the most part you will be visiting anchorages. As further north, anchoring with a long line ashore is the norm in many places. Berthing in the harbours is stern or bow-to using your own anchor except where laid moorings are supplied.

Main charter bases

Göcek A small village in the north corner of the Gulf of Fethiye that has developed into an important charter base. Transfer time is around 30 minutes from Dalaman Airport,

A typical two-week intermediate itinerary is as follows:

Göcek – Kekova – Göcek

Total 160 miles

Starts at Göcek.

Skopea Liman/ Deep Bay	Anchor with a long line ashore or bow-to the jetty off the restaurant.
Skopea Liman/ Kapi Creek	Sail to Wall Bay for lunch. End up in Kapi Creek. Restaurant.
Gemiler Adasi	Anchor in Karacaoren Buku for the night. Restaurant.
Kalkan	Stern or bow-to. Restaurants.
Lay day	Arrange a trip to Patara and/or Xanthos.
Kas	Stern or bow-to. Restaurants.
Kekova Roads	Anchor for the night in Ucagiz. Restaurants.
Lay day	Potter around and return to Ucagiz or Gokkaya.
Kas	
Kalkan	
Gemiler Island	Yachts often leave very early in the morning to get up this difficult stretch of coast. Anchor with a long line ashore to the island.
Skopea Liman/ Tomb Bay	Anchor with a long line ashore or stern or bow-to the jetty off the restaurant.
Göcek	

Land excursions

Fethiye	Home to a few sarcophagi and a large rock tomb behind. The market in the town is colourful.
Patara	A huge city now mostly covered in sand. You pass by it on the way down the coast. Taxi from Kalkan.
Xanthos	The ancient capital of Lycia in a wooded valley. Surrounded by numerous sarcophagi. Taxi from Kalkan. Recommended.
Kale Koy	A small castle and miniature theatre amid a vast necropolis. Yachts anchor off in the bay below. Recommended.
Salikent Gorge	A deep gorge with a river running down through it, local villages and stunning scenery.

Yacht pontoon off restaurant in Kale Koy in Kekova

the short transfer time making it a popular place for charter fleets.

Fethiye The large town in the east corner of the gulf. There are charter fleets at Fethiye Marina or in nearby locations around Fethiye Bay. Transfer time from Dalaman Airport is around 45 minutes.

Finike A small charter fleet sometimes based here.

Sailing area

Yachts tend to potter around the NW side of the Gulf of Fethiye amongst the islands and bays and then head either NW towards Marmaris or SE towards Kekova. The coast is, as elsewhere, mountainous and largely wooded in pine.

Onward routes

Marmaris A popular one-way route for many charterers. Around 70–80 miles.

Kemer or Antalya Celebi Marina A one way route that although not popular, poses no problems. Around 140–150 miles.

Other charter areas

Kusadasi A small charter fleet operates out of Kusadasi. Izmir Airport is nearby with

about a 1 hour transfer. Most charters are skippered charter although bareboats are available. Yachts either head north towards Cesme or south to Bodrum.

Kemer/Antalya Celebi Small numbers of charter yachts operate out of these two marinas. Antalya Airport is nearby with about a 30 minute transfer. Most charter is skippered charter although bareboats are available.

Lycian sarcophagi near Kekova

Other Mediterranean Destinations

MALTA

Some bareboat and skippered charter is available out of Marsamxett. For a one-week charter there is just about enough to do around the two main islands, but for the adventurous and for longer charters most people will head for the southern coast of Sicily. The crossing to Sicily can be made in a long day starting early in the morning though for the return trip be careful to budget in a day's grace in case the weather is not clement for the trip – you don't want to be late getting the boat back to the charter base.

CYPRUS

There is limited bareboat and skippered charter out of Larnaca and Limassol Marina in the southern (Greek) half of Cyprus. One of the problems with this area is that there are very few places to visit along the coast. For what really amounts to day-sailing or a bit of coastal cruising the area has a long settled summer season.

SAILING GUIDES AND CHARTS

Italian Waters Pilot Rod Heikell. Imray. Covers Malta.

Turkish Waters and Cyprus Pilot Rod Heikell. Imray.

North Africa Pilot RCC Pilotage Foundation/ Graham Hutt. Imray. Covers Tunisia in detail.

Imray Mediterranean Almanac ed. Rod Heikell. Imray.

For further information try an internet search and sailing magazines or a charter agent.

TUNISIA

There is some limited skippered charter out of El Kantaoui and Monastir. Charter has never really taken off in Tunisia for no good reason. The country is relatively stable, there are wonderful cruising areas and interesting things to do and see ashore.

Gulf of Corinth chapel

ATLANTIC ISLANDS

CANARIES

The Canaries have experienced an explosion in tourist numbers in the last couple of decades and in recent years have become increasingly popular as a sailing area. Its chief advantage is a year-round season with the winter being the most popular. This winter season has led to a number of charter companies setting up here with bareboat and skippered charter. A number of RYA courses are also run here.

The islands are really only suitable for the more experienced charterer to go bareboating here as the trade winds can be boisterous at times, the seas are reasonably big Atlantic rollers and the distances between some of the islands necessitate overnight trips.

Infrastructure ashore is well developed with numerous marinas dotted around most of the islands. Because the Canaries are a popular destination for package holidays there are restaurants and bars everywhere and you won't have any problems provisioning the boat or finding somewhere to eat out.

BEFORE YOU GO

For
✔ Settled weather patterns and a long year-round season.
✔ Exciting sailing in the trade winds.
✔ Short distance from Europe for winter sailing.

Against
✘ Crowded in the popular winter season and marinas often full.
✘ Long passages between the islands.
✘ Crowded ashore with winter sun devotees and some tacky resorts to house them.

Types of charter
❖ Bareboat
❖ Skippered charter
❖ Sailing schools

Suitable for
❖ Intermediate to experienced.

Graciosa in the Canaries

Mindelo market in the Cape Verdes

SAILING GUIDES AND CHARTS

Atlantic Islands Anne Hammick. RCC Pilotage Fund/Imray. Covers Canaries, Cape Verdes and Azores.

Reeds Nautical Almanac. Adlard Coles Nautical. Covers Azores.

CAPE VERDES

There is a small bareboat charter fleet at Mindelo on Sao Vicente in the Cape Verdes group that also offers skippered charter. This is an area on the frontier of chartering and away from well-trodden sailing routes. It offers unspoiled anchorages and a friendly and interesting life ashore. In the cafés and restaurants you will come across some of the finest and most talented music in Africa.

The minus to chartering here is that the trades blow strongly with acceleration zones between the islands. It's an area for experienced charterers only.

AZORES

The Azores are the gems of the Atlantic Islands. The people are overwhelmingly friendly and the scenery is spectacular. Atlantic sailors arriving from the Caribbean will often say that these are the most beautiful and interesting islands they have visited.

There is limited bareboat and skippered charter around the Azores with the minus again being the relatively long distances between the islands. Some whale and dolphin watching expeditions run from here as well. It is an area for experienced charterers and there is always a long Atlantic swell in the waters around the islands.

CARIBBEAN:

VIRGIN ISLANDS, LEEWARDS & WINDWARDS

Sailing around these islands is tradewind sailing at its most civilised with constant easterly winds bending the palm fronds on the beach. When you arrive in an anchorage you will generally have little difficulty finding island-style bars and restaurants. Some of them are absolute gems and you will have to tear yourself away to explore other places.

In other places there is a more sophisticated scene ashore and you can wine and dine in chic restaurants with excellent cuisine, though at a price. Many of the places in the Caribbean have acquired an almost mythological status such as Basil's Bar on Mustique and Nanny Cay in the BVIs and are must-visits for some.

The whole Caribbean experience from the Virgin Islands in the north to Grenada in the south is a pot-pouri of experience. Some of the islands like Dominica and Grenada have wonderful hinterland with thick rainforest clothing the steep slopes. Everywhere there is warm turquoise water with temperatures that invite you to float around or snorkel over coral. Sub-aqua divers can explore deeper water from any of the many dive operators around the islands. There are marinas with all facilities and anchorages away from it all.

The Caribbean has an active racing scene and many of the regattas are world class affairs with racing pros helming the latest go-fast designs. Many of these regattas also have a charter boat division so you can participate in the races on an equal footing. Some of the charter companies will put together special racing packages including measurement and racing fees. Amongst the more famous are the BVI Spring Regatta, Heineken Regatta and of course Antigua Sailing Week. See the Introduction chapters for a list of regattas.

WHEN TO GO

High season is in the winter from December to March. The islands are drier in the winter although you will still get significant showers with the trades bringing moist air in from the Atlantic, especially over the higher islands further down the chain. Peak high season is December to February which of course coincides with the Christmas holiday break. Arguably some of the best weather is later in the season from February through till May when the weather is drier than earlier on and the easterly trades have settled down. Temperatures are all in the range 25–30°C and although the humidity is high, it is alleviated by the trades blowing over the islands and is not as uncomfortable as it can be near larger land masses. Sea temperatures are in the range 22–28°C with temperatures getting warmer from north to south.

Early season October to mid-November. This is at the tail end of the hurricane season and so a weather eye needs to kept for the possibility of hurricanes developing. November is generally safe. The easterly trades blow at around 15–20 knots with some squalls bringing rain.

High season Mid-November to March. This is peak holiday season and for those in search of winter sun this is the best period. Over the Christmas period there are the 'Christmas trades' which tend to blow a good deal harder than the regular trades, often up to 25–30 knots with associated squalls.

Late season March to May. This is arguably the best time to go sailing in the Caribbean as the weather has settled down with the easterly trades blowing at a manageable 12–18 knots and less rain than earlier on. For the racing fraternity there is the attraction of various regattas including the famous Antigua Sailing Week in April.

Low season The Tropical Storm and hurricane season officially runs from June to November and this is the least favoured time to go sailing in the Caribbean for obvious reasons. In fact June and even July are pleasant months to sail here and the risk of tropical storms is relatively low. Later on in August through to October the risk of tropical storms is much higher and this is also the wet season to boot so there is relatively little charter going on. If you are chartering at this time you need to liaise closely with shore crew and keep a close watch on the weather. If there is any possibility of a hurricane brewing then you will most likely need to leave the boat and find shelter ashore.

BEFORE YOU GO

For
✔ Consistent trade winds and warm temperatures year round.
✔ Translucent seas at the temperature of warm soup and good snorkelling over the reefs.
✔ Plentiful anchorages and good holding.
✔ Potter around an island or two or do longer passages down through the island chain.
✔ Lots of sandy beaches and enough bars and restaurants to satisfy most.

Against
✘ Popular areas crowded in high season.
✘ Trade winds can be boisterous at times between the islands.
✘ Care needed in the hurricane season (June to November).
✘ Formalities can be time consuming, going from island to island.

Types of charter
❖ Sailing schools
❖ Flotilla
❖ Clubs
❖ Bareboat
❖ Skippered charter
❖ Luxury charter

GETTING THERE

Scheduled international flights from Europe and the USA fly all year round to many of

At Antigua	Av max °C	Av min °C	Highest recorded	Relative humidity	Days 0.1 mm rain	Sea temp °C	Wind direction & force
Jan	28	21	32	65%	12	26	NE 4-5
Feb	29	21	33	66%	9	25	ENE 4-5
Mar	29	21	34	59%	9	25.5	ENE 4
Apr	30	22	34	59%	8	26	ENE 4
May	31	23	36	60%	10	26.5	E 4
Jun	31	24	37	63%	13	27	E 3-4
Jul	31	24	37	64%	14	28	ESE 3-4
Aug	31	24	37	66%	16	28	ESE 3-4
Sep	32	23	36	66%	13	28	SE 3-4
Oct	31	23	34	66%	14	28	E 4
Nov	29	23	37	68%	16	27.5	ENE 4
Dec	28	22	33	67%	13	26	NE 4-5

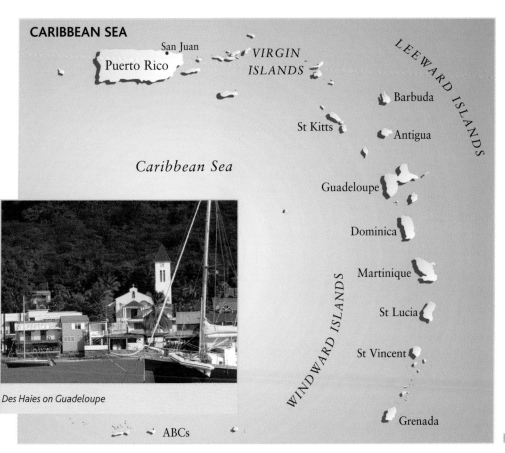

CARIBBEAN SEA

San Juan

Puerto Rico

VIRGIN ISLANDS

LEEWARD ISLANDS

Barbuda

St Kitts

Antigua

Caribbean Sea

Guadeloupe

Dominica

Martinique

WINDWARD ISLANDS

St Lucia

St Vincent

Des Haies on Guadeloupe

ABCs

Grenada

the major islands. Puerto Rico is the main hub for flights from the USA. USVI, St Martin, St Kitts, Antigua, Guadeloupe, Martinique, St Lucia and Grenada all have airports with regular international flights from the USA and Europe. In the winter there are a number of charter flights running from Europe to some of these airports (principally Antigua, St Lucia and Grenada) in addition to scheduled flights. There are also international flights to Barbados and from there you can catch inter-island flights to places like St Vincent.

If you need to get between the islands then it is wise to book in advance for inter-island flights. To get to BVI you will need to fly to one of the main hubs like St Martin or St Lucia and take an inter-island flight to BVI from there. Likewise to get to St Vincent for a charter you will likely fly to Barbados and get an inter-island flight from there. There are no real inter-island ferry services except between St Vincent and Grenada and the USVI and BVI.

WHEN YOU'RE THERE

Visas and documentation

Members of the EU and most non-EU countries including America, Canada, Australia, New Zealand, Norway, Austria and Switzerland do not require visas but must have proof of a return ticket or proof they are departing on a yacht and will leave from elsewhere. Charterers arriving to pick up a yacht for a one- or two-week holiday will have no problems getting in or out from the countries above. Nationals of other countries, particularly countries like Russia and some of the old Soviet bloc countries that are not part of the EU, should check on the visa requirements for the country they are flying into.

In some cases proof of competence to handle a yacht will be asked for and you need to ask the charter company about requirements. Most charter companies will require some sort of qualification for more difficult areas. All other boat documentation will be provided by the company. It can take

ESSENTIAL INFORMATION

Capital(s) *Virgins*: Charlotte Amalie in USVI, Road Town in BVI.
Leewards: Phillipsburg in Sint Maarten, Marigot in St Martin, St John's in Antigua, Basse-Terre in Guadeloupe, Roseau in Dominica.
Windwards: Castries in St Lucia, Fort-de-France in Martinique, Kingstown in St Vincent, St Georges in Grenada, and Bridgetown in Barbados.

Time zone UT + 4

Language English serves in most of the islands although in the French islands some French is useful and likewise Dutch in the Dutch islands.

Telecommunications Automatic dialling. Country codes Antigua 268, Guadeloupe 590, Dominica 767. GSM phones supported throughout the Caribbean though charges are high. Card phones. Some charter companies offer hire sat-phones for their boats. Internet cafés and wifi in larger centres and marinas.

Electricity French, Dutch and British islands 230V 50Hz. Other islands 220V 60Hz.110V in USVI and also in some of the other islands.

several hours for clearance of the charter documentation before you leave. It is normal for the representative of the charter company to arrange this and to advise on procedures at subsequent harbours.

If you intend to visit several countries in the Caribbean chain then you will have to deal with customs and immigration officials in those countries yourself if you are on a bareboat charter. In some cases this can be a little frustrating and time consuming, although straightforward in practice. Most pilot books or your charter company can advise on procedures and costs.

Health

Medical services Are generally adequate in the larger islands though for any major emergency it would be best to evacuate to the USA or back to Europe if possible. The

French and Dutch islands have some reciprocal medical care for EU nationals. Charterers must take out private medical insurance for the trip and most charter operators can arrange this along with travel insurance.

Water In most places the water is potable, but it is likely that delicate stomachs will react to local micro-organisms in the water and for a few days some people will have a mild case of the runs. In some places water is collected rain water and may cause some problems. Those with delicate stomachs and babies should drink bottled water.

Trading schooner, Grenada

Money and banks
The different countries in the region use different currencies. The Eastern Caribbean dollar which is tied to the US dollar is used in St Kitts, Nevis, Antigua, Dominica, St Lucia, St Vincent and Grenada. The Euro is used in St Martin, St Barts, Guadeloupe, and Martinique. The US dollar is used in the Virgin Islands. However the US dollar is common currency in all of these countries and prices will often be in US dollars as well as any local currency. In St Martin (Dutch side) you can get US dollars from ATMs.

In the populated centres of the islands there are banks and ATMs which work with most credit and debit cards like Visa and Mastercard. On a boat you will likely be spending a bit of time away from populated centres so it pays to stock up with some local currency or dollars where you can. Most of the larger restaurants and shops accept Visa or Mastercard.

Eating and drinking
Eating out is a variable feast. In the popular areas restaurants will serve an 'international' fare which can be anything from steaks to pastas, fish and chips to salads, jerk chicken to rotis. Influences vary but are generally Mediterranean, mostly Italian and French, local Creole cuisine although it is better executed in some places than others, good fish done in a variety of ways, pizzas both American style and thin-base

Italian style, gumbo and fish stews, and that lunch-time staple the roti. The latter is akin to the Indian roti or chapati wrapped around a mild beef, chicken or vegetable curry and is the best fast food going in the Caribbean.

To find decent and good value restaurants can take some time and you would do well to take local recommendations. Too many of the restaurants serve badly executed food for the same price as a restaurant down the road that takes time and trouble over the ingredients and the cooking.

The local tipple of the islands is, not surprisingly, rum and you can hardly visit the Caribbean without sampling a rum punch or for the brave ti-punch which is simply rum, a little cane sugar syrup and a squeeze of lime. Wines are imported into the islands and prices are reasonable. The French islands feature French wines while the others have New World wines as well. Beer is produced locally around the islands with Carib, Red Stripe and Wadadli common, although there is also a wide range of imported beers as well.

Provisioning
Most of the islands import nearly everything including much of the fruit and vegetables, so prices not surprisingly have a premium. In the French islands much of what you buy

SAILING GUIDES AND CHARTS

Grenada to the Virgin Islands Jaques Patuelli. Imray. Covers the Windwards, Leewards and Virgins comprehensively in one volume.

Cruising Guide to the Virgin Islands Simon & Nancy Scot. Cruising Guide Publications.

A cruising Guide to Puerto Rico: Including the Spanish Virgin Islands Stephen J Pavlidis. Seaworthy Publications.

Cruising Guide to the Leeward Islands Chris Doyle. Cruising Guide Publications. Good coverage of marinas and anchorages and things ashore.

Cruising Guide to the Leeward Islands Stephen J Pavlidis. Seaworthy Publications.

Streets Guide Anguilla to Dominica Donald M. Street Jnr. iUniverse.com Inc.

Streets Guide Martinique to Trinidad Donald M. Street Jnr. iUniverse.com Inc.

Cruising Guide to the Windward Islands Chris Doyle. Cruising Guide Publications. Good coverage of marinas and anchorages and things ashore.

Cruising Guide to the Windward Islands Stephen J Pavlidis. Seaworthy Publications.

Charts for the area are good and easily available. British Admiralty charts, US DMA charts, Imray Iolaire yachting charts and Nautical Publications all provide good coverage of the area.

is imported from France whereas in the other islands most of the staples and tinned goods are American in origin. In the larger centres there are good supermarkets with a wide range of goods where you should stock up for the leaner areas ahead. Smaller places will have a local shop but this will inevitably have little on the shelves.

In the larger islands there are good markets with fresh fruit and vegetables, island bread, home-cooked cakes and home-made relishes and sauces, clothes, and local knick-knacks that are usually better than the tat in tourist shops. It's worth going as much for the colour and the buzz as for

shopping. Try the market at Marigot on St Martin, at St George's on Antigua, Point a Pitre on Guadeloupe, St Pierre on Martinique, Castries Market on St Lucia and St George's in Grenada.

Costs

As most food items are imported they will cost more than in Europe or the USA. Typically food costs are 15% to 30% more than the equivalent items in Europe and the USA, though you can save money on basic food items that are not immediately recognisable compared to home-grown labels. Depending on supply some items may not be in the shops until 'next week', though that can be an 'island time' next week.

Eating out can range from US$25 to $35 a head in more modest restaurants to a lot, lot more in the chic establishments on many of the islands. It's pretty easy to tell from the menu outside what sort of costs you are looking at. Local food like rotis and pizzas are generally cheaper and there are some restaurants in the modest range that produce very good food sourced from local ingredients for the price.

Rum and rum-based drinks are cheap and you can buy a good rum like Appletons or Pussers rum at bargain prices. Wines are reasonably priced as is the local beer. If you are out drinking then prices vary considerably depending on the establishment and a beer in a simple beach bar in Antigua is going to cost around US$2, a lot less than a beer on the waterfront in St Barts (US$5). Personally I go for the beach bar.

Hire cars around the islands are fairly expensive at around US$45–50 per day. Local buses are relatively cheap although often crowded and taxis are expensive. On some of the islands share-taxis, usually vans with additional seats, operate on a more or less fixed route.

Crime and personal safety

There is some theft from boats around the islands although this generally involves dinghies and outboards. Most charter companies will supply a stainless steel cable or chain to lock up the dinghy when going ashore. At night dinghies should ideally be hoisted up on davits or on the side of the boat and locked. Ashore there is little theft although it pays to take normal precautions and take a minimum of cash and leave jewellery, expensive watches and handbags behind. Cameras are also a popular target so take just a small still or video camera and not the whole Steven Spielberg kit.

On some of the islands, notably USVI, Antigua, Guadeloupe, Dominica, Martinique, St Vincent and Grenada it pays to stay out of the capital at night. There have been enough instances of aggravated robbery to make these no-go areas in the late evening and night. In all areas take advice form the charted operator on how safe an area is.

There have also been sporadic instances of night time robberies from yachts, particularly in the Windward Islands especially St Vincent and St Lucia. Again check with your charter company for the latest security advice.

Main Caribbean regattas

Late Jan	Port Louis Grenada Sailing Festival
Early Feb	Tobago Carnival Regatta
Mid-Feb	St Croix International Regatta
Late Feb	RORC Caribbean 600. Offshore Race around Caribbean.
Early Mar	St Maarten Heineken Regatta
Late Mar	St Thomas Rolex Regatta
Early Apr	BVI Spring Regatta
Late Apr	Antigua Sailing Week

Some yachts get worried about Boat Boys in the Caribbean, but refer back to the Introduction for coping with Boat Boys in the anchorages. Most are honest and helpful characters and in some places like Portsmouth on Dominica they double as security guards at night to make sure undesirables don't hassle yachts.

Navigating in coral

There are a few cardinal rules for navigating in coral:

1 Never come into an anchorage or harbour fringed by coral at night. It takes just one navigation light out of order to severely complicate the whole endeavour. Most charter companies require you to be in before dark.

2 By day try to approach coral with the sun fairly high in the sky and preferably behind you. For anchorages on the leeward side of the islands this means you should be in before 1500-1600.

3 Fortunately many of the anchorages on the leeward side are not encumbered by coral but even so you will need to be in before 1700 latest. Sunset around 1730-1800 is best viewed from the cockpit when at anchor with a drink in your hand.

4 Electronic navigation charts are not to be trusted for accurate navigation through coral (or any other dangers to navigation). The Mk 1 eyeball is the preferred method.

5 A pair of polarised sunglasses will make a big difference to your ability to pick out coral.

6 In general dark blue is deep, light blue is OK, turquoise start to get worried, yellow and brown you need to be somewhere else. When it is cloudy it gets more difficult to see depths as the clouds cause shadows on the bottom and it can be hard to distinguish colours and features.

7 Always have someone experienced up front conning you through coral and work out a simple set of hand signals for communicating.

VIRGIN ISLANDS

The Virgin Islands are the chain lying more or less west to east from the Spanish Virgins off Puerto Rico in the west to the US Virgins and the British Virgins in the east. Of the three groups the British Virgins (BVI) are far and away the most popular charter destination. Some charters operate out of the US Virgins (USVI) and from the marinas on the east side of Puerto Rico from where you can sail across to the Spanish Virgins.

The BVI are popular because the Sir Francis Drake Channel is a cruising area well sheltered by the outer islands from the Atlantic swell and enclose a spectacular area peppered with islands, (there are more than sixty if you count the very small ones) that is tailor-made for charter. Add to this mix wonderful turquoise water and sandy beaches, a landscape littered with black granite boulders and fringed by coral reefs, and some wonderful bars and restaurants ashore and it is no wonder that the islands are known as 'Nature's Little Secret'.

Snorkelling around the clear waters is a normal part of the day here. The names of some of the places around the islands, Dead Chest Island, Smugglers Cove, Throw Away Wife Bay, The Baths, give a *Treasure Island* flavour to the topography and the names of bars ashore, *The Soggy Dollar Bar*, *Foxys*, *Bitter End Yacht Club*, *Mad Dogs*, and of course *Pussers* with the famous 'Painkiller' based on its famous rum, give you some hints to what happens of an evening ashore.

The USVI has a more limited charter area and many of the charter boats from Charlotte Amalie will cross over into the BVI. The Spanish Virgins off the east coast of Puerto Rico are the least developed. The US navy has long used the islands as a base and for target practice, but in recent years has retrenched, leaving areas for yachts to cruise. They are a simpler place with the same wonderful turquoise water and forested slopes, but without as many bars and restaurants around.

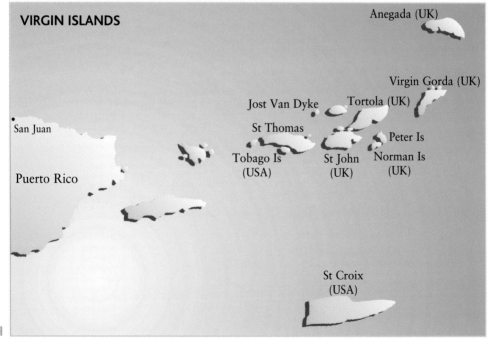

VIRGIN ISLANDS

Anegada (UK)

Virgin Gorda (UK)

Jost Van Dyke   Tortola (UK)

St Thomas

San Juan   Peter Is

Tobago Is   St John   Norman Is
(USA)   (UK)   (UK)

Puerto Rico

St Croix
(USA)

CHARTER AREAS

BVI

The BVI is far and away the most popular area and the best set up for yacht charter. The islands are stunningly beautiful and the sailing in protected waters outstanding, so it is not surprising that it is difficult if not downright impossible to get away from it all and the likelihood is that you will meet up with numerous other charter yachts around the islands. It also means that there is good infrastructure everywhere and some of the best watering holes in the world.

USVI

The USVI has less to offer as a cruising area so not surprisingly charter boats often cruise part of the BVI as well.

SPANISH VIRGINS

These are the least spoiled of the islands with just a small amount of charter. There are wonderful anchorages away from it all and a few places like Culebra where you get

Note

Non-US visitors to the USVI and Puerto Rico require an American visa. Normally this will be a multi-entry visa. Travellers to US territory must also complete Advance Passenger Information – an ESTA. Go online to https://esta.cbp.dhs.gov/esta/esta.html where you can complete the online form.

Most visitors to the BVI do not need a visa in advance, but you will not be able to sail to the USVI from BVI if you do not have a multi-entry visa. Charterers sailing from the USVI can visit the BVI without a visa. Take advice from your charter operator or agent on visa requirements.

a run ashore. Yachts can sometimes do one-way trips from Puerto Rico to the USVI.

Wind and sea
The easterly trades blow steadily throughout the year although over Christmas and New Year they can be blustery and stronger than normal – the so-called 'Christmas Trades'. The islands themselves form a natural barrier stopping the worst of the Atlantic

swell so that the Sir Francis Drake Channel is a sheltered body of water. Mind you, when the trades do kick in above average there can be a bit of a chop on the water.

Currents are variable around the islands, but as most navigation is by the Mk 1 eyeball and the distances between anchorages are short, they are not bothersome.

Suitable for...

The Virgins are suitable for the adventurous beginner though you will need to have some knowledge of navigating around coral. For the less experienced there is a flotilla option or on bareboat it may be useful to take a skipper for at least a couple of days – consult with your charter company. For the more experienced bareboat sailor the sailing is exhilarating with decent winds over relatively flat water. Families with non-sailors might want to consider a 50-50 holiday with part of the time spent in a beach house and exploring ashore.

Harbours and anchorages

There are a number of marinas around the BVI and USVI, but mostly you will be picking up a mooring buoy or anchoring. Charges are made for mooring buoys and in some places you will not be allowed to anchor and must pick up a buoy if one is available. In the season you may have to have an alternative anchorage in mind if your first choice is full.

Care is needed in some of the anchorages around the BVI and USVI if a big sea is running outside or a northerly buster pushes a swell in. It is up to the skipper to decide whether somewhere is safe or not and if necessary to chug off to a safer spot. Fortunately there are lots of anchorages within relatively short distances in the BVI. In the Spanish Virgins there are numerous wonderful anchorages and there is always plenty of room to anchor.

Main charter bases

BVI: The main charter base is at Road Town on Tortola where probably 80% of charter boats are based. There are also bases at places like Sopers Hole, Maya Cove and Beef Island.

USVI: Charlotte Amalie.

Puerto Rico east coast: Charter bases at Puerto del Rey in Fajardo and San Juan.

Sailing area/suggested itinerary

From Tortola (Road town)

Approx 60 miles

One-week charter from Road town exploring the Sir Francis Drake Channel

Day 1	Road town	Sail down to Sopers Hole and pick up a mooring or anchor. There is also a small marina. Dinner at Pussers or the Jolly Roger.
Day 2		Sail across the channel to the Indians for lunch and then onto The Bight on Norman Island. Try the floating bar/restaurant, the 'William Thornton'.
Day 3		Sail over to Peter Island for lunch and then onto Cooper Island for the night. Restaurant ashore.
Day 4		Beat up the channel to the southwest end of Virgin Gouda and pick up a mooring off The Baths. Go to Savanna Bay a little way up for the night or to Virgin Gorda Marina near Spanish Town.
Day 5	Lay day	Explore Spanish Town or return to The Baths.
Day 6		Last exhilarating sail downwind all the way to Road town.
Catch the flight back		

LEEWARD ISLANDS

The Leeward Islands will conjure up some well known names like Antigua and St Barts but they also include some lesser known gems like Guadeloupe and Dominica. The Leewards are the drier islands of the Caribbean chain running down the eastern perimeter of the Caribbean Sea and consequently are more popular than the Windwards further south. They are also more developed than most of the Windwards and consequently there are more restaurants and bars ashore.

The islands all have a charm and 'feel' of their own. St Barts is upmarket and the restaurants and bars ashore, not to mention the boutiques, would not be out of place in chic parts of Paris. Dominica is more homespun with eco-tourism the mainstay of tourism. Antigua has a mix of good restaurants and bars and is home to superyachts and the racing fraternity who congregate here for Race Week. Guadeloupe is the dark horse of the group with the intriguing town of Point a Pitre and lots of good anchorages with a French touch to the cuisine.

The island chain runs around an arc of several hundred miles and most are independent countries that you must clear in and out of. Because of the distances involved and formalities for clearing in and out, most charterers will stick to just a few of the islands. Around Antigua charterers will sail around Antigua and Barbuda with maybe trips to St Kitts and Nevis or south to Guadeloupe. From Guadeloupe charterers will probably want to sail to Dominica and around Les Saintes and Marie-Galante. Charterers on bigger bareboat and skippered yachts will be able to cover greater distances although part of chartering in the Leewards is getting a good sail in before dusk and then going ashore for a meal and entertainment ashore.

CHARTER AREAS

ST MARTIN

A number of charter companies are based here, mostly on the French side around Marigot, and yachts will cruise around St Martin and down to St Kitts and St Barts.

ANTIGUA

A number of charter companies operate out of Falmouth, English Harbour and Jolly Harbour. Yachts cruise around Antigua and Barbuda and sometimes down to Guadeloupe. Falmouth is a major hub for superyacht charter.

GUADELOUPE

Charter yachts operate out of Point a Pitre and cruise around Guadeloupe, Les Saintes and sometimes down to Dominica.

Rum Cruise

Along the lines of the Classic Malts Cruise in Scotland there is now the Rum Cruise leaving from Antigua and cruising down through the Leewards and Windwards to St Lucia. Along the way the cruise visits some of the famous old rum distilleries scattered throughout the islands in the company of dedicated rum connoisseurs Paul and Marguerite Jackson. Many of these little known distilleries produce exceptional 15 or 20 year old matured rums in wonderfully exotic locations.

The cruise is probably best suited to intermediate to experienced sailors as there are some longish legs on the cruise. Go to www.horizonyachtcharters.com.

Yachts can sometimes do one-way charters between Antigua and St Martin by arrangement with the charter company.

Wind and sea

The easterly trades blow steadily throughout the year although over Christmas and New Year they can be blustery and stronger than normal – the so-called 'Christmas Trades'. Between the islands the sea rolls in clear across the Atlantic so there is a large swell to deal with. On the lee side of the islands there will be calm patches and less sea where the wind is blocked and at either end of the islands there will be increased winds where it blows around either end.

Currents are variable but mostly west-going and where the wind meets the current at a bit of an angle (going north out of Deshaies on the northern end of Guadeloupe is one notorious area) there can be large confused seas and breaking crests.

See the Caribbean Introduction for advice on the hurricane season.

Suitable for...

The Leewards are suitable for the more experienced bareboat sailor in order to cope with the winds and seas between the islands and for some tricky navigation in coral. The less experienced should take a skipper for at least part of the charter to get used to the area and can work out an itinerary which, say, involves just sailing around Antigua where there are a lot of good anchorages. Experienced sailors will revel in the trade-wind breezes and exciting sailing between the islands.

Harbours and anchorages

There are a number of marinas around the major islands, but for the most part you will be anchoring off and going ashore by dinghy. Around St Martin there are a number of attractive anchorages and it's not far to Anguilla or St Barts. If you want a bit of peace and quiet head for Anguilla and if you want ultra-chic head for St Barts. Around Antigua there are numerous anchorages on the leeward side and unusually on the windward side. For peace

Sailing area/suggested itinerary

From Antigua (English Harbour)

Approx 200 miles

Two-week charter from English Harbour down to Guadeloupe and back.

Day 1	**English Harbour** Go for a short shakedown cruise to Falmouth, literally next door.
Day 2	Falmouth to Deshaies on Guadeloupe. Exhilarating off-wind sail.
Day 3	Lay day in Deshaies.
Day 4	Sail down the lee side of the island to Rivière Sens Marina near Basse-Terre.
Day 5	Sail across to Les Saintes.
Day 6	Lay day in Les Saintes or sail to Marie-Galante.
Day 7	Sail back up the lee side of Guadeloupe to the anchorages at Les Trois Tortue or near Pigeon Island.
Day 8	Deshaies again (it's worth it).
Day 9	Sail across to Falmouth on Antigua.
Day 10	Sail up Goat Head Channel to Five Islands.
Day 11	Pop into Jolly Harbour to top up with water and diesel.
Day 12	Back to English Harbour.

This leaves a couple of days in case any adverse weather is encountered.

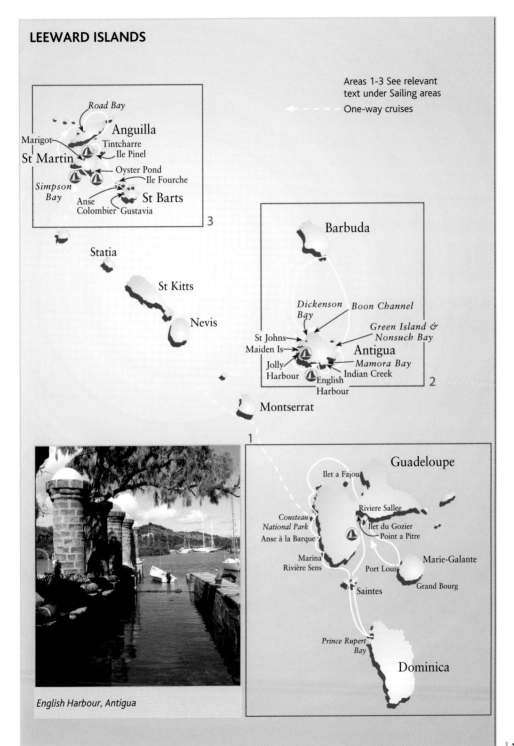

LEEWARD ISLANDS

Areas 1-3 See relevant text under Sailing areas
One-way cruises

Anguilla
Road Bay
Marigot
St Martin
Tintcharre
Ile Pinel
Oyster Pond
Ile Fourche
Simpson Bay
Anse Colombier
Gustavia
St Barts

3

Statia

St Kitts

Nevis

Barbuda

Dickenson Bay
Boon Channel
Green Island & Nonsuch Bay
St Johns
Maiden Is
Jolly Harbour
Antigua
Mamora Bay
Indian Creek
English Harbour

2

Montserrat

1

English Harbour, Antigua

Guadeloupe
Ilet a Fajou
Riviere Sallee
Cousteau National Park
Ilet du Gozier
Anse à la Barque
Point a Pitre
Marina Rivière Sens
Port Louis
Marie-Galante
Saintes
Grand Bourg
Prince Rupert Bay
Dominica

St Martin (Marigot)

Approx 75 miles

One-week charter from Marigot to Anguilla and St Barts.

Day 1	Sail from Marigot to Road Bay on Anguilla. Anchor off and choose a restaurant ashore.
Day 2	Sail a short distance up to Little Bay and pick up a mooring buoy. Stay the night or return to Road Bay.
Day 3	Sail down to Grand Colombier and pick up a mooring buoy.
Day 4	Sail down to Gustavia and anchor off or go on the quay if there is room and there is not too much swell. Spend the night in Gustavia or look around and then return to Grand Colombier.
Day 5	Short hop up to Simpson Bay. Anchor off in the bay and go ashore where there are any number of bars and restaurants.

Land excursions

St Martin	all-singing and dancing resort areas with casinos, nightclubs and restaurants and bars. It is a bit tacky in places.
Barbuda	is a natural wonderland with clear clear water and a huge colony of frigate birds.
Guadeloupe	has a substantial area of natural rainforest and it's well worth taking a hire car around the island.
Montserrat	is the smoking active volcano across the water from Antigua and the best way to see it is from Antigua by helicopter.
Dominica	has a thick carpeting of rainforest and there are all sorts of excursions you take. The Indian River trip is easy and in Portsmouth, but try to go to the Carib Indian reservation as well.

and quiet away from the hurley-burley of Falmouth yachts can cross to Barbuda. Around the large island of Guadeloupe there are lots of good anchorages and the offshore islands of Les Saintes and Marie-Galante.

Main charter bases
St Martin Simpson Bay Lagoon and Marigot.
Antigua English Harbour, Falmouth and Jolly Harbour.
Guadeloupe Point a Pitre.

Onward routes
One-way routes can be organised between St Martin and Antigua and sometimes between the BVIs and St Martin/Antigua. These longer inter-island trips need more

experienced crew and you will need to budget for a few extra days in case you are held up by boisterous weather.

WINDWARD ISLANDS

The Windward Islands stretch from Martinique at the northern end down to Grenada in the south. These islands are to some extent more remote and less developed than the Leewards and the Virgins, though all things being relative, there are pockets of sophistication scattered throughout the Windwards. The islands are more mountainous than the Leewards and the steep slopes were unsuitable in days gone by for cultivating sugar cane so they are still largely covered in rainforest. The islands are wetter than the Leewards as the high peaks tend to hook the rain clouds and empty them as they pass over. The high land also affects the easterly trades and on the lee side will often block the wind so you will be motoring in the shadow of the land.

The island chain runs around an arc of several hundred miles and most are independent countries that you must clear in and out of. They also have probably the most colourful and interesting national flags in the Caribbean. Just as in the Leewards, because of the distances involved and formalities for clearing in and out, most charterers will stick to just a few of the islands. From Le Marin on Martinique charterers will either sail south to St Lucia or north up the coast of Martinique to Dominica at the bottom of the Leewards. From St Vincent charterers will sail around the Grenadines and down to Bequia and the Tobago Cays. From Grenada most will sail around Grenada itself which has more than enough anchorages to do that, with maybe a trip up to Carriacou and the Tobago Cays.

The area is really suitable for the more experienced charterer as several of the passages between the islands, from Martinique to St Lucia, St Lucia to St Vincent and Grenada to Carriacou, involve reasonable distances with a healthy ocean swell rolling in off the Atlantic. Charterers on bigger bareboats and skippered yachts will be able to cover greater distances, although you need to keep an eye on the weather and budget in enough time to comfortably get back to the base. As in the Leewards the idea is to get a good sail in before dusk and then go ashore for a few drinks and a meal.

CHARTER AREAS

MARTINIQUE

Nearly all charter companies are based in Le Marin, the huge lagoon on the southern end of the island. Yachts will cruise south to St Lucia or north up the coast of Martinique to Dominica.

ST LUCIA

Small charter fleet at Rodney Bay.

ST VINCENT

Charter yachts operate out of Blue Lagoon on the south of the island. From here most yachts will head south for the Grenadines to Bequia, the Tobago Cays and maybe Carriacou. There are more than enough places to vary the itinerary when returning back up to St Vincent.

GRENADA

Charter yachts operate out of St Georges or True Blue Bay. Yachts can cruise around the much indented south coast of Grenada or venture north to Carriacou and the Tobago Cays.

Yachts can sometimes do one-way charters between Martinique and St Vincent and Grenada and St Vincent by arrangement with the charter company.

Wind and sea

The easterly trades blow steadily throughout the year although they tend to be a little

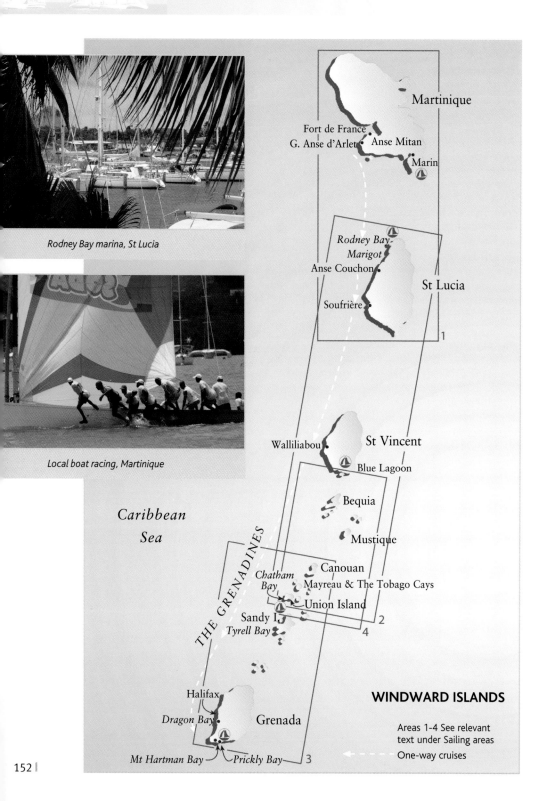

Rodney Bay marina, St Lucia

Local boat racing, Martinique

Martinique

Fort de France
G. Anse d'Arlet • Anse Mitan
Marin

Rodney Bay
Marigot
Anse Couchon

St Lucia

Soufrière

1

Walliliabou • St Vincent

Blue Lagoon

Bequia

Caribbean
Sea

Mustique

Canouan

Chatham
Bay   Mayreau & The Tobago Cays

Union Island

Sandy I.   2

Tyrell Bay   4

Halifax

Dragon Bay

Grenada

Mt Hartman Bay — Prickly Bay   3

WINDWARD ISLANDS

Areas 1-4 See relevant
text under Sailing areas
- - - ➤ One-way cruises

152

stronger over Christmas and New Year like the 'Christmas Trades' further north and die down somewhat in April and May. Between the islands the sea rolls in clear across the Atlantic so there is a large swell to deal with. On the lee side of the islands there will be calm patches and less sea where the wind is blocked and at either end of the islands there will be increased winds where it blows around either end. In places like the northern end of St Vincent and the southern end of Grenada this channelled wind can be appreciably stronger and raise nasty seas.

Currents are variable but mostly west-going and where the wind meets the current at a bit of an angle (again the northern end of St Vincent and the northern end of Grenada are notorious) there can be large confused seas and breaking crests.

See the Caribbean Introduction for advice on the hurricane season.

Suitable for...

The Windwards are suitable for the more experienced bareboat sailor in order to cope with the winds and seas between the islands and for some tricky navigation in coral. The less experienced should take a skipper for at least part of the charter to get used to the area and can work out an itinerary which, say, involves just sailing around Martinique or Grenada where there are a lot of good anchorages close by. Experienced sailors will revel in the tradewind breezes and exciting sailing between the islands.

Harbours and anchorages

There are a number of marinas around the major islands, but for the most part you will be anchoring off and going ashore by dinghy. Some of the anchorages have mooring buoys you can pick up and a charge will be made for these.

Around Martinique there are numerous anchorages and if you get the chance anchor off St Pierre although it can be difficult. Head north to Dominica for some peace and quiet and wonderful excursions ashore through the rainforest. To the south St Lucia has numerous wonderful anchorages including off The Pitons which feature on the national flag.

Bequia

Land excursions

Martinique	Drive inland for some delightful villages and verdant tropical forest. Visit to Jardin de Balata.
St Lucia	It's worth taking a tour (hire a car or take an organised trip) around the island where there are some wonderful beaches and wild areas on the windward coast. The market in Castries makes a good morning excursion.
Carriacou	Still has a number of yards building old-fashioned Carriacou schooners.
Grenada	Tour the island and visit the organic chocolate factory. Also wild beaches on the windward side and a wonderful waterfall where you can swim in the pool at the bottom.
Trinidad	Organise a side-trip to Trinidad which celebrates Carnival (February) like nowhere else in the Caribbean.

Sailing area/suggested itinerary

From Martinique to St Lucia

Approx 90 miles to Soufrière and back. Approx 270 miles to Tobago Cays and back. Approx 160 miles on one way trip Le Marin to Tobago Cays and St Vincent.

One-week charter from Marigot to Anguilla and St Barts

Day 1	Short sail out to Ste Anne and anchor off.
Day 2	Sail across to Rodney Bay on St Lucia. Anchor off in the bay or go into the marina in the lagoon.
Day 3	Sail down the coast to Marigot Bay. Anchor off in the outer part of the creek or go into the marina. Try J-J's Paradise for dinner.
Day 4	Sail down to Soufrière Bay and anchor off La Soufriere or go on the dock.
Day 5	Lay day. Visit Sulphur Springs and Diamond Gardens.

Here you need to make a decision about sailing down to St Vincent or pottering around St Lucia before returning to Martinique. The sail to St Vincent involves longish passages and can be challenging. Here we continue onto St Vincent.

Day 6	Sail across to St Vincent and down the coast to Blue Lagoon. There have been a number of incidents in the anchorages on the west side of St Vincent and they are best avoided.
Day 7	Sail down to Bequia.
Day 8	Sail down to the Tobago Cays.
Day 9	Lay day.
Day 10	Sail back up to Blue Lagoon on St Vincent.
Day 11	Sail back to Rodney Bay on St Lucia.
Day 12	Sail back to Le Marins on Martinique.

Two days factored in for weather on this longish itinerary. For a shorter itinerary just return from Day 5 back to Rodney Bay and then Ste Anne and Le Marin on Martinique. It is also possible to do a one-way trip from Le Marin to the Tobago Cays and back to Blue Lagoon on St Vincent.

From St Vincent (Blue Lagoon) to the Grenadines

Approx 100 miles

10-day charter from Blue Lagoon down through the Grenadines to Union Island and back

Day 1	Sail down to Admiralty Bay on Bequia. The anchorage is usually crowded but with a bit of perseverance you can find a mooring or a spot to anchor.
Day 2	Sail to Mustique. Pick up a mooring and have a drink in Basil's Bar.
Day 3	Sail down to Tobago Cays and anchor. Marine Park fee payable per person.
Day 4	Lay day in Tobago Cays.
Day 5	Sail down to Petit St Vincent and anchor.
Day 6	Sail across to Clifton on Union Island. Lunch stop at Palm Island.
Day 7	Sail back up to Charlestown on Canouan. Lunch stop at Mayreau.
Day 8	Sail to Admiralty Bay on Bequia.
Day 9	Sail back to Blue Lagoon.

If you want to do more distance you can sail further down the chain to Tyrell Bay on the south side of Carriacou.

At St Vincent most will head south to Bequia and the Grenadines including the Tobago Cays where you anchor inside a horseshoe reef looking out to the Atlantic swell beating onto the reef.

Through the Grenadines there is a refreshing mix of simple eateries ashore and more sophisticated places such as Basil's Bar on Mustique or the Portofino on Bequia.

Around Grenada there are any number of anchorages and the new upmarket marina at St George's. In most places there are restaurants ashore from the humble to the more sophisticated like the Dodgy Dock in True Blue Bay.

Main charter bases
Martinique Le Marin. Fort de France.
St Lucia Rodney Bay Marina.
St Vincent Blue Lagoon.
Grenada True Blue Bay. St George's.

Other Caribbean Destinations

Around the Caribbean basin there are a number of other smaller charter destinations which offer a wilder and less developed Caribbean than the Lesser Antilles from the Virgins to the Windwards do.

CUBA

Once the playground for Americans, it is likely in the future that Cuba will open up to tourism in a big way. At present Cuba is promoting tourism to get foreign currency in to help out the island's ailing economy and get American dollars in – take American dollars in cash when you go. It should be remembered that Cuba is the largest island in the Caribbean and the indented coast and offshore islands offer a huge cruising area.

At present there are a number of charter companies offering bareboat and skippered charter in a limited area. Even on a bareboat charter here you will probably have to have a skipper or 'advisor' on board because of the difficulty of navigating through the coral. Some of the passes are truly breathtaking as you squeak through between the coral on either side.

On the south coast there are charters out of the marina at Cayo Largo and on the north coast there are charters from around the resort areas east of Havana. There are few marinas or yacht harbours and provisioning and getting fuel and water is largely via the hotels. There are restaurants at the resort areas and others around the coast and larger islands, but there will certainly be more in the future.

What Cuba offers is a huge Caribbean island with all that implies, semi-tropical temperatures and warm waters, reefs and

cays, marine life aplenty and good fishing, trade winds, an interesting cuisine and Cuban rum, all with virtually no yachts around at all, for the present anyway. In the future it will undoubtedly become a more popular area.

Like other parts of the Caribbean you should avoid Cuba during the hurricane season from June to November although the really bad months for hurricanes are August to October. The easterly trades that blow over the rest of the Caribbean also blow along the northern and southern coasts of Cuba. Outside the reefs considerable seas pile up, but inside the reefs which can run out for 2–3 miles, there is fairly calm water in the lagoons.

You can fly direct to Havana from Europe although not at present from the USA. Transport within Cuba is by internal flights or by road. For information on yacht charters consult the internet and the sailing magazines or a charter agent.

CENTRAL AMERICA

The Caribbean coast of Honduras, Belize and Panama is literally edged in shallow coral reefs and cays. Sailing-wise it is a whole unexplored area and a number of owner-operators charter out of these countries. All charter here is skippered charter and no wonder if you look at a chart of the area. The navigation behind the reefs would test anyone's skill.

This charter area is for anyone looking for an adventurous holiday away from more crowded charter areas. Somewhere like the San Blas islands off the coast of Panama offers an unforgettable experience. The Kuna Indians are semi-autonomous from mainland Panama and life here revolves around the coral cays with communication largely by dug-out canoe and hardly a restaurant in sight. On the other hand you can eat your fill of fresh crayfish and crab and snorkel around coral reefs with no one else in sight.

Selling molas in the San Blas Islands, Panama

Cruising Honduras and Belize you can take a shore-side excursion to Mayan ruins and local Indian communities. There are also mini-eco-tours to take through the jungle where you are likely to see plants including lots of orchids, insects and tropical birds that have all but disappeared from more urbanised areas.

Most of the skippered charter, much of it in catamarans because of the shallow waters inside the fringing reefs, will be found on an internet search. Some are advertised in magazines and on agents, books as well, but the majority are by owner-operators who have decided to base themselves along this wonderful coast and find advertising on the internet the easiest option. Most of them will advise you on where to fly to and will likely organise a transfer to the boat.

USA

This is the most powerful and richest country in the world. There are a lot of misconceptions about the USA and most visitors will find that ideas about the country quickly evaporate. The people you will meet ashore are inevitably friendly and generous with help and advice. It's the sort of place where if you ask where a supermarket or restaurant is then the person will likely drive you to it. At the very least they will make sure you know how to get there safely and will often recommend the crab or lobster at xyz restaurant and tell you which bar the local yachties hang out in. It's cruising made easy.

The USA is quite simply a vast country with a long Atlantic and Pacific seaboard. The climate, topography and local culture varies with the latitude and longitude and cannot be pinned down in any generalised way. Charter areas are scattered all along the eastern and western coasts as well as in the Great Lakes which straddle the USA and Canada. The latter are really vast inland seas and it is a bit of a misnomer to call them lakes. Because of the size of the continent it is impossible to make generalisations about weather conditions and the sort of coast and harbours you will come across. For specific charter areas the relevant information will be included although in abbreviated form for some areas. Many Americans regard the Bahamas and the Caribbean as their charter area of choice and many charter companies operating there are American.

WHEN TO GO

This is covered under each charter area section.

GETTING THERE

The USA has an extensive network of major international airports and smaller domestic airports with regular scheduled and charter flights operating everywhere. No country is better served by international and connecting flights. The relevant international and domestic airports are given under each charter area.

WHEN YOU'RE THERE

Visas and documentation

Non-American citizens must carry their passports. Remember to take your passport (Americans included) if you are sailing across to the Bahamas from Florida, to Mexico from California, or to Canada from the Pacific

Northwest. Most European passport holders including UK citizens do not require a full visitor's visa for a stay of 90 days or less although to get a visa waiver you must complete an online Travel Authorisation form 72 hours in advance of travel. Go online to https://esta.cbp.dhs.gov/esta/esta.html where you can complete the online form.

You will require an e-passport (with a chip) or a machine readable passport (MRP) to visit the USA. Citizens of some countries like South Africa, Israel, Russia and some of the old eastern bloc countries will require a visa in advance. You should check on the web or with the US consulate if you are unsure.

Proof of competence to handle a yacht will not normally be required although you will have to satisfy the charter company you have sufficient experience to take out a bareboat. Some proof of competence may be required for longer passages such as going across the Gulf Stream to the Bahamas or sailing around Bahia in Mexico. It depends on the charter

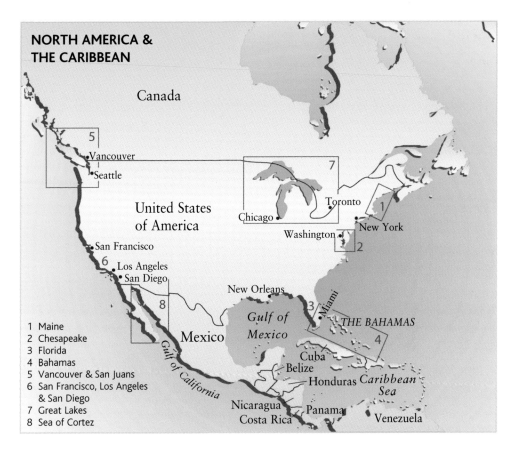

NORTH AMERICA & THE CARIBBEAN

Canada

Vancouver
Seattle

United States of America

Chicago

Toronto

Washington

New York

San Francisco

Los Angeles
San Diego

New Orleans

Gulf of California

Mexico

Gulf of Mexico

Miami

THE BAHAMAS

Cuba
Belize
Honduras   Caribbean Sea

Nicaragua   Panama
Costa Rica   Venezuela

1 Maine
2 Chesapeake
3 Florida
4 Bahamas
5 Vancouver & San Juans
6 San Francisco, Los Angeles
   & San Diego
7 Great Lakes
8 Sea of Cortez

company and their assessment of your competence. All other boat documentation will be provided by the charter company. To go fishing all states require you to have a fishing permit which can usually be obtained locally for a small fee for your stay.

Health
Medical services Are everywhere very good. It is essential that you have health insurance to travel to the USA as health care here is the most expensive in the world. Most insurance companies will add a premium to normal health insurance cover for the very high costs of care in the USA. You would be exceptionally foolish to travel in the USA without fully comprehensive health insurance and most charter companies will insist that you take out a full policy as part of their booking conditions.

ESSENTIAL INFORMATION

Capital Washington

Time zone UT -5 to -8 depending on the state. Pacific standard time in California is -8 hours. Eastern standard time in New York is -5 hours. DST +1 in summer Apr–Oct.

Language English. Spanish common in some areas.

Telecommunications Automatic dialling. Country code 1. Public telephone service. You will need a quad-band GSM phone in the USA to operate on all GSM bands though a tri-band will work for most operators. Many places have wifi and there are also internet cafés in most larger places.

Electricity 110V 60Hz

BEFORE YOU GO

For
✔ Large choice of cruising areas from the Pacific Northwest to Chesapeake to the Bahamas and the Florida Keys.
✔ Easy communications and excellent facilities in most places.
✔ Friendly people and lots of interesting things to see ashore.
✔ Good seafood.
✔ Comparatively inexpensive once you are there.

Against
✘ Some areas crowded in the high season.
✘ Some areas require experienced navigators.
✘ Limited cruising area in a few places.

Types of charter
❖ Flotilla/ sailing in company
❖ Bareboat
❖ Skippered charter
❖ Luxury charter in some areas

Money and banks
The unit of currency is the globally recognised US dollar, (the greenback) that can be used in almost any country in the world for goods and services. It is usually not worth buying dollars before you go. Cash advances on major credit cards, Visa and Access (MasterCard), and on charge cards like American Express and Diners Club, can be made and most ATM machines accept Visa or Access.

Banks are open 1000–1500 Mon–Fri although there may be variations in the summer between states. ATM machines are the best way of getting money in the USA with no hassles.

Eating and drinking
America is not often thought of as being a gourmet destination, but in my opinion and that of others it has very good food and in many places a wide range of ethnic restaurants serving wonderful inexpensive food. West coast food is now a recognised style of cuisine and clam chowder and crab-cakes around Maine and Chesapeake have long been famous. All along the coast seafood is excellent and generally fresh and cooked in interesting ways.

From north to south and east to west the USA has a wide range of regional cooking and it has adopted all the styles of its melting pot of immigrants over the years. You can get affordable Japanese, Southeast Asian, Italian, Mexican, Creole, and good old American home cooking as well. Portions are always large as reflected in the girth of many Americans and institutions like the American breakfast are serious affairs. And of course there are those American favourites like hamburgers and fried chicken although it pays to stay away from the brand names which now encircle the world and go to smaller establishments where this fare is infinitely better.

Remember that a tip is expected in bars and restaurants, usually around 15% of the bill. If you don't tip it is just plain embarrassing for all concerned, you will get dirty looks from staff and customers alike, and it means less in the pay packet for the waiter or waitress at the end of the week. When in Rome etc.

Californian wine is eminently quaffable and some of it is very good although it is generally not cheap in restaurants. Avoid the brands commonly exported and go for smaller vintners. American beer is usually light lager and more of a refreshing cool drink than an alcoholic beverage. There are other stronger dark beers in some areas if you prefer a change to the ubiquitous Budweiser, Miller and Schlitz. Spirits are widely available and cocktails are popular in most places.

Provisioning
All provisions are easily found in larger towns and tourist spots although big supermarkets are usually out of town a bit. The smaller supermarkets will be able to supply nearly everything you want anyway. Delicatessens have a whole range of tempting treats in the way of cold meats and salamis and cheeses.

Many of the larger charter companies and some of the smaller ones can provision the boat up for you on arrival. Normally you get either a list on which to tick off the items you want or a range of menus from basic to luxury with the items you get in each clearly stated. Getting the charter company to provision for you rarely costs too much more than doing it yourself and can let you get away early from the charter base. In any case there will be lots of opportunity in most places to restock the larder.

Costs

The overall cost of living is low to medium. Typical costs for eating out depend on the sort of place you go to with small no-frills restaurants or cafés being very good value and up-market restaurants being quite expensive. For breakfasts go to a diner where a large breakfast will cost around US$5–$10 each. Lunch and snacks in a pizza place, Chinese or Southeast Asian restaurant with a set menu or a salad bar will cost around $10–$15 a head for large portions. Evening meals in a restaurant can range from $20 a head for a cheap Japanese or Mexican meal with a beer to $50–$80 a

head for more upmarket cuisine with wine. In between there are numerous variations, but on the whole good quality cheap food, including good seafood, is easily found at a price to suit your pocket.

Provisioning is relatively cheap for all items and meat and fresh fruit and vegetables are abundant and good quality.

Transport is relatively cheap with air fares being the lowest in the world per air mile and rail and coach travel also good value. Car hire is the cheapest in the world with a compact normally costing around $20 per day although with deals arranged beforehand car hire can be lower. Insurance must be added to these prices and varies from state to state. Hire bikes including mountain bikes are available in some places at low cost.

Crime and personal safety

Although some areas in the USA have a reputation for violent crime and especially mugging, out of large urban areas crime is not a big issue. In places like New York, Washington, Annapolis, Miami, Los Angeles and San Diego you need to be careful when out and about, especially at night. Don't flash money around, don't look as if you are lost, don't wear expensive jewellery and don't venture into any part of the city which is known to have a reputation for crime. If the worst happens and you are mugged do not get excited and make sudden movements and just hand your money and valuables over. The mugger will most likely be armed with a knife (guns are rarer despite the numbers in the USA) and probably be just as scared as you – he only wants to get away with the dosh as quickly as possible.

When you leave the boat in harbour or at anchor to go ashore make sure it is securely locked and that any obvious temptations on deck have been stowed below. Leave the dinghy somewhere secure and chain it up if necessary. If you have an outboard on the dinghy ensure it is padlocked on. Most marinas have security guards and it is unlikely you will have problems when berthed for the night.

SAILING GUIDES AND CHARTS

Sailing guides for the areas are readily available in the USA and can often be purchased from the charter company when you book the holiday. The relevant guides are mentioned for each area in that section.

Defence Mapping Agency (DMA) charts are widely available throughout the USA. There are many locally produced charts which have been cut down to A2 or A3 format and bound together to make useful chart-books for yachts. Many of these chart-books have harbour and anchorage plans, aerial photographs, notes on things to see and do ashore, and even good restaurants to go to. They can usually be found locally or ask the charter company you are booking with if this sort of publication is available.

EAST COAST USA

FLORIDA AND THE BAHAMAS

Florida and the Bahamas are lumped together here because charter boats from Florida cross the Gulf Stream to cruise around the Bahamas.

WHEN TO GO

The season is year round although in August to October at the height of the hurricane season you may be disinclined to try your luck.

Low season May to mid-November. Paradoxically the summer months here are the low season as this is the wettest time of the year with slightly higher humidity. It is also the hurricane season which officially lasts from June to November. Hurricanes usually pass to the south of Florida and the Bahamas in June and July and the worst months are August to October. The trades tend to be east to southeast in the summer. Thunderstorms are common.

High season December to April. The mild winter temperatures make this a wonderful place to sail in the winter and water temperatures are still high. In fact the winter sea temperature is more refreshing than the high summer sea temperatures which make swimming a bit like being in warm soup. The easterly trades tend to be from the northeast at 10–15 knots. There can be winter gales influenced by depressions moving across the bulk of the USA to the north and these can bring strong southerly winds, commonly southeast, and rain and cooler temperatures.

GETTING THERE: KEY WEST

There are numerous daily scheduled and charter flights to Miami and Orlando from most important European and Pacific airports. There are some international flights to Tampa on the west coast. There are numerous domestic flights to Miami, Fort Lauderdale, Ley West, Marathon and Orlando on the east coast, and to Tampa and Clearwater on the west coast.

	Av max °C	Av min °C	Highest recorded	Relative humidity	Days 0.25 mm rain	Sea temp °C	Wind direction & force
Jan	23	16	29	66%	9	22	NE-E-SE F3-4
Feb	24	16	31	63%	6	23	E-SE F4
Mar	26	18	33	62%	7	24	E-SE F3-4
Apr	27	19	34	64%	7	25	E-SE F3-4
May	29	22	34	67%	12	28	E-SE F3-4
Jun	30	23	34	69%	13	30	SE-E F3
Jul	31	24	36	68%	15	31	SE-E F3
Aug	31	24	36	68%	15	32	SE-E F3-4
Sep	31	24	35	70%	18	30	SE-E F3-4
Oct	28	22	34	69%	16	28	NE-E F4
Nov	26	19	31	64%	10	25	NE-E F4
Dec	24	17	33	65%	7	23	NE-E-SE F4

FLORIDA & THE BAHAMAS

St Petersburg

Florida

• Palm Beach

Grand Bahama

Marsh Harbour

Fort Lauderdale

Miami •

Bimini Islands

Great Abaco

Key Biscayne

Berry Islands

Key Largo

Eleuthera

Key West

Islamorada

Nassau

Andros

B A H A M A S

Exumas

Cat Island

San Salvador

Cuba

Ragged Island Range

Long Island

Crooked Islands

CHARTER AREAS

Charter yachts operate on both the east and west sides of Florida although most charter is concentrated around the east side and the Florida Keys. It is a popular charter area with excellent diving and fishing in the clear waters. It also offers a wide choice from the sheltered waters of the Intracoastal Waterway to offshore across the Gulf Stream to the Bahamas. The Bahamas just 80 miles or so off the coast are renowned for diving and fishing. Because much of the water around the Florida keys and the Bahamas is shallow many charter yachts have shoal draught keels and catamarans are also popular for exploring the waters where deeper draught craft have difficulty getting to.

Wind and sea

The prevailing wind in this area is the easterly trade winds. In the summer the winds blow from the east to southeast at around 10–15 knots although the effects are lessened closer to the Florida coast and here there are often variable winds. Thunderstorms are common in the summer and can bring strong winds for a short period. The summer is the wet season and a fair amount of rain falls in July to October. The hurricane season lasts from June to November although August to October is the high risk period for the Florida coast and the Bahamas. Hurricanes have hit this area and in August to October a close listening watch should be kept on the radio and to weather forecasts. Weather forecasts are excellent for the area and you will be warned well in advance of any hurricane likely to hit Florida. One thing you can be sure of is that you do not want to encounter the fury of a full blown hurricane on a boat and the best policy in the event of a hurricane heading your way is to get the boat into a marina and head inland.

In the winter the prevailing trades blow predominantly from the northeast at around 10–15 knots although, as above, the effect is lessened close off the coast of Florida. At times a cold norther can blow down the coast from the north to northwest and may at times reach gale force. Northers usually blow when the pressure starts to rise for the permanent winter anticyclone over America. Strong southeast gales can also blow when depressions move out into the Atlantic from the American land mass.

Seas in this area range from nearly flat in the Intracoastal Waterway to quite rough when strong winds blow against the north-going Gulf Stream. In Hawk Channel outside the keys seas are light to moderate. Over the Gulf Stream things can get very

rough with a strong northerly and it is advisable to monitor weather forecasts carefully. Some charter companies will ban yachts going to the Bahamas if bad weather is likely.

Suitable for...
The possibilities around the Florida keys and the Bahamas offshore mean the area has something for everyone. Beginners can potter around the Intracoastal Waterway and out into Hawk Channel in settled conditions. Experienced sailors and crew can get some miles in crossing to the Bahamas and back again to Florida. There are a few semi-flotillas/sailing in company holidays although not the organised flotillas of the Mediterranean. There are bareboats of all types and skippered charter from smaller yachts up to very large yachts. There are also instruction courses offered by some of the charter companies ranging from learning to sail courses up to certified ASA (American Sailing Association) and RYA courses.

Harbours and anchorages
Harbours range from marinas with every facility laid on to smaller yacht harbours and boat piers. Most marinas have all facilities including hot showers, restaurants and shops within the marina, and swimming pools. Even smaller less flashy harbours and piers will have some facilities and you will find the locals there go out of there way to help you. Anchorages vary from mud around the mangrove creeks to sand on the outer keys and Bahamas. In the mangrove swamps there are lots of mosquitoes and noseeums so take plenty of insect repellent. The locals reckon that the mosquitoes here come with napkins.

Main charter bases
The main charter bases on the east coast are in the marinas around Miami and Fort Lauderdale and along the main keys at Key Largo, Islamorada and Key West. Many of the marinas here are along the Intracoastal Waterway and there are charter bases at

many of these. It is usually possible to arrange one way charters between bases for an additional cost. On the west coast of Florida most charter yachts are near Tampa. There are domestic flights to Key West and Marathon on the east coast and to Tampa, Clearwater/St Petersburg Airport.

From Miami Airport there are airport shuttle services to downtown Miami and to most Key destinations. Normal coach services and airport limousine services (read taxi) also operate along the coast. Probably the best way to do things is to have a hire car waiting at the airport and drive to your destination. It is sometimes possible to leave the car at the charter base after a few days and arrange to have another waiting there on your return. From Miami it is a leisurely drive to Key Largo and a bit longer to Key West depending on traffic.

Sailing area

On the eastern side there is a threefold choice of how you sail down the coast and keys. The Intracoastal Waterway runs down between the Keys and the coast. Sheltered by the Keys, it is comparatively flat water and there are numerous marinas and anchorages.

This area is shallow in places and care is needed outside the channel. The channel itself is clearly marked with yellow triangles to starboard and yellow squares to port when heading south. The road bridges connecting the keys open for boats so that you can get out into Hawk Channel. Between the Keys and the outer fringing reef is Hawk Channel which offers better sailing and deeper water. The outer fringing reef stops the worst of the swell but not the easterly trades. It is also possible to sail outside the fringing reef but there is little point to this. It's worth leaving a

SAILING GUIDES AND CHARTS

The Bahamas – Abaco Ports of Call & Anchorages Tom Henschel. Mile High Publishing.

The Cruising Guide To Abaco Bahamas Steve, Jeff & John Dodge. Imray.

Cruising Guide to the Florida Keys Capt. Frank Papy.

Richardson's Marine Florida Keys And Bimini Chartbook and Cruising Guide

A suggested one-week itinerary from Miami to Key West

Miami – Key West

total 135 miles

A cruise down the Florida Keys. Starts at Miami

Elliot Key	In Biscayne Bay. Anchor off the beach. Swim and explore the island.
Key Largo	Leave via Angelfish Creek to the Hawk Channel for a good sail south. Anchor behind Rodriguez Key or go into Marina del Mar for some nightlife.
Islamorada	Visit the Pennekamp Coral Reef State Park for snorkelling. Go to Holiday Isle Marina at Windley Key for the night. Restaurants.
Duck Key	Sail to Hawks Cay Resort. Good beach and swimming.
Newfound Harbour	Anchor off Little Palm Island. Restaurant. Visit Big Pine Key to see the world's smallest deer.
Key West	Good snorkelling at Looe Key Marine Sanctuary. Go to Lands End Marina for the night. Restaurants and bars aplenty.
Key West	Explore the island and don't forget to visit Hemingway's house and the bar he frequented.

A suggested one-week itinerary around the Abacos in the Bahamas

Marsh Harbour around the Abacos and return

60 miles

A cruise around the Abacos starting and finishing at Marsh Harbour

Day 1	Relax around Marsh Harbour with a good seafood dinner.
Day 2	Sail across to Hopetown on Elbow Cay.
Day 3	Sail up to Great Guana Cay and relax – there is seven miles of sandy beach. Some activity ashore or just snorkel in the clear waters.
Day 4	Lay day. Go ashore to Nippers for a drink.
Day 5	Sail to Treasure Cay. Anchor off or go into the marina.
Day 6	Sail back to Marsh Harbour with maybe a stopover for lunch in Great Guana Cay.

For longer periods yachts can go further in the Abacos to Sandy Cay in the south and Green Turtle Cay and Manjack Cay in the north. Most sailors here rapidly adapt to 'island time' and end up covering less distance than planned and getting in more swimming and more drinks ashore than planned.

day free for an excursion by Air-Boat on the Everglades.

Crossing to the Bahamas involves longer distances and some overnight sailing. It is around 50 miles to Bimini on the western side of the Bahamas where you can clear customs. From Bimini to somewhere like Great Stirrup Cay is 75 miles. After pottering around your chosen part of the Bahamas it is then necessary to get back to Bimini, clear out, and re-cross the Gulf Stream to the east coast. Really it is inadvisable to take less than two weeks over a Bahamas cruise because of the distances involved. In the Bahamas you will find lots of local colour, but it is the local colour under the water which is the big attraction. The shallow waters allow snorkelling around not far off the bottom and the clear waters and coral reefs are home to a wide variety of marine life. There are tropical fish everywhere.

The Bahamas have had a reputation as a drug smuggling area that yachts should keep clear of. These days the vigilant American coastguard has eliminated much of the drug smuggling activity around here, but you will still need to be careful and it is best to stick to the more popular areas and if possible sail in company with another yacht.

On the west coast of Florida there are lots of small islands and mangrove creeks to explore. The area is less developed than the east coast and there are fewer tailor made marinas and yacht facilities. The birdlife here is prolific with ibis, cormorants, pelicans, osprey and herons. This being Florida, there are also alligators.

CHESAPEAKE BAY

Chesapeake Bay is an enclosed waterway extending over 200 miles from Norfolk in Virginia to past Baltimore in Maryland. It is much indented with a number of rivers and creeks running into it and it has numbers of islands and islets. Much of it is very shallow and care is needed with your pilotage so you don't get stuck in the mud too often. The area is popular in the summer with considerable numbers of local boats around and there are numerous marinas and boat harbours to pull into for provisions and eating out. Eating out is part of the reason for being here with excellent crab, fish, and shrimps on offer in all sorts of yummy ways.

The season here lasts from April to October. May and June and again in September are reckoned the best months to sail here. Being inland it can get very hot in July and August and winds are the least reliable during high summer. For the most winds are from the south to southwest at 10–12 knots although there are numerous days of calm or very light winds. Thunderstorms are fairly frequent in the summer and may be accompanied by strong winds, often from west to northwest. There are tides in the area with the strongest currents in the narrow channels at the southern end around Annapolis. Most navigation is straightforward with buoys, beacons or withies marking the channels. One thing to look out for is the large numbers of buoyed crab pots all around the area making it essential to keep an eye out most of the time. However the crab is so good ashore you won't begrudge the chore of zigzagging around crab pots.

Chesapeake Bay has a wonderful mixture of cities and towns with all amenities and good maritime museums and even better seafood restaurants. Marinas here offer just about every conceivable facility including good showers and toilets, restaurants and bars, and most have swimming pools. There are smaller towns, some with small marinas or piers, and lots

Washington	Av max °C	Av min °C	Highest recorded	Relative humidity	Days 0.25 mm rain	Sea temp °C	Wind direction & force
Apr	18	7	35	45%	11	7	S-SW F3
May	24	12	36	48%	12	11	S-SW F3
Jun	28	17	39	52%	11	17	S-SW F2-3
Jul	31	20	41	53%	11	20	S-SW F2-3
Aug	29	19	41	53%	11	22	SW-NE F2-3
Sep	26	15	40	53%	8	20	NE-E F3
Oct	19	9	36	50%	9	16	NE-E F3-4

SAILING GUIDES AND CHARTS

Cruising the Chesapeake: A Gunkholers Guide
Bill Shellenberger. International Marine.

of anchorages behind islands or up creeks. Many of the boats here have lifting keels as getting stuck in the mud when exploring creeks and inlets is a common experience. Around the remoter areas the vegetation is luxurious and the bird life prolific including egrets, herons and kingfishers. There are even supposed to be otters up some of the creeks. The heat and the thick vegetation does give rise to a few pests and 'noseeums' are a problem so pack a good insect repellent. Towards the end of the summer there are frequently lots of jellyfish around, ruling out swimming and probably one of the reasons a lot of marinas have pools.

There are a lot of places of note to visit around the Chesapeake. From the south, Annapolis is considered by some Americans to be the boating capital of the USA and has a good maritime museum and is home to the American Naval Academy. The old historic centre of the city is well worth a visit and there are shops and boutiques aplenty. Around this area there are lots of examples of old maritime Chesapeake with many of the waterfront areas restored and in use for transient boaters exploring the area. Places like St Michaels and Oxford should not be missed. At the northern end of Chesapeake Bay it is possible to sail right up the Potomac to Washington DC although it is likely you will be more seduced by the charms of smaller places before the White

House claims your attention. Baltimore, the capital of Maryland at the northern end of Chesapeake Bay can also be visited by boat.

Most charter companies are clustered around Annapolis although there are companies operating out of the northern end of the Bay as well. There are international and feeder flights to Annapolis and internal communications by rail and coach are good. Alternatively get a hire car.

MAINE

The coast and islands in the state of Maine between Boston and Nova Scotia make up a spectacular cruising area although not one for the inexperienced. The area has its share of rocks and reefs, but the real problem is fog which can roll off the sea at any time. It is also not spectacularly warm here with temperatures in July and August an average $24°-26°C$ in the day and $14°-16°C$ at night although it can feel chillier than this.

The two main cruising areas are Penobscot Bay and its islands or Casco Bay further south. Both bays are dotted with islands. Many of these are uninhabited or have just an original house or two on them. Around the islands navigation is fairly straightforward although there are shallow areas, rocky reefs and ridges, and the tides which can cause appreciable races between the islands. Fog is common through spring and summer when the prevailing southerlies bring moist warm air up over the cold Labrador current.

Facilities are limited except in the centres of population which are few and far between. There are international flights into Boston and feeder flights from New York.

WEST COAST USA

The west coast of America has a number of varied charter areas. Charter bases are in the San Juan Islands just under the Canadian border, San Francisco, Los Angeles and San Diego. The cruising conditions and climate vary considerably between the northern and southern areas with charter in the north confined to the summer and charter in the south extending over a longer period.

SAN JUAN ISLANDS AND SEATTLE

Puget Sound wrapping around the San Juan Islands just under the border with Canada is a huge much indented cruising area. It is a popular area for yachting, but it is possible to get away from it all. Effectively the area is increased by Vancouver and Vancouver Island just over the border and customs clearance between the USA and Canada is easy and quick. The islands are sheltered from the worst of the Pacific swell by Vancouver Island and Olympic Peninsula which enclose Puget Sound and extends down to Seattle. There are so many indentations around the coast and islands it is always possible to find shelter.

The season runs from May to September although in the spring and autumn (fall) it can get chilly at times. It also rains a lot, a grey drizzle that doesn't show up in the statistics as much as it does when you are there. Day temperatures are pleasantly warm and at times it can get very hot as a glance at the table shows. The best time to be here is from June to September. Winds can be light and variable in July and August with more consistent winds in June and September. At times there will be a blow off the Pacific, more frequent in the spring and autumn than high summer.

Navigation amongst the islands is fairly straightforward except for strong tidal streams which can reach 4-5 knots in places like the Spieden Channel. Tides are around 4.3 metres at springs. The area is well covered by yachtsman's guides and if these are not on the charter yacht then get hold of a copy before you set off.

The islands are a wild area with lots of good walking and the opportunity to get away from it all. Dense forest covers much of the area and a number of the islands and adjacent coast are national park. Much of the area was and some of it still is logging country and there are old logging towns scattered around the area. The

SAILING GUIDES AND CHARTS

Evergreen Pacific San Juan Islands Cruising Atlas Charts and aerial photos. Available locally.

Emily's Guides to the San Juan Islands Set of three guides. Available locally.

At Seattle	Av max °C	Av min °C	Highest recorded	Relative humidity	Days 1 mm rain	Sea temp °C	Wind direction & force
May	18	8	33	56%	12	11	S F2-3
Jun	21	11	37	54%	9	12.5	W/S F2-3
Jul	22	12	38	51%	4	14	W-SW F3
Aug	23	13	36	54%	5	14	NW-W-SW F3
Sep	19	11	33	61%	8	12.5	W-SW F3
Oct	15	8	28	73%	13	11	SW-S F2-3

Spinnaker option for light airs

region is actually semi-tropical rainforest in parts with a dense forest canopy under which lichens, mosses and ferns grow. There are lots of marked hiking paths and it is well worth allotting some time out from sailing for rambles ashore. The birdlife is prolific, including eagles and herons, and there are elk and bears in places. The waters are home to all sorts of marine life including whales (orcas or killer whales frequent the area), dolphins and seals.

There are a number of yacht marinas, piers in places or laid moorings in the bays. Otherwise you are on your own and anchoring. Facilities are limited away from the centres of population but there is usually somewhere you can get to for provisions and a bite ashore if you need it. All charter is bareboat or skippered and operates out of Seattle, Friday Harbour, Anacortes and a few other places. It is also possible to sail down from charter bases in Vancouver to the islands.

There are international and domestic flights into Seattle and Vancouver and some smaller connecting flights and seaplanes. Internal travel and communications are good whether by train, coach or car.

LOS ANGELES AND SAN DIEGO

The warm summers and temperate winters make this a more amenable charter area than the San Juans in the north, but while the climate is better, the cruising area is greatly restricted. You can basically go north or south along the coast. There are a few off-lying islands but no enclosed cruising area like Puget Sound or the area inside Vancouver Island. It is also hampered by the Pacific swell rolling in along the coast which provides good surfing conditions off the beaches, but makes coastal passages in light winds uncomfortable and restricts the number of anchorages to those where an indentation provides shelter from the swell.

Winds in the summer are normally a sea breeze blowing onto the coast which rarely gets above 20 knots. Cruising from Los Angeles is usually south to San Diego taking in Catalina Island, Newport, Dana Point,

At San Diego	Av max °C	Av min °C	Highest recorded	Relative humidity	Days 1 mm rain	Sea temp °C	Wind direction & force
Mar	18	10	37	66%	7	14.5	NW-W F4
Apr	19	12	36	68%	4	15	NW-W F4
May	19	13	37	71%	3	15.5	NW-W F4
Jun	21	15	36	72%	1	17.5	NW-W F3-4
Jul	23	17	38	73%	1	18	NW-W F3-4
Aug	23	18	34	73%	1	19	NW-W F3-4
Sep	23	17	43	72%	1	19	NW-W F3-4
Oct	22	14	36	71%	3	18	NW-W F3-4
Nov	21	11	34	67%	4	17	NW-W F3-4

SAILING GUIDES AND CHARTS

Charlie's US Pacific Coast Charlie's Charts.

Planning where to go is part of the fun

Oceanside and Mission Bay along the way. Cruising from San Diego is either north to Los Angeles and Catalina Island or you can go south to Mexico and Ensenada and the Los Coronados Islands. It is worth taking a few days just to potter around San Diego Bay. There are numerous yacht marinas along the coast and mostly laid moorings in the few usable anchorages. The harbours and anchorages are popular in the summer and things can get very crowded. Marina del Rey in Los Angeles is the largest marina in the world. It is possible to cruise in the winter but the Pacific swell rolling in tends to get bigger and there is always the possibility of the dreaded Santa Ana winds which blow over gale force and cause a large swell to beat onto the coast.

Communications are easy. Los Angeles Airport has international flights from all over the world. There are connecting flights to San Diego although it is a short trip by land. Trains and coaches serve the cities and towns although a hire car simplifies things greatly and hire cars in the USA are probably the cheapest in the world.

THE SOUTH PACIFIC

FRENCH POLYNESIA, TONGA, FIJI, VANUATU, AND NEW CALEDONIA

FRENCH POLYNESIA (Society Islands)

French Polynesia covers a vast area of the Pacific with several island groups including the Marquesas, Tuamotus, Îles Sous le Vent and the Society Islands which includes the best-known island of Tahiti. The name Tahiti has such connotations that it almost stands for the whole group. It has long been a magnet for northern Europeans of romantic persuasions and this includes many yachtsmen, but although there is some yacht charter out of Tahiti, most yacht charter is out of Raiatea in the Îles Sous le Vent.

SOUTH PACIFIC ISLANDS

The islands of the Iles Sous Le Vent (including Raiatea, Tahaa, Bora Bora and Huahine) and the Society Islands (Tahiti and Moorea) are of volcanic origin rising abruptly from the sea and are surrounded by fringing coral reefs. The scenery is spectacular and there is much to do and see ashore. The islands have been fairly well developed over the years for land-based tourism so expect good facilities ashore and restaurants of a high standard and likewise a high price outside of the main centres.

WHEN TO GO

The season is year round although many charter yachts do not run between January and March, the worst cyclone months and the wet season. High season is generally considered to be June to August and mid-season April to May.

BEFORE YOU GO

For
- ✔ Some of the most spectacular islands in the Pacific.
- ✔ Excellent navigation aids.
- ✔ Good snorkelling and warm waters.
- ✔ Consistent trade winds.
- ✔ Visit black pearl farms and ancient Polynesian sites.

Against
- ✘ Expensive ashore.
- ✘ Long haul flights needed to get there.
- ✘ Can be rainy and squally when SPCZ dips down across the islands.

Types of charter
- ❖ Bareboat
- ❖ Skippered charter

Suitable for
- ❖ Intermediate and experienced sailors.

ESSENTIAL INFORMATION

Capital Papeete

Time zone UT -10

Language Tahitian and French. Some English spoken.

Telecommunications Direct dialling. Country code 689. Quad band mobile phones work here depending on your supplier. Wifi and internet cafés.

Electricity 220V 50Hz

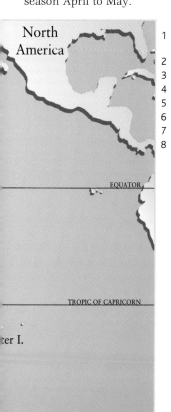

North America

1 Tahiti & Society Islands
2 Tonga
3 Hawaii
4 Micronesia
5 Vanuatu
6 New Caledonia
7 Western Samoa
8 Fiji

EQUATOR

TROPIC OF CAPRICORN

ter I.

The prevailing trade winds blow across the islands from an easterly direction at around 15–20 knots in the wet season (May to August) and 10–15 knots in the dry season (September to April). It should be remembered that cyclones do sometimes hit the Society Islands during the months of

At Papeete	Av max °C	Av min °C	Highest recorded	Relative humidity	Days 2.5 mm rain	Sea temp °C	Wind direction & force
Apr	32	22	33	78%	10	28	NE-E-SE F4
May	31	21	33	78%	10	28	NE-E-SE F4
Jun	30	21	32	79%	8	27	E-SE F4-5
Jul	30	20	32	77%	5	26	E-SE F3-4
Aug	25	20	31	77%	8	26	NE-E-SE F4
Sep	25	21	31	76%	10	26	NE-E-SE F4
Oct	26	22	32	76%	11	26	E-SE F4-5
Nov	31	22	32	77%	13	27	NE-E-SE F4
Dec	31	22	33	78%	14	27	NE-E-SE F4

SOCIETY ISLANDS

SAILING GUIDES AND CHARTS

Charlie's Charts: French Polynesia.

Guide to Navigation and Tourism in French Polynesia Bonnette/Deschamps.

November to May with January and February being the worst months. Temperatures are tropical with around 30°–32°C in January and December and 28°–30°C in June and July.

GETTING THERE

Tahiti is served by international flights from some European and US international airports and from Sydney and Auckland. Internal flights operate to many of the islands including Raiatea.

WHEN YOU'RE THERE

Visas and documentation

Visas are not required from most countries including EU countries, the USA and Australasia if you are not staying more than 30 days. A valid passport is required for entry.

The skipper of the boat will need a certificate of competence such as the RYA International Certificate of Competence.

Sailing area

Charter yachts operate mostly from Raiatea and some from Papeete. Most of the sailing is between the islands including Moorea, Huahine, Raiatea, Tahaa, Bora-Bora and Tahiti itself. The fringing coral reefs provide protection from the seas once you are inside them and there are numerous anchorages. The channels through the passes and inside the barrier reefs are all well buoyed. Between the fringing reefs and the high jungle-clad volcanic islands the vistas are awe-inspiring and it won't take too long before old images of Gauguin, of Fletcher Christian and his Bligh, of a dozen Hollywood movies set in the south Pacific wriggling out of your subconscious. The islands are truly wonderful places and evocative of everything a South Sea paradise should be.

Because of the dangers of sailing amongst coral and the sometimes boisterous trade winds this area is suited to intermediate and experienced sailors for bareboats. There are often variable currents around the reefs, up to 3–4 knots in places, and this means you must keep an eye on your navigation. The channels through the reefs are well marked and buoyed using IALA System A. Going through a reef entrance for the first time, with breakers and surf on either side of the pass, needs steady nerves and concentration. Less experienced sailors should take a skippered charter or at least a skipper for some of the time until they get used to the area.

For the most part you will be anchoring or picking up moorings. There is a marina on Raiatea and Marina Taina and the municipal marina in Papeete. There are a few jetties in places, usually off hotels or restaurants. Ashore costs are high and eating out in a restaurant can cost anything from €20 to €30–50 a head. With the French influence the food is of course very good in places. Provisioning is likewise not cheap but is excellent with a lot of good French imported items.

TUAMOTUS AND MARQUESAS

Most charter to these two island groups is skippered charter and the yachts are generally larger than your average bareboat.

Tuamotus These are a group of nearly 80 atolls stretching for over a thousand miles across the South Pacific. Many of the atolls are inhabited and some have small airstrips. The atolls were formed when over time the central island sank into the ocean leaving just the coral barrier reef. Getting in through the passes of the atolls and navigating inside requires considerable care and you will need to have faith in your skipper. What the atolls do have is some of the most remarkable diving in the Pacific and most charter boats heading to the Tuamotus will have tanks and compressors on board so you can dive over the reefs. Even if you don't do sub-aqua, the snorkelling is superb.

Moorea

Marquesas This group of high islands is tucked on the edge of the vast Pacific and if you get the chance to charter here then you should take it. The high mountainous islands are breath-taking and the Marquesan Polynesians, and a few Europeans, live a simpler life to their cousins in Tahiti. This is getting back to nature sort of stuff and if you are looking for sophisticated restaurants and night clubs this is not the place for you. If you are looking for stunning scenery and a welcoming low-key way of life and some good though simple restaurants, then try to get here.

Like the Tuamotus, charters here are skippered charter and the charter boats are usually fairly large and consequently somewhat more expensive.

TONGA

Tonga is made up of three main island groups between approximately 18° and 22°S. Charter boats mainly operate from the Vava'u group in the north. All sailing is either skippered or bareboat and sailing in company with a lead boat to keep an eye on things can be arranged. The area is one of outstanding beauty with a multitude of wonderful anchorages amongst the islands and behind the reefs. It has become more popular in recent years so there are numbers of yachts around but you can get away from the crowds with a bit of planning.

WHEN TO GO

The season is essentially in the southern hemisphere winter which is outside of the typhoon months. The most popular months are from August through till October. It does rain here when the South Pacific Convergence Zone (SPCZ) dips down over Tonga, but the rain will usually disappear within a day or two. Even when it's raining, the air and sea temperatures are tropical.

The prevailing easterly trade winds, somewhere between northeast and south-

east, blow consistently across the islands between April and October at around 15–20 knots and less predictably so from November to March. Typhoons occasionally pass through the islands with the worst

Tonga

At Nelafu	Av max °C	Av min °C	Highest recorded	Relative humidity	Days 1 mm rain	Sea temp °C	Wind direction & force
Apr	30	24	33	76%	14	28	N-NE-E F4
May	29	23	32	76%	12	28	E-SE F4
Jun	29	23	32	73%	7	27	E-SE F4-5
Jul	29	23	33	75%	9	26	E-SE F4-5
Aug	29	24	32	73%	9	26	E-SE F4
Sep	29	23	32	75%	11	26	E-SE F4-5
Oct	29	24	34	76%	14	26	E-SE F4
Nov	30	23	33	75%	16	27	E-SE F4-5
Dec	29	23	33	77%	19	27	E-SE F4-5

months being from January to March. Temperatures are tropical year round with 28°–30°C in December and January and 25°–26°C in June and July.

GETTING THERE

Tonga is served by international flights from New Zealand, Australia, and Fiji. Flights from Europe and the USA can connect through any of these hubs. Internal flights connect the H'apai and Vava'u groups.

WHEN YOU'RE THERE

Visas and documentation
Visas are not required from most countries including EU countries, the USA and Australasia if you are not staying more than 30 days. A valid passport is required for entry.

Sailing area
Charter yachts operate around the northerly Vava'u group of islands where there are literally scores of wonderful anchorages. The actual sailing area is not huge and because there are so many anchorages within a short distance you can sail as much or as little as you like. Because of the danger of navigating amongst coral and the possibility of the southeast trade winds sometimes turning to the SW-W-NW, especially in the dry season and so making

ESSENTIAL INFORMATION

Capital Nuku'alofa

Time zone UT + 13

Language Tongan and English

Telecommunications Direct dialling. Country code 676. Quad band mobile phones work here depending on your supplier. Wifi and internet cafés.

Electricity 230V 50Hz

Sailing by in the Vava'u group

Suggested itinerary

From Neiafu around the Vava'u group

Approx 50 miles

Day 1	Arrive on the yacht in Neiafu. Dinner and drinks ashore.
Day 2	Depart Base for Port Maurelle on Kapa Island.
Day 3	Sail across to Hunga Island and anchor overnight in the Coral Garden.
Day 4	Lay day on Hunga or sail to some of the day anchorages around Hunga before returning to the Coral Garden.
Day 5	Sail across to Tapana Island. Pick up a mooring if one is free or anchor. Book dinner at Paella.
Day 6	Lay day at Tapana or sail to Ofu further east.
Day 7	Sail back to the anchorage under Nuku Island or to Port Maurelle.
Day 8	Have a look in nearby Swallows Cave and anchor off Mala Island for dinner ashore.
Day 9	Sail back to Neiafu and organise a whale watching trip for the last day.
Day 10	Whale watching.

Land excursions

Whale watching	Not so much a land excursion as a one-off chance to see Humpback whales close up and to swim with them. A quite extraordinary excursion and one of the few places in the world that you can do this.
Island tour	Hire a taxi for the day to do a tour of the island and see local inland villages and local crafts like weaving falas.
Friday night regatta	In the season there is a yacht race around a short course in Neiafu harbour organised by the Moorings and local businesses. Very informal and a lot of fun to take part in.

normally safe anchorages untenable, this area is not suited to inexperienced skippers for bareboats. Intermediate sailors worried about navigating in coral should take on a skipper, at least for part of the charter. The islands and anchorages themselves are a paradise and ashore there is much to enjoy. A traditional Tongan feast is usually part of an itinerary although it is pretty much a set-piece for tourists in the main centres.

SAILING GUIDES AND CHARTS

Cruising Guide to the Vava'u Island Group in the Kingdom of Tonga The Moorings. You can also download an older version of this guide from www.tongasailing.com/tonga_charters.htm

Sailingbird's Guide to the Kingdom of Tonga Charles Paul & Katherine Pham-Paul. Sailingbird Publications.

Other Pacific Islands

SAMOA

Samoa is divided into Eastern and Western Samoa, the eastern group of islands being administered by the USA. The western group has some skippered charter around the islands and reefs although not a lot. The Samoan Islands, lying between 13°–15°S of the equator, have a tropical climate and like many of the other south Pacific islands are blessed by constant trade winds from the southeast. The scenery, anchorages and life ashore are wonderful and every bit as good as other islands in the south Pacific.

For information see the internet or a charter broker.

(For temperatures and climate see the chart for Tonga.)

FIJI

Fiji has a huge cruising ground with an estimated 300 or more islands. The islands are volcanic and steep-to with wonderful fringing coral reefs. It has some skippered and luxury charter but no bareboat charter as such. The continuing friction between the Fijian and Indian populations and the last coup by the army in 2006 under Colonel Bainimarama unsettled tourism in Fiji and

this persists to the present day in the larger urban settlements. Fortunately most yacht charter is well out of the way of this and life goes on as normal in the outer islands.

Charter yachts operate from Suva, Lautoka, Viti Levu and Musket Cove in the Malolo group of islands. There is enough cruising around the islands and reefs off the western side of Viti Levu to keep anyone happy. This is also the leeward side of the prevailing easterly trades and consequently the drier side as most of the rain falls on the easternmost islands. The wind has also lessened by the time it gets to the western side of the group and is mostly 10–15 knots from the NE-SE. Yachts normally cruise around the Mamanutha group and the Yassawas lying more or less north-south on the western side of Viti Levu. There are few facilities apart from the resort at Musket Cove and a few other resort hotels where there are restaurants. It is customary in Fiji to go ashore to meet the head of the village and this affords a good introduction to island life and you just may get invited for dinner. Needless to say the diving is superb around the islands and the fishing is good.

The best season is May to October and there is little charter during the cyclone season from November to March which is

At Suva	Av max °C	Av min °C	Highest recorded	Relative humidity	Days 1 mm rain	Sea temp °C	Wind direction & force
Apr	29	23	34	77%	19	27.5	E-SE F4
May	28	22	34	79%	16	26.5	E-SE F4
Jun	27	21	32	74%	13	25.5	E-SE F3-4
Jul	26	20	32	73%	14	25	E-SE F3-4
Aug	26	20	32	74%	15	24.5	E-SE F3-4
Sep	27	21	32	73%	16	25	E-SE F4
Oct	27	21	34	73%	15	25.5	E-SE F4
Nov	28	22	34	74%	15	26	E-SE F3-4
Dec	29	23	36	74%	18	27.5	E-SE F3-4

SAILING GUIDES AND CHARTS

A Yachtsman's Fiji Michael Calder. Cruising Classroom.

South Pacific Anchorages Warwick Clay. Imray.

also the wet season. There are international flights to Nadi International Airport on the western side of Viti Levu and internal flights to Suva and Musket Cove.

There are bareboat (with a guide) and skippered yacht charter available. For information see the internet or a charter broker.

VANUATU

The island chain of Vanuatu sits sandwiched between Australia and Fiji on the edge of the Coral Sea. There is some skippered charter out of Port Vila on Efate Island. The prevailing winds are the southeast trades and temperatures are much similar to Fiji (see climate chart). The best season is May to October and the islands are in the path of cyclones during the season from November to March. There are international flights into Port Vila.

For further information see the internet or a charter broker.

NEW CALEDONIA

There is bareboat and skippered charter out of Noumea and normal itineraries go to the Loyalty Islands or the Isle of Pines to the south. One-way itineraries are possible. The island is a French Overseas Territory and much of the charter is organised by French companies. In fact it was from here that French secret agents chartered a yacht to sail to New Zealand to sink the *Rainbow Warrior*. The climate is typically tropical and the winds are the prevailing SE trades. There are international flights into Noumea and internal flights to many places.

For further information try the internet, French sailing magazines or a charter broker.

MICRONESIA

Situated in the NW Pacific just above the equator the island chain of Micronesia offers abundant sailing and diving opportunities. There are a number of small charter operations offering skippered charter and sail-dive charter. Most operations are out of Palau and from here there are so many possibilities it is probably best to just sit back and allow the skipper to organise an itinerary. International flights into Palau.

For information try American and SE Asia boating magazines or a charter broker.

AUSTRALASIA

AUSTRALIA

Australia, the 'Lucky Country', is now a popular destination for holidays with a huge varied geography and a climate ranging from the semi-tropical in the south to the dry arid desert in the middle to tropical in the north. Much of the coast of this continent is not well suited to sailing and the popular areas are all on the east coast.

There is so much to see and do in this country that many charterers from the northern hemisphere will include a yacht charter as part of a longer holiday in the country. Notions of Australia often revolve around easy-going sun-tanned men wearing sun-hats with dangling corks and swigging from a 'tinny' and visitors are often surprised at the cosmopolitan and sophisticated nature of the country and the people. It is a special place and between the topography and the people there are few who do not enjoy the ex-perience and want to return again.

Australia has several established charter areas, but although a popular holiday destination it is only comparatively recently that the notion of chartering in Australia for those in the northern hemisphere has become popular. The main charter area is the Whitsunday Islands lying within the Great Barrier Reef approx-imately half way along the Queensland coast. The Whitsundays encompass some 70 islands counting the very small ones and it is really the only cruising area in Australia where you can sail around a group of islands and find secure anchorages. The Whitsundays lying just north of the Tropic of Capricorn have a tropical climate and the season is year round. There are also charter bases at Sydney and Brisbane where the climate is less equatorial and more geared to the seasons.

BEFORE YOU GO

For
✔ Long sailing season and tropical temperatures in the Whitsundays.
✔ Good steady sailing winds over most of the season.
✔ Some of the best diving over coral in the world off the Barrier Reef.
✔ Friendly and helpful locals.
✔ Good seafood and cosmopolitan cuisine around Sydney.

Against
✘ Long flight times from European countries.
✘ Internal flights necessary to get to the Whitsundays.
✘ Shorter season at Sydney.

Types of charter
❖ Sailing in company
❖ Bareboat
❖ Skippered charter
❖ Luxury charter

Suitable for
❖ Adventurous beginners to experienced sailors.

WHEN TO GO

Whitsundays The season in the Whitsundays is year round and high season tends to be geared to peak holiday periods: Easter, school holidays, and Christmas and New Year are designated peak periods. In the Whitsundays you get higher temperatures during the southern hemisphere summer from November to April (around 26–30°C) and slightly less wind than the winter. From May to October temperatures are slightly less than the summer (around 22–28°C) but

At Townsville	Av max °C	Av min °C	Highest recorded	Relative humidity	Days 0.25 mm rain	Sea temp °C	Wind direction & force
Jan	31	24	40	70%	15	28	E-SE F4-5
Feb	31	24	43	68%	12	27	E-SE F4
Mar	30	23	35	68%	10	27	E-SE F4
Apr	29	21	36	62%	6	26	SE F4
May	27	18	32	60%	5	24	S-SE F4
Jun	25	16	31	60%	4	22	S-SE F4
Jul	24	15	29	58%	3	21.5	E-SE F3-4
Aug	25	16	32	59%	3	21	E-SE-S F4
Sep	27	19	34	61%	2	22.5	NE-E-SE F4
Oct	28	22	34	64%	4	24	N-NE-E-SE F4
Nov	29	23	38	66%	5	25	N-NE-E-SE F4
Dec	31	24	38	69%	12	26	N-NE-E-SE F4

the winds are on average slightly stronger than the summer.

Brisbane/Sydney Further south at Brisbane and more so at Sydney the summer and winter periods are more pronounced and the southern hemisphere summer (November to April) is the favoured period.

GETTING THERE

There are numerous scheduled flights to Sydney, Brisbane and Cairns Airports from most large inter-national airports around the world. There are internal connections to most other major destinations in Australia.

To get to the Whitsundays most people opt to fly to Proserpine or Hamilton Island where a bus, taxi or water taxi will take you to the charter base. Some charter companies may deliver the boat to Hamilton Island. It is also possible to take a hire car to the adjacent mainland or get a coach or train to Proserpine.

Flight times from Europe are around 20 hours and from the USA around 10–12 hours. In my experience it is best to have a brief stopover somewhere en route rather than flying direct. A stopover will usually diminish the effects of jet-lag commonly found on long flights from Europe to Australia.

WHEN YOU'RE THERE

Visa and documentation

All visitors to Australia require a valid visa (except for New Zealanders) which must be obtained before arrival. Visas are normally easily obtained within a short time. EU and US passport holders can easily get an e-visa online. Go to www.immi.gov.au.

You will need a certificate of competence for bareboats. Other relevant paperwork for the charter yacht will be prepared by the charter company on your arrival and a full briefing on the yacht and area will be given.

Health

Immunisation Only required if coming from an infectious area.

Quarantine Australia has very strict quarantine laws and you are not allowed to bring in many foodstuffs or even transport them between states.

Medical services There are good medical services in even quite small places and

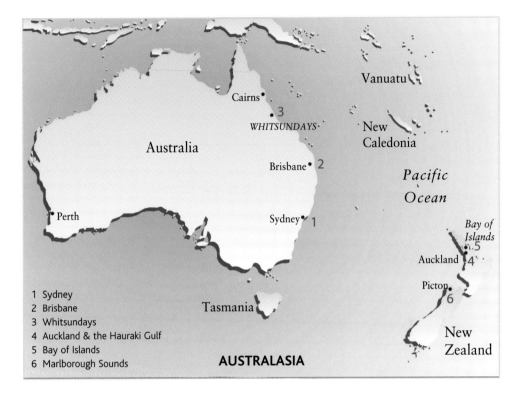

1 Sydney
2 Brisbane
3 Whitsundays
4 Auckland & the Hauraki Gulf
5 Bay of Islands
6 Marlborough Sounds

AUSTRALASIA

efficient land and air ambulance services. It is essential to take out private medical insurance that includes repatriation in the case of major illness. Although medical fees are not excessive, costs will mount up over time and a medical insurance policy is only sensible.

Water Water is generally safe to drink everywhere.

Money and banks

The unit of currency is the Australian dollar and rates of exchange are reasonably stable. There is little point in obtaining Australian currency before you enter the country.

Banks are open 1000–1600 Monday to Friday. Money can often be exchanged in other places such as travel agents or charter operators. All major credit cards and charge cards can be used in the larger towns and tourist resorts. ATM machines can be found in the cities and larger resorts and work with most credit cards.

ESSENTIAL INFORMATION

Capital Canberra

Time zone (there are three time zones) East coast UT + 10

Language English and Strine

Telecommunications Automatic dialling. Country code 61. Phone cards in many places. GSM phones supported throughout Australia. Internet cafés and wifi.

Electricity 220V 50Hz AC

Eating and drinking

Eating out in Australia is excellent with considerable influence from the major immigrant groups from Southeast Asia and Europe. In the larger centres good Thai, Malaysian, Japanese, Vietnamese and Chinese food will be found along with

SAILING GUIDES AND CHARTS

There are numerous guidebooks on cruising in Australian waters and on specific areas. The following may be useful:

Australian Cruising Guide Alan Lucas. Imray. A general guide to cruising around Australia.

Cruising the Coral Coast Alan Lucas. Covers the area inside the Barrier Reef in detail.

100 Magic Miles (and chart). Produced by the charter operators in the Whitsundays and covers the area in detail. DVD also available.

Australian charts provide excellent coverage and there is also a series of charts with aerial photographs of harbours and anchorages widely available.

European orientated restaurants such as Italian, Greek, Spanish and French. Many of these influences have been Aussified with interesting mixes of ingredients and cooking styles. The basis, the raw ingredients for the different cuisines, is excellent with an especially good variety of seafood. One excellent Australian institution resulting from the once draconian licensing laws is the BYO (bring-your-own) restaurant which allows you to bring along your own wine or other alcoholic beverage and, for a small corkage fee, drink it in the restaurant with the meal.

Australians are known as beer drinkers although in fact Australian beer is overrated being mostly of the bland lager types common in Europe and the USA. Australian wine is excellent as most people know and keenly priced so that you can sample excellent wines at reasonable prices.

Provisioning

Provisioning is easy almost everywhere although in the smaller places you will obviously not get the choice available in larger towns with supermarkets. Most of the charter companies can arrange a provisioning service and will provide a list of items before you get to the boat so that you can select what you want to have on board before arriving.

Costs

The overall cost of living is average, perhaps slightly below the European average. Eating out depends on where you are and can vary from around £15 a head to double that for a good restaurant. Remember with BYO restaurants you substantially reduce the overall cost by avoiding the high mark-up most restaurants put on beverages. In terms of value for money the eating out is good value. Beer is around 75p a bottle and wine around £6–8.

Local transport is average for coaches and internal flights. Taxis are moderate. Hire cars are around £18–20 a day.

Crime and personal safety

Australia is a safe country to travel in and the likelihood of violence or robbery away from the large cities is remote. Theft from boats is infrequent and few precautions are necessary, especially around the Whitsundays.

CHARTER AREAS

WHITSUNDAYS

Situated on the east coast of Australia near the southern end of the Great Barrier Reef and just over 400 miles north of Sydney and 200 miles north of Brisbane. There are said to be 70 islands in the group although realistically there are only just over a dozen that can be usefully used along with the adjacent mainland coast. Many of the islands now have resorts on them although a number have been designated as nature reserves and are deserted.

Consequently you can mix-and-match your cruising to take in anchorages where you must rely on your own resources and resorts where there are good facilities and restaurants. The Whitsundays are arguably the best cruising area in Australia with an

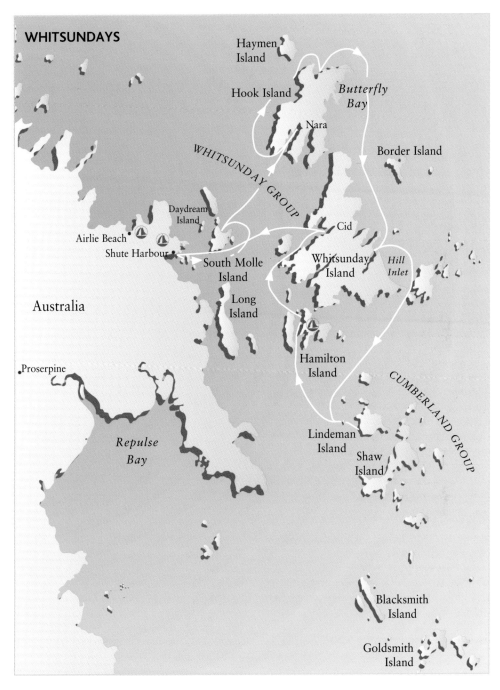

WHITSUNDAYS

Haymen Island

Hook Island

Butterfly Bay

Nara

Border Island

WHITSUNDAY GROUP

Daydream Island

Airlie Beach

Shute Harbour

South Molle Island

Cid

Whitsunday Island

Hill Inlet

Australia

Long Island

Hamilton Island

Proserpine

Repulse Bay

Lindeman Island

Shaw Island

CUMBERLAND GROUP

Blacksmith Island

Goldsmith Island

archipelago of islands that you can sail around and a good number of anchorages of all types offering protection depending on the wind. Trips to the Great Barrier Reef itself can be organised by excursion boats or seaplane. Like any ideal sailing and charter area, you will not of course be on your own.

Wind and sea

With the Great Barrier Reef protecting the area of sea sandwiched between the reef and the mainland there are no really big seas rolling in. However, even across the sea area between the reef and the islands the regular southeast trade wind can at times cause sufficient seas to make some anchorages untenable. The prevailing southeast trades are the predominant wind although it blows at varying strengths and may at times be interrupted by northerly winds. During the dry season from March to October the southeast trade winds are most regular at around 15–20 knots. Often the southeast trades will blow for a week or more before dying down for a few days when northerlies may blow. March to May is the windiest time when the trades blow strongly and there is the possibility of gale force winds at times. The occasional cyclone sometimes cuts through the area at this time.

Between November and April the southeast trades are less prevalent and not as strong at around 10–15 knots and there will be northerly winds as well at around 10–15 knots. There are also days of calm weather. This is the traditional wet season although most rain falls at night. During this time there are more usable anchorages around the Whitsundays because of the alternating winds and the likelihood of more days of calm.

Suitable for...

The area is suitable for intermediate to experienced sailors although the charter companies cater for everyone here and can organise an itinerary for the less experienced and provide a guide/skipper for a few days until you feel comfortable. The dry season from March to October when the southeast trades are stronger and predominant is for more experienced sailors as the number of safe anchorages is reduced during this period and the sailing is somewhat harder.

Harbours and anchorages

There are few harbours as such and for the most part you will be on moorings or at anchor. A number of the resorts and the charter companies have jetties or moorings for visitors and you will be advised on these by the charter company. As indicated, anchoring options depend on the wind and again the charter companies are well versed in detailing safe anchorages depending on wind and sea. There are a number of all-weather anchorages around the islands as well. Contrary to popular opinion you will not be anchoring on coral around the Whitsundays with most of the bottom being sand or mud and this is in many ways a blessing for the charterer as anchoring amongst coral is not always a simple process. If you want to go diving on the reef a dive-boat or seaplane is the sensible and environmentally sound option.

Main charter bases

The main charter base is at Shute Harbour on the mainland coast and at Airlie. However yachts can be delivered to Hamilton Island where there is an airport. It is about a 45-minute transfer from Proserpine Airport to Shute Harbour and around a 15 minute transfer from Hamilton Island Airport to the boat if delivered to the island.

Sailing area

The Whitsundays make up a cruising area in which you can easily sail between the islands in a short time and change your mind and head off somewhere else should the weather change or just on a whim.

Other areas

Brisbane There is some limited bareboat and skippered charter out of Brisbane.
Sydney There is limited bareboat and skippered charter out of Sydney, principally from Pittwater Harbour 15 miles north of Sydney. The area comprises Pittwater harbour itself, Cowan Creek and the Hawkesbury River. There is ample opportunity to cruise around the three-headed area with many indentations and creeks although a one week cruise is probably best. It does not of course offer the clear water and tropical conditions of the Whitsundays.

A typical 6 day cruise is as follows:

Shute Harbour – Shute Harbour

Total 80-90 miles

Day 1 **South Molle Island** Moorings available off South Molle Resort. Good walking ashore. Restaurant.

Day 2 **Hook Island/Nara Inlet** Fjord-like inlet. Sea eagles and waterfalls after rain.

Day 3 **Whitsunday Island/Hill Inlet** Sail around Hook Island. Anchor at Butterfly Bay for lunch. Bring up in Hill Inlet for the night. Wonderful beach and oysters.

Day 4 **Hamilton Island** Stop in the Lindemans for lunch. Restaurants and facilities ashore at Hamilton.

Sea-plane tour to the Barrier Reef. Bottles can be arranged or snorkel and reef-walk.

Day 5 **Whitsunday Island/Cid Harbour**

Day 6 **Shute Harbour**

Land excursions

Most charterers should spend some time looking around the wonderful landscape that is Australia. The flora and fauna is spectacular and unique and the country as a whole shatters the senses with its immensity. To see the well-known sights, an organised excursion is easiest as this is a big, big country. If you are short on time, flying is the only way to get around. If you have more time don't omit less well-known sites which can be every bit as spectacular and generally more interesting than the popular bits of Australia like Ayres Rock (Uluru) or Alice Springs. And don't forget to spend some time in Sydney which is a lively cosmopolitan place sited on a wonderful complex of harbours.

Airlie Beach, Whitsundays

NEW ZEALAND

Despite the fact there are more yachts per head of population than anywhere else in the world, chartering in New Zealand is relatively new. Most of this has got to do with the distances to these two islands tucked between Australia and Antarctica and the flying time involved to get there from the northern hemisphere. It doesn't really matter whether you go east-about or west-about to get there from Britain as the flying time is approximately the same. But with the increasing popularity of holidays in New Zealand over the last decade, so yacht chartering has increased in popularity and there are now a number of yacht charter companies in several locations. The main charter areas are in the North Island around Auckland and the Hauraki Gulf, the Bay of Islands further north, and in the South Island within the Marlborough Sounds. The climate in the north is semi-tropical with the season running through the southern hemisphere summer from November to April and in the South Island a slightly shorter season.

WHEN TO GO

The season around Auckland and the Bay of Islands runs for the southern hemisphere summer between mid-October and mid-April. The season in the Marlborough Sounds is tighter, with the charter season operating November to March.

Early season Mid-October to end November. Temperatures are around 16–20°C with temperatures dropping in the evening to 10–14°C.

High season December to end of February. Around Christmas is the most popular period. Temperatures are around 21–24°C in the day although at times they will get up to 30°C. The southern sun is fierce and seems hotter than closer to the equator. Temperatures at night are around 15–17°C.

BEFORE YOU GO

For
- ✔ Magnificent and dramatic scenery and wide open spaces afloat and ashore.
- ✔ Settled summer season with semi-tropical temperatures.
- ✔ Friendly and helpful people ashore.
- ✔ Good fishing and good seafood ashore if you fail to catch your own.

Against
- ✘ Long flight to get there (24 hours flying time from the UK, 12 hours flying time from west coast USA).
- ✘ Unsettled conditions in the spring and autumn.
- ✘ It rains more than the locals admit.

Types of charter
- ❖ Sailing in company
- ❖ Bareboat
- ❖ Skippered charter

Suitable for
- ❖ Intermediate to experienced sailors.

Wind patterns are most predictable with sea breezes at around 10-15 knots prevailing.

Late season March to mid-April. Temperatures start to drop to spring levels of around 15–20°C and the wind can be bitingly cold at times. There is a chance of gales coming in off the Southern Ocean.

GETTING THERE

There are numerous scheduled flights to Auckland Airport from most large international airports or onward flights from Sydney in Australia. There are internal connections to other parts of the country. For Auckland the international

At Bay of Islands	Av max °C	Av min °C	Highest recorded	Relative humidity	Days 0.25 mm rain	Sea temp °C	Wind direction & force
Oct	16	9	22	66%	17	16	NW-W-SW F4
Nov	19	12	27	64%	15	17	N-NW-W-SW F4
Dec	21	14	32	64%	12	18.5	NW-W-SW F4
Jan	23	16	32	62%	10	20	All dir. F3-4
Feb	23	16	32	61%	10	20	NE-E-S F4
Mar	22	15	30	65%	11	20.5	All dir. F4
Apr	19	13	27	69%	14	19	All dir. F4

flight dumps you 45 minutes from the harbour. For the Bay of Islands you can fly to Kerikeri and get a shuttle bus to Pahia or hire a car and make a leisurely trip over a couple of days to Pahia and Opua. For the Marlborough Sounds you can fly to Nelson or Wellington and connect from there. For Europeans it is best to have a short stopover somewhere en route to dilute jet-lag effects.

WHEN YOU'RE THERE

Visa and documentation
Most visitors to New Zealand will get a three month visa on entry. All EU and US nationals and many other countries do not require a visa but if in doubt check on the NZ immigration website www.immigration.govt.nz.

For the charter boat you will require a certificate of competence. Other relevant paperwork for the charter yacht will be prepared by the charter company on your arrival and a full briefing on the yacht and area will be given to you.

Health
Immunisation Only required if coming from an infectious area.
Quarantine New Zealand has very strict quarantine laws and you are not allowed to bring in many foodstuffs or animal products including some souvenirs made from animal skins etc.

ESSENTIAL INFORMATION

Capital Wellington

Time zone UT + 12 DST +1 hour Oct–April

Language English and Maori

Telecommunications Automatic dialling. Country code 64. Phone cards in many places. GSM phones supported throughout New Zealand. Internet cafés and wifi.

Electricity 220V 50Hz AC

Medical services There are good medical services throughout the country and efficient land and air ambulance services. Private medical insurance should be taken out in case of an accident involving an extended stay in hospital.
Water Water is generally safe to drink everywhere.

Money and banks
The unit of currency is the New Zealand dollar and rates of exchange have been reasonably stable over the last five years. There is little point in obtaining New Zealand currency before you enter the country.

Banks are open 1000–1600 Monday to Friday. Money can sometimes be exchanged at travel agents or charter operators. All major credit cards and charge cards can be

SAILING GUIDES AND CHARTS

There are a number of locally produced guides.

Royal Akarana Yacht Club Coastal Cruising Handbook Produced by the Royal Akarana Yacht Club.

Northland Coast: A Fishing and Cruising Guide William Owens. David Bateman publ.

Hauraki Gulf: A Fishing and Cruising Guide William Owens. David Bateman publ.

New Zealand Cruising Guide – Central Area Murray and Koh.

The New Zealand Hydrographic Office produces good scale charts of all areas and these are widely available in New Zealand.

used in the larger towns and tourist resorts. ATM machines can be found in the cities and larger resorts and work with most credit cards.

Eating and drinking

Eating out in New Zealand is good with wonderful raw ingredients and some influence from immigrant groups. By and large, cuisine away from the cities and large resorts tends to the English model. Meat or fish and three veggie, although the superior ingredients make it more tasty than in England. In some places there are some excellent fish restaurants and some interesting kiwi variations on the standard cuisine.

Like the Australians, New Zealanders are known as beer drinkers although the beer just isn't that great. However, New Zealand wine, particularly the whites, are world class.

Provisioning

Provisioning is easy almost everywhere although in the Bay of Islands and Marlborough Sounds you will be away from anything resembling a hamlet for much of the time so it is essential to provision up when you can. Most of the charter

companies can arrange a provisioning service and will provide a list of items before you get to the boat so that you can select what you want to have on board before arriving.

Costs

The overall cost of living is slightly below the European average and is generally good value for money. Eating out depends on where you go and varies from around £10 a head in simple establishments to £20–30 a head in a good restaurant. Wine is around £8 and up a bottle in a restaurant but BYOs mean you can buy a reasonable bottle for £5 in a 'bottle-store' and take it along yourself. Beer is around £1 a half litre. Provisioning is relatively cheap with local variations on hard and soft cheeses, good cured meats and other processed items. Fresh fruit and vegetables are amongst the best in the world and inexpensive. Fresh meat (including the ubiquitous mutton) and fresh fish is available everywhere as are oysters and mussels. Public transportation is mostly by bus or mini-bus and is reasonable. Taxis are moderate in cost. Hire cars start at around £20 a day. Mountain bikes can be hired in many places.

Crime and personal safety

New Zealand is a safe country to travel in and the likelihood of violence or robbery away from the large cities is remote. Theft from boats is infrequent and few precautions are necessary.

CHARTER AREAS

AUCKLAND AND THE HAURAKI GULF

This is the much indented natural harbour around Auckland and numerous off-lying islands. This is the heart of sailing in New Zealand and there are numerous local races just about every day as well as international races like the recent Louis Vuitton Pacific

Cup. There are several marinas and a whole host of anchorages around the coast and islands. At the hub is Auckland with a wide choice of restaurants and bars.

Wind and sea
New Zealand sits on the edge of the great Southern Ocean and is on the edge of systems coming off the bottom of Australia. These systems track through fairly regularly in the spring and autumn so you get on average one every seven days or so. This means a front will come through bringing predominantly westerly winds. Some of these can be strong and even gale force, but generally move through within a day or two.

In the summer highs are more persistent and you will often have days where the prevailing winds are sea breezes. The sea breeze fills in from the NNE-N by lunchtime and generally gets up to 10–15 knots. At night a southerly land breeze may blow, rarely getting above 10 knots. If you have to get somewhere remember mornings are often calm and you will be able to motor.

Suitable for...
The area around Auckland is suitable for inexperienced to experienced sailors. There is sufficient sheltered water for the inexperienced to get about safely and a good choice of safe anchorages. The charter companies can provide a guide/skipper for a few days until you feel comfortable if necessary. The Marlborough Sounds are more suited for experienced sailors.

Harbours and anchorages
There are marinas around the Auckland area and up the coast to Opua. Around the Hauraki Gulf you will generally be anchoring once you have left a marina base. The same applies in the Bay of Islands once you leave Opua Marina.

There are anchorages everywhere with good all-weather anchorages available. Some anchorages have moorings, but mostly you will be using your own anchor. The bottom is mostly mud or sand.

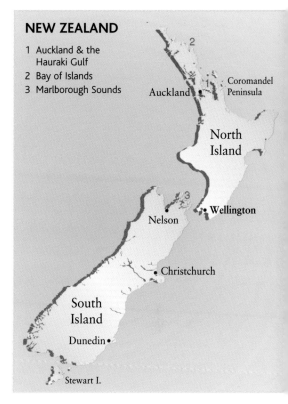

NEW ZEALAND
1 Auckland & the Hauraki Gulf
2 Bay of Islands
3 Marlborough Sounds

Main charter bases
Westhaven Marina Right in the heart of Auckland. The main charter base for the Hauraki Gulf.
Gulf Harbour Marina At Whangaparoa about 1 hours drive north of Auckland.

Sailing area
The cruising area around the Hauraki Gulf includes a mix of populated areas with their facilities and the native bush which clothes the hillsides.

BAY OF ISLANDS
The Bay of Islands is just what its name states, a large bay, really a gulf, with around 30 islands dotted about it although there are really only a dozen that provide useful anchorages. It is blessed by a sub-tropical climate and there is diving aplenty and wonderful walks through the native bush ashore. In 1978 the Bay of Islands was

191

A typical 7 day cruise itinerary is as follows

Auckland/Westhaven Marina back to Westhaven Marina

150 miles (Great Barrier)

Day 1	Leave Westhaven Marina for lunch at Islington Bay on Rangitoto. Overnight at Onetangi Bay on Waiheke Island. Restaurant and wonderful walks ashore on the island.
Day 1	**Coromandel Peninsula** Anchor overnight at Te Kouma harbour.
Day 1	**Great Barrier Island/Port Fitzroy** Good diving. Seafood restaurants with good crayfish, scallops, mussels, etc.
Day 1	**Great Barrier Island/Port Fitzroy** or go to Tryphena or Whangaparaoa.
Day 1	**Kawau Island** Overnight at Bon Accord Harbour. Visit Governor Grays Mansion House. Good walks through the bush.
Day 1	**Gulf Harbour Marina/Whangaparaoa** Restaurants.
Day 1	**Westhaven Marina**

For a shorter itinerary, the leg to Great Barrier Island can be omitted.

Land excursions

There are numerous organised tours to sites like Rotorua to see bubbling mud pools and geysers, white-water rafting in North Island rivers, trekking, bungee jumping (New Zealand is the home of this particular madness) or just to see the sights. Alternatively hire a car or camper-van and make your own way around. New Zealand has probably the greatest geographical diversity of any country I know.

formally declared a maritime and historic reserve and this has ensured that development has not blighted it. There are a few restaurants scattered around but mostly you are on your own and must cater for yourself. An area for those who like to go sailing and get away from it all.

Wind and sea

In the summer proper the prevailing winds are land and sea breezes. The sea breeze will fill in mid-morning from the NNE-E and usually gets up to 10–15 knots by mid-afternoon. At night there may be a light S-SW land breeze but it rarely gets above 5–10 knots. There may sometimes be a sea fog when warm tropical air meets the cooler seas around the east coast. In spring and autumn things are less settled and at the edges of the season there are likely to be gales. Often the wind will suddenly turn from the NE to the SW and blow with some force.

Seas in the area are generally fairly flat and there are more sheltered anchorages than you can shake a stick at. In some of the more exposed areas there can be a big swell coming up from the south, but on the whole it is possible to get behind an island or islands and out of the swell. There may also be a swell that lasts through the night from the NE sea breeze, but there are so many well sheltered anchorages that this shouldn't be a bother.

Suitable for...

Intermediate to experienced sailors. There are a lot of places to go to and it is relatively simple to tailor an itinerary that covers as much or as little ground as you want to cover.

Harbours and anchorages

There is just one marina at Opua in the Bay of Islands. There are few harbours and in

Opua Marina in the Bay of Islands

most of these you will have to anchor off or pick up a mooring anyway. Some care is needed entering river harbours where the bar at the entrance and depths over it change over time. There are anchorages everywhere. The bottom is generally sand or mud.

Main charter bases

Opua This can be reached by car, bus or an internal flight from Auckland to Kerikeri and shuttle bus from there.

Sailing area

A myriad choice of bays and inlets. The area is tidal so some care is needed over tidal ranges (around 3 metres at springs) but depths are such that you will have no problem anchoring safely in most bays and creeks. Islands like Urupukpuka, Motorua, Robertson, and Motuatohia all have all-weather anchorages. More adventurous sailors can go north to Cavalli Island and Whangaroa Harbour.

OTHER AREAS

Marlborough Sounds

Most charter yachts operate out of Picton which is the only marina in the area. The Sounds are well-sheltered but can be subject to severe gusts off the high land and to katabatic winds at night. The scenery and surroundings are outstanding with few comparable places in the world. Most of the steep hills are covered in native bush. There are a few restaurants scattered around the area but on the whole you must cater for yourself – the fishing incidentally is superb. They also produce some of the best Sauvignon Blanc in the world here. The season is slightly shorter than in the sub-tropical north with Christmas again being the most popular time.

You can get an internal flight to Picton or Blenheim from major cities or there is a ferry from Wellington to Picton.

SOUTHEAST ASIA

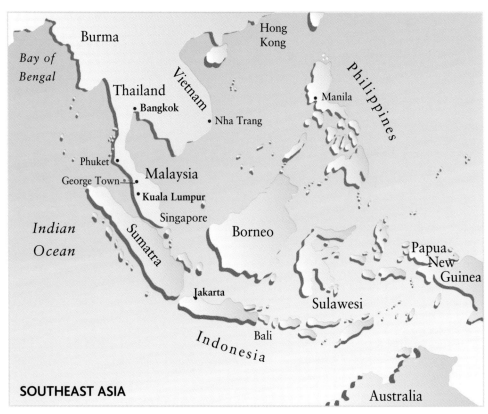

Burma

Bay of
Bengal

Thailand

Bangkok

Nha Trang

Vietnam

Hong
Kong

Manila

Philippines

Phuket

George Town

Malaysia

Kuala Lumpur

Singapore

Indian
Ocean

Sumatra

Borneo

Papua
New
Guinea

Jakarta

Sulawesi

Indonesia

Bali

SOUTHEAST ASIA

Australia

Longtail boat off Phuket

THAILAND

A relatively new charter area with all charter centred around Phuket on the west coast. Although the west coast of Thailand is relatively short, the much indented coastline and numerous islands combine to make up an extensive cruising area. While it is possible to cruise during either the northeast monsoon (November to April) or the southwest monsoon (May to October), the northeast monsoon period is the favoured time for sailing in Thailand and you will find charter companies will probably close down for part of the southwest monsoon period. The attractions of sailing in Thailand are evident to anyone who has seen photographs of the area or read even a little about the country and its culture. The geography is spectacular, the people are gentle, the culture and cuisine exotic but accessible and the sailing is not at all bad.

WHEN TO GO

There are two distinct seasons corresponding to the two monsoon periods although some divide the year up into three periods with the cool dry season from November to February, the hot season from March to June and the rainy season from July to October. The favoured season is during the northeast monsoon between November and April and the less favoured is the southwest monsoon between May and October.

Northeast monsoon November to April. This is the dry season and consequently the least humid season. Average temperatures range from around 31–32°C in November and December to 34–38°C in April. Temperatures are only a few degrees less at night around Phuket. The average humidity at midday is around 50–58% over the season. The northeast monsoon will have settled down by mid-November and lasts through until mid-April with a consistent pattern. The best months are reckoned to be December, January, and February.

BEFORE YOU GO

For
✔ Spectacular islands and coast with sheer limestone pinnacles covered in tropical jungle.
✔ Good sheltered sailing area with lots of anchorages.
✔ Tropical temperatures and warm waters for swimming.
✔ Exotic and welcoming culture ashore.
✔ Good food although too spicy for some.

Against
✘ Moderately long flights from Europe and USA.
✘ Crowded with tripper boats around popular places like Ko Phi Phi.
✘ Too humid for some.
✘ Waters often murky with river silt making swimming uninviting until offshore.

Types of charter
❖ Flotilla
❖ Bareboat
❖ Skippered charter
❖ Luxury charter

Suitable for
❖ Adventurous beginners to experienced sailors.

Southwest monsoon May to October. This is the wet season and those unused to the tropics will find the humidity difficult to handle. Average temperatures range from 34–38°C in May to 31–32°C in October although temperatures will often reach 39–40°C. The average humidity is around 58–70% over the season. Although the humidity figures appear not to be that much higher than the Mediterranean countries or countries lying in the far northern or southern hemisphere, the actual effect is a little uncomfortable during the height of the rainy season. The worst months are

At Phuket	Av max °C	Av min °C	Highest recorded	Relative humidity	Days 0.1 mm rain	Sea temp °C	Wind direction & force
Jan	31	24	34	57%	5	27	NE-E F3-4
Feb	32	24	36	54%	3	28	NE-E F3-4
Mar	33	25	34	56%	6	29	NW-NE-E F3-4
Apr	33	25	34	61%	12	29	NW-W F3-4
May	31	25	36	68%	21	29	NW-W-SW F3-4
Jun	31	25	37	68%	19	28	W-SW 3-4
Jul	31	25	37	68%	19	28	NW-W-SW F4
Aug	31	25	37	68%	20	28	W-SW F4-5
Sep	30	24	36	70%	22	27.5	NW-W-SW F4
Oct	30	24	34	70%	23	28	NW-W F3-4
Nov	30	24	37	67%	16	28	N-NE-E F3-4
Dec	31	24	33	62%	9	26.5	NE-E F4

ESSENTIAL INFORMATION

Capital Bangkok

Time zone UT + 7

Language Thai. Some English spoken in tourist areas.

Telecommunications Automatic dialling in the larger centres. Country code 66. Most mobile phones work here depending on your supplier. Wifi and internet cafés

Electricity 220V 50Hz AC

reckoned to be July, August and September. **Note:** Phuket actually has a double rainy period with most rain falling in May and again in October. On average it will rain for more than 20 days in the month during these two months.

GETTING THERE

There are numerous scheduled flights to Bangkok and Phuket international airports from most major European and American airports and also from most major airports around the Pacific rim. Few charter flights operate as most of the major airlines flying scheduled flights can provide competitive prices for long-haul flights. Direct flight times from Europe are around 12 hours, from the USA around 12–18 hours depending on where you fly from, and from Australia around 8 hours.

From Bangkok to Phuket there are regular daily internal flights which take around an hour for a direct flight.

WHEN YOU'RE THERE

Visas and documentation
Most visitors to Thailand including all EU, USA & Canada and Australasians will get a 30 day visa on arrival. Most others will get a 15 day visa. Check with your charter operator on the period you will get a visa for or if there are any special requirements.

The skipper of the boat will need a certificate of competence such as the RYA International Certificate of Competence.

Health
Immunisation There are no requirements but the following vaccinations should be obtained: cholera, typhoid, tetanus booster,

hepatitis A (preferably Havrix or otherwise gammaglobulin).

Malaria The incidence of malaria in Thailand has increased in recent years with some resistant strains in the north. This does not affect Phuket where the incidence of malaria is low to non-existent. If advised take an appropriate malaria prophylactic. The best way to avoid malaria is to avoid being bitten, so cover up in the evenings, use a good (more than 30% DEET) repellent and a coil or plug-in fumigant.

Medical services Range from adequate or good in cities and tourist resorts to poor in out-of-the-way places. It is essential to take out private medical insurance and if the charter operator cannot arrange this, then most of the larger travel agents or other agencies can. Ensure the insurance covers repatriation in the case of major illness.

Water Visitors should not drink local water and this includes ice. Although the water is safe to drink in some areas, the visitor on a short stay should avoid it. This also means not eating fruit and vegetables washed in the water. For the most part any problems will be a reaction to local micro-organisms in the water to which you are not accustomed. There is however a risk of more serious waterborne diseases in some areas. Bottled water or juices are available everywhere although there is the practice of filling bottles with ordinary tap water in some places.

Note: AIDS and HIV related illness has increased dramatically in Thailand in recent years and given Thailand's reputation for easily obtained sexual favours, all precautions should be taken and safe sex must be practised.

Money and banks

The unit of currency is the *baht* and rates of exchange are stable (the *baht* is tied to the US dollar). There is no point in obtaining *baht* before you go as you will get as good a rate of exchange in Thailand as anywhere else.

Banks are open 0830-1530 Monday to Friday. Exchange offices and travel agents operate outside these hours. All major credit cards and charge cards can be used in the cities and larger tourist resorts. Some smaller places may not accept your *Visa* or *Mastercard* even though they have a sticker up to say they will, but try a little persuasion before you give up. ATM machines can be found in the cities and larger tourist resorts and work with most credit cards.

Eating and drinking

Some love Thai food and others are not so keen. In general it is spicy and often hot with a lot of garlic and the small fiery peppers called *phrik khii nuu* (mouse-shit peppers). In the hot soups and curries ask for it without the hot peppers unless you like exceptionally hot dishes. In most places, even on street stalls, the food will be cooked freshly to order and you can often point out what you want to go into it. Dishes often contain chicken, beef, pork or fish. Around Phuket there is an excellent choice of seafood and it should not be missed. Dishes are often flavoured with lemon grass, ginger, coriander, lime juice and coconut milk. There are a lot of Chinese influences on much of the food. Rice is the normal accompaniment although noodles are also popular.

Beer and rice whiskey are the two normal drinks. Most visitors tend to stick with the beer of which the most popular brand is *Singha*. Rice whiskey is not expensive, tastes marginally like white rum and should be tried before you order a bottle.

Provisioning

Most provisions can be found in and around Phuket Island and where there is any concentration of charter yachts, the more entrepreneurial Thais offer a provisioning service. It is worth going ashore in a settlement of any size to wander around the market and you can usually buy fish off passing Thai fishermen. Most yachts will take on basic provisions like bottled water, fruit and vegetables, juices, beer, a few staples and canned goods, enough for three to five days, as you will probably eat out for the rest of the time.

Costs

The overall cost of living is low. To a large extent it depends where you eat out. A meal at a street stall (and they can be excellent) can cost as little as £1.50 per head while a meal in a more upmarket restaurant or hotel can be £10–15 per head. In general meals in hotels tend towards a more western approach to food for which you pay over the odds. Small restaurants have excellent local dishes at very reasonable prices. Beer is surprisingly expensive at around £1.50–2.00 a bottle. Local whiskey is around £5 a bottle.

Local transport is very cheap in Thailand. It may be by *tuk-tuk*, the three-wheeler furies which charge around, by *songthaew*, small pick-up trucks with bench seats, or by normal taxi. Normal bicycle rickshaws are also found. Whatever method you choose, be sure to establish the price before you get in and haggle over the drivers' initial price. Hire motorbikes are around £5 a day although this is a dangerous way to get around.

Crime and personal safety

In general you will have few problems in Thailand as long as you stick to the Phuket area. Piracy has been mentioned in the past off the Thai coast, but this is mostly off the east coast and no recent incidents have been reported off the west coast for some time. Some of the crew on Thai fishing boats in the area may look piratical, but they are a friendly lot who will help rather than hinder your cruise. Theft from boats is relatively infrequent but take all precautions and lock the yacht securely when going ashore.

Ashore there have been some incidents of drugged cigarettes, drinks or sweets being offered to people who wake up some time later minus their possessions, but on the whole little of this goes on around Phuket. Nonetheless precautions are in order in some of the bars.

CHARTER AREAS

PHUKET

Situated on the west coast of Thailand, Phuket is used as a generic name to cover Phuket Island, Phang Nga Bay and the islands scattered around this area. It is a spectacular area with high limestone cliffs, steep-to islands and lush tropical forest. The area offers a mix of resorts and deserted unspoilt bays. Some of the islands and anchorages are simply spectacular, fantastic jutting pillars topped by dense jungle and undergrowth. Ashore, the resorts vary from chic exclusive hotels to more downmarket affairs and anywhere there are a few tourists a restaurant will be found nearby.

Wind and sea

The prevailing wind in the area depends on the monsoon season.

The wind blows from the northeast during the northeast monsoon and this is the favoured time to sail in this area when the wind is blowing off the land. It has a diurnal component and generally gets up around midday, blows at Force 4–6, and dies at night. With the wind off the land seas are small and rarely get over a metre in height. There may be days of calm at the beginning and end of the season but otherwise there is little disruption to the pattern.

The wind blows from the southwest during the southwest monsoon period and there can be squalls and thunderstorms at times. The southwest wind tends to blow more consistently day and night and pushes a heavy sea onto the coast across the Indian Ocean. Many of the anchorages along the coast are dangerous to use during the southwest monsoon. During July–August there is a small risk of a typhoon affecting the area.

Suitable for...

During the northeast monsoon when wind patterns are settled and predictable the area

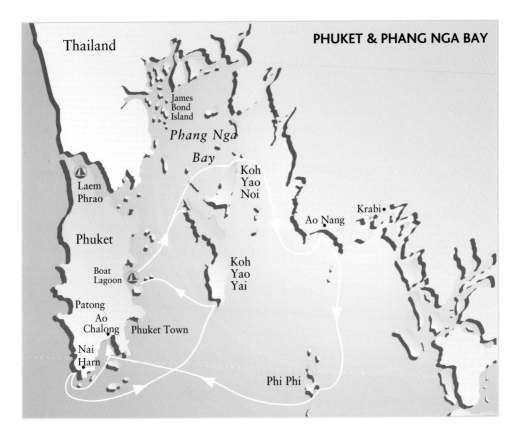

is suitable for intermediate and experienced sailors. A small flotilla operates from near Phuket and this is a good way to get to know the area. Within Phang Nga Bay there is ample cruising for a two week period in well sheltered waters. For bareboat charterers who want to go further afield there is the west coast of Phuket and the Similan and Surin Islands.

During the southwest monsoon, cruising is much restricted and most yachts will content themselves with a cruise around those parts of Phang Nga Bay that afford shelter from the southwest wind. This period is for experienced sailors.

Harbours and anchorages

There are few harbours as such and for the most part you will be on moorings or at anchor. The area is mostly fairly shallow and approaches to anchorages require some care over navigation. A number of rivers empty into or near Phang Nga Bay and this makes the water a milky green and the bottom difficult to see. Out amongst the islands the water is clearer and you will more easily see the bottom and pick up dangers to navigation like shallows, rock and coral. The anchorages are for the most part in fairly shallow water and you will have no problem with the holding which is predominantly mud or sand.

The anchorages are spectacular and vary from steep-sided cliffs to white sand beaches. They are not to be missed.

Main charter bases

The main charter bases are around Phuket with yachts at Boat Lagoon Marina and Yacht Haven near Phuket and at Laem Phrao. Phuket is around one hour from Bangkok on a direct flight and it is about 15 minutes to Laem Phrao and 30 minutes to the Boat Lagoon from the airport.

A typical 10-day cruise (allowing time for transfers to and from Bangkok and some sightseeing) is as follows:

Boat Lagoon (Phuket) to Boat Lagoon

Total 110 miles

Day 1	**Arrive Boat Lagoon** Relax around the restaurants and bars in the marina.	
Day 2	**Koh Yao Noi** Anchor off the NW side of the island.	
Day 3	**Ao Nang** Anchor off the beach. Restaurants.	
Day 4	Lay day. Cruise around Krabi and the Koh Dam group of islands.	
Day 5	**Phi Phi Islands** Anchor for the night in Tonsai Bay. Restaurants.	
Day 6	**Ao Chalong** A large bay on the bottom of Phuket. Anchor off. A long row ashore. Restaurants and nightlife.	
Day 7	**Nai Harn Bay** Good for swimming. Phuket Yacht Club ashore offers upmarket restaurants and bars or there are some less expensive restaurants.	
Day 8	Lay day	
Day 9	**Koh Yao Yai** or **Koh Rang** Good beaches.	
Day 10	**Boat Lagoon**	

Sailing area

The sea area between Phuket on the west and the mainland on the east makes up the main cruising area. The coast is much indented and the bay is peppered with islands. Most yachts will do a circuit of the bay and islands and then can extend the cruise to the west coast of Phuket and the Similan and Surin Islands if more sea miles are wanted. One of the features of the area are the *hongs*, rock tunnels, caves and chimneys that have been eroded from the

SAILING GUIDES AND CHARTS

There are several guides affording information on cruising in Thailand. The following may be useful:

Sail Thailand Thai Marine Leisure/ Colin Piprell. Artasia Press. Covers the area around Phuket.

Andaman Sea Pilot Image Asia.

Indian Ocean Cruising Guide Rod Heikell. Imray. Covers the area around Phuket.

Admiralty charts provide adequate cover for the area around Phuket. Thai charts provide more detail.

cliffs. There are many which can be explored by dinghy from nearby anchorages.

EAST COAST THAILAND

There is some bareboat and skippered charter off the east coast of Thailand around the offshore islands and along the coast. Those who sail in this area rate it highly and within the area there are tranquil bays with wonderful sandy beaches and developments ashore with bars and restaurants so you can mix and match your experiences.

Most charter is out of the resort islands of Koh Chang or Koh Samui, both of which have been long known to backpackers as little island paradises with clear turquoise water and friendly inhabitants. Today they are a great deal more developed than they were, but in a boat you can get away from the hotels and bars to bays the shore-based tourists can't reach.

Koh Chang An archipelago of islands lying close to the Thai border with Cambodia. The season is basically during the northeast monsoon from October to April when the wind direction is predominantly from the northeast through east with some southeast

Land excursions

Most charterers flying in through Bangkok will want to spend a couple of days here on the way to or from Phuket. There is much to see and do here, much more than you can cram into a couple of days and that's not counting just wandering around the markets and shops or going upriver on a longtail boat. If you have longer there are many other excursions, with the trip to the northern highlands at Chiang Mai being one of the most popular.

at times. The archipelago is sheltered from the seas kicked up by the northeast monsoon because it is tucked under the shoulder of Cambodia. Sailing here is bareboat or skippered and bareboat sailing is suitable for intermediate to experienced sailors although the less experienced could take a skipper for a few days to acquaint themselves with the area.

Koh Samui This archipelago of islands lies off the east coast of Thailand approximately opposite Phuket on the west side. The season here is during the southwest

monsoon from May to October when the mainland coast of Thailand protects the archipelago from the seas kicked up by the southwest monsoon. Like Koh Chang the sailing here is bareboat or skippered and the bareboat option is suitable for intermediate and experienced sailors.

Pattaya A number of bareboats and skippered charter operate out of Ocean Marina near Pattaya close to Bangkok. Try doing an internet search or look at the southeast Asia yachting magazines for more information (see p.205).

Phi-Phi Island near Phuket

MALAYSIA

A charter area on the west coast of Malaysia centred around Langkawi Island just under the Thai border. There are said to be over a hundred islands in the Langkawi group, but only if you count some very small islets. While it is possible to cruise during either the northeast monsoon (November to April) or the southwest monsoon (May to October), the northeast monsoon period is the favoured time for sailing in Malaysia and you will find charter companies will probably close down for part of the southwest monsoon period. There are many attractions to sailing in this area. The many spectacular islands, friendly people and delicious cuisine is difficult to better in Asia.

WHEN TO GO

There are two distinct seasons corresponding to the two monsoon periods. The favoured season is during the northeast monsoon between November and April and the less favoured is the southwest monsoon between May and October.

Northeast monsoon November to April. This is the dry season (although paradoxically it can be wet at Langkawi and Penang from September to December) and consequently the least humid season. Average temperatures range from around 31–32°C in November and December to 33–37°C in April. Temperatures are only a few degrees less at night. The average humidity at midday is around 66–71% over the season. The northeast monsoon will have settled down by mid-November and lasts through until mid-April with a consistent pattern. The best months are reckoned to be December, January and February.

Southwest monsoon May to October. This is the hot season and later the wet season and those unused to the tropics will find the humidity difficult to handle. Average temperatures are around 33–37°C from May through to October although temperatures will often reach 39–40°C. The average humidity is around 79–81% over the season. The humidity is uncomfortable at first throughout this season. The worst months are reckoned to be July, August and September.

BEFORE YOU GO

For
- ✔ Exotic culture and wonderful food.
- ✔ Spectacular limestone scenery.
- ✔ Year-round tropical temperatures and warm waters.

Against
- ✘ Too hot and humid for some.
- ✘ Murky water not suited to snorkelling.

Types of charter
- ❖ Bareboat
- ❖ Skippered charter
- ❖ Luxury charter

Suitable for
- ❖ Adventurous beginners to experienced sailors.

ESSENTIAL INFORMATION

Capital Kuala Lumpur

Time zone UT + 8

Language Bahasa Malay. English is widely spoken.

Telecommunications Automatic dialling in the larger centres and tourist resorts. Country code 60. Good service throughout the country. Most mobile phones work here depending on your supplier. Wifi and internet cafés.

Electricity 220V 50Hz AC

At Penang	Av max °C	Av min °C	Highest recorded	Relative humidity	Days 0.25 mm rain	Sea temp °C	Wind direction & force
Jan	32	23	37	68%	8	27.5	N–NE–E F4
Feb	33	23	36	64%	7	28	NE–E–SE F4
Mar	33	23	37	64%	11	28.5	NW–NE–E F3-4
Apr	33	24	37	66%	14	29	W–NW–N F3-4
May	32	23	36	66%	16	29	SW–W–NW F3-4
Jun	32	23	36	67%	12	28.5	SW–W–NW F3
Jul	32	23	35	67%	12	28.5	SW–W F3
Aug	32	23	36	67%	15	28	SW–W–NW F3-4
Sep	31	23	37	69%	18	28	SW–W–NW F3-4
Oct	32	23	34	70%	21	28	NW–W F3-4
Nov	31	23	35	71%	19	28	N–NE–E F3-4
Dec	32	23	35	68%	11	27	N–NE–E F3-4

GETTING THERE

There are numerous scheduled flights to Kuala Lumpur and Penang from most major European and American airports as well as from most major airports around the Pacific rim. Few charter flights operate as most of the major airlines flying scheduled flights can provide competitive prices for long-haul flights. Direct flight times from Europe are around 12 hours, from the USA around 12–18 hours, and from Australia around 8 hours.

From Kuala Lumpur and Penang there are internal flights to Langkawi, around one hour from Kuala Lumpur and 30 minutes from Penang.

WHEN YOU'RE THERE

Visas and documentation

Most visitors to Malaysia from Europe, the USA and Commonwealth countries will automatically get a visa on entry for 30 or 60 days.

Tuk-tuks in Malaysia

Fishing boats, Langkawi

You will likely require a certificate of competence to skipper a bareboat but check with your charter company. Other relevant paperwork for the charter yacht will be prepared by the charter company on your arrival.

CHARTER AREAS

LANGKAWI

Situated on the west coast of Malaysia just under the Thai border, Langkawi is the principal charter area with, it is said, over 100 islands. It is a spectacular area with high cliffs, steep-to islands and lush tropical forest. Penang is the peninsula formerly known as Georgetown to the south of the Langkawi group. Apart from Penang there are few large centres of population and most of the other settlements can be fairly described as villages. Kuah on Langkawi island is the closest you get to a town after Penang. Around the island there are a number of marinas set in wonderfully exotic locations. Rebak Marina is only connected by a small ferry to the main island of Langkawi. The islands and anchorages are spectacular with jutting pillars of rock, fjord-like inlets dripping with vegetation, and deserted white sandy beaches. Ashore things vary between chic exclusive hotels with hot and cold running everything to simple fishing villages and simple but tasty local restaurants.

Charter here is bareboat, skippered or luxury charter. The area is suitable for the less experienced through to intermediate and experienced sailors. The less experienced can potter happily around the anchorages and harbours while the more experienced can circumnavigate the main island and head down to Penang, stopping at Pulau Payar National Park on the way for some diving.

SAILING GUIDES AND CHARTS

Andaman Sea Pilot Image Asia.

Indian Ocean Cruising Guide Rod Heikell. Imray. Covers Langkawi and Penang.

Admiralty charts provide adequate cover for Langkawi and Penang. Malaysian charts provide more detail but are difficult to obtain.

Other Southeast Asia Destinations

Apart from Thailand and Malaysia where charter is well developed, there are a number of small operations in other southeast Asian countries. Some of these are on converted traditional craft like the *pinisi* or *bugis* in Indonesia or *junks* in Vietnam. Some of the charter is just about getting away from it all and cruising through seascapes that are like nothing anywhere else in the world while others concentrate on sail-dive. For information on charter in the area try a search on the internet, a charter broker or one of the following south east Asian boating magazines (web addresses given here):

Asia Pacific Boating
www.asia-pacificboating.com
Action Asia (travel magazine distributed worldwide) www.actionasia.com

INDONESIA

There are a number of small charter operations here. There are some converted *bugis*, traditional Indonesian schooners, cruising the coast around Nusa Tenggara, the Moluccas and Sulawesi. There are other operations out of Bali and from near Jakarta. A few luxury yachts will sometimes do charters around the area depending on demand and there are sometimes some smaller privately skippered charter yachts.

PAPUA NEW GUINEA

There are a few owner-operated charter boats sailing around this area. Sail-dive is popular and mostly operates off the east coast where the diving is said to be world class.

VIETNAM

There are some recently built *junks* operating sail-dive charters around Nha Trang and during the NE monsoon around the Mekong delta. These boats are purpose built and offer a fair degree of comfort and of course the chance to sail on a junk rigged boat.

PHILIPPINES

There are a number of sail-dive charters operating out of Manilla and Bacuit Bay and at least one skippered sailing yacht available for charter in Marina del Nido in Bacuit Bay. The scenery is outstanding and the diving over remote reefs outstanding.

Patong Beach on Phuket

INDIAN OCEAN

Of the three major oceans, the Indian Ocean is the least trammelled by yachts. It is a place to get away from it all. The various charter locations around the Indian Ocean are exotic and little known and for some just a little scary. In fact, the people are welcoming and the culture not as intimidating as it might seem from afar. The Red Sea, the Seychelles and the Maldives encompass a diverse group of countries.

Diving is a major attraction to the Indian Ocean. Whether you just snorkel or are an experienced sub-aqua diver, the diving here is superb and from a yacht you can just slip over the side in an anchorage and watch tropical fish of all colours and hues swimming over the coral reefs. In most places the sea is like a marine soup with a kaleidoscope of colour everywhere.

Apart from the diving, the sailing is good in the tropical monsoon weather and the northern Indian Ocean has a deserved reputation as a benign sea weather-wise. The northeast monsoon blows from November to March and rarely above Force 4–5. Around the Seychelles the northwest monsoon (a variant on the northeast monsoon) is also a gentle wind that makes for good sailing around the main Home Islands group.

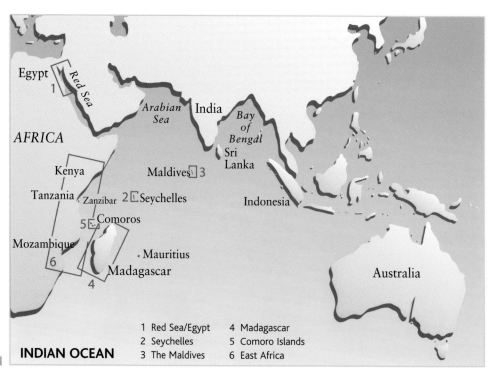

INDIAN OCEAN

1 Red Sea/Egypt	4 Madagascar
2 Seychelles	5 Comoro Islands
3 The Maldives	6 East Africa

RED SEA: EGYPT

Yacht charter in Egypt is exclusively in the Red Sea and is as much to do with diving as to do with sailing. Marine life over the coral reefs along the Egyptian Red Sea coast is world renowned with some authorities baldly stating that there is nothing like it elsewhere. Whatever the arguments, there is no doubting it has some of the top dive sites in the world.

Charter yachts operate mostly from Hurgadha and nearby marinas and to a lesser extent from Safaga and Port Ghalib. Nearly all charter is skippered and given the difficult nature of these coral strewn waters, this is the best way to go. It also gives you a source of local knowledge on board who can direct you to the best dive sites, to the most comfortable anchorages close to the dive sites, and to alternative dive sites should the weather prevent you getting to a chosen place or prevent you anchoring there. There may be the possibility of bareboat charter if you have experience sailing in coral in other areas.

Sailing in this area can be rewarding, but can also be a battle against the strong prevailing northerlies. Navigating amongst the coral is complicated because of the extent and irregular nature of the reefs which are quite different in the Red Sea to the more common outlying reefs around islands and typical atoll patterns found in the Caribbean, Indian Ocean and Pacific. In addition the islands and coast are low-lying in many places and because visibility is often bad when the wind whips sand off the desert to create hazy conditions, navigation between reefs and islands is difficult to say the least.

SAILING GUIDES AND CHARTS

Red Sea Pilot Elaine Morgan & Stephen Davies. Imray.

Wonders of the Red Sea David Fridman and Tony Malmqvist. ISIS. Red Sea marine life. Published and available in Egypt.

A number of locally produced books on dive sites and marine life are available in the larger tourist areas.

At Hurgadha	Av max °C	Av min °C	Highest recorded	Relative humidity	Days 0.1 mm rain	Sea temp °C	Wind direction & force
Jan	21	10	27	39%	1	20	N-NW F5
Feb	23	11	31	40%	1	18.5	N-NW F5
Mar	26	14	34	38%	2	19	N-NW F5
Apr	31	18	41	30%	1	21	N-NW F5
May	36	17	44	28%	0.1	22.5	N-NW F5
Jun	38	24	44	20%	0	24	N-NW F5
Jul	39	26	47	13%	0	25	N-NW F5
Aug	40	26	46	24%	0	26.5	N-NW F5
Sep	37	25	43	27%	0	26	N-NW F5-6
Oct	33	21	39	34%	0	25	N-NW F5
Nov	28	16	37	38%	1	23.5	N-NW F5
Dec	23	12	31	42%	1	21.5	N-NW F5

The season in the northern Red Sea is virtually all year round, with high season in the northern European winter when temperatures in this area are more moderate. It can even be cold at night.

All of the yacht charter companies here can arrange diving courses, advanced instruction, and of course take you to the reefs to go diving. In the end this is the only real reason to come here as the sailing, while challenging, is not really good enough on its own. The diving, though, is superlative.

For further information consult sailing and diving magazines, the Moorings, or a charter broker.

Felucca in Egypt

SEYCHELLES

In the early days there was only really skippered charter around the Seychelles but in the last 20 years several bareboat fleets have been set up in the Seychelles and it is possible to sail yourself around the islands. All charter is out of the capital and principal port Victoria on the main island of Mahe. There are numerous scheduled flights into the capital from most parts of the world and tourist facilities on the island are already extensively developed so there is no problem getting around and finding somewhere to eat out.

The Seychelles are made up of over a hundred islands ranging from the larger granite based islands to typical coral atolls though most charter is around the Home Islands and there is more than enough to see and do here. There are basically two seasons; the hot season from December to May and the cool season from June to November. The hot season coincides with the northwest monsoon or Cross Monsoon and the cool season with the SE trades. The prevailing direction of the wind in the hot and cool seasons effectively determines which anchorages can be used and which reef entrances are safe.

Bareboat charterers will sail around the group of islands to the north of Mahe including Praslin and La Digue. Longer trips to the coral atolls around the Amirantes and Aldabra groups will be by skippered charter and usually only on the larger and faster superyachts because of the distances involved. Apart from Port Victoria, there are only a few piers at the large hotels to tie up to and for the most part you will be anchoring off on white coral sand.

At Port Victoria	Av max °C	Av min °C	Highest recorded	Relative humidity	Days 0.1 mm rain	Sea temp °C	Wind direction & force
Jan	28	24	31	78%	15	28	NW-N F3
Feb	29	25	32	76%	10	28	NW-N F3-4
Mar	29	25	32	74%	11	28	W-NW-N F3
Apr	30	25	33	74%	10	29	All dir. F3-4
May	29	25	33	74%	9	28	S-SE-E F4-5
Jun	28	25	32	75%	9	27	S-SE-E F4-5
Jul	27	24	30	76%	8	26	S-SE-E F4-5
Aug	27	24	31	75%	7	26	S-SE F4-5
Sep	28	24	31	75%	8	26	S-SE-E F4-5
Oct	28	24	31	75%	9	26	SE/NW-N F4
Nov	29	24	32	74%	12	27	SE/NW-N F3
Dec	28	24	33	78%	15	28	NW-N F3

The attractions of the Seychelles are many. In the equatorial region air and sea temperatures vary only a little through the year as can be seen from the chart. Winds here are normally a pleasant 10-20 knots and gales are rare. The beaches are superb white sandy swathes, the vegetation that fecund tropical abundance edged by palms, the birdlife is unique in places, the diving is superb, the food is wonderful and the Seychellois warm and friendly. The only drawback is it can be expensive for services and eating out, but on a boat you can mix and match eating on board and eating out to even things up.

For further information search the internet and try the sailing magazines or a charter broker.

Seychelles. All granite and turquoise water

MALDIVES

Like the Egyptian Red Sea coast, the Maldives are a sail-dive destination rather than a straight yacht charter destination. All charter here is skippered charter and the yacht is used as a base to get between dive sites. This gives divers a big advantage over hotel-dive holidays as you can get around a number of sites, taking everything you need with you.

The Maldives are a string of atolls stretching for over 450 miles north to south. They are all atolls (the word atoll comes from the Maldivian language). There are international flights to the capital Malé and most charter is based here and operates around the atolls to the north and south of the main island.

The diving is superb and this is what people come here for. The people are friendly, the atolls attractive in that low-lying atoll sort of way (the islands are rarely more than 2.5 metres high), and the food

SAILING GUIDES AND CHARTS

Indian Ocean Handbook Rod Heikell. Imray. Has a sma section on the Maldives

adequate to good. The climate varies between the cool season from November to April and the hot season from June to October, but it rains here quite a lot all of the time with May–June and November being the wettest months. The monsoon season roughly corresponds with the cool season during the NE monsoon and the hot season the SW monsoon. During the SW monsoon it can get very rough getting between the atolls so if you are prone to being seasick pick the NE monsoon period.

For further information try sailing and dive magazines or a charter broker.

MADAGASCAR, COMORO ISLANDS AND EAST AFRICA

A number of skippered and crewed charter yachts shuttle around this part of the world taking in Kenya, Zanzibar, the Comoros and Madagascar. Usually you join the yacht for part of the trip depending on the season. The Seychelles are also often included in this charter patch.

Facilities in this part of the world are not everywhere well developed for tourism with the exception of Kenya. Consequently you really need a large and well-found yacht that can carry most things it needs and an experienced skipper for this part of the world. Large catamarans are frequently used partly because of their ability to get in close to the shore in coral fringed anchorages and to make use of some reef

entrances which could be tricky for deep draught yachts.

For further information try an internet search, sailing magazines or a charter broker.

SOME UNUSUAL & FAR-FLUNG CHARTER DESTINATIONS

The following brief collection of unusual destinations covers some far-flung locations scattered around the globe. There are probably a lot more, and it surprises me still to find yacht charter operating in some places I have voyaged to or stopped over in on overland treks. Recently I came across a sail-dive charter yacht in Massawa in Eretria on a voyage down the Red Sea. And on a visit to Vietnam I came across a skippered charter *junk* operating out of Nha Trang on a sail-dive basis and during the northeast monsoon around the Mekong River. Many of these charter operations are fragile affairs run by cruising yachtsmen who have taken a liking to some exotic location and who set up for a year or two before moving on. Others are well established operations that have been in place for years.

Tracking down some of these far-flung charter operations takes time and effort. Often there are no packages and not always a good contact office for booking the charter. For those interested I suggest one of two options.

The first option is to take some time — a fair amount of time usually — and do a thorough internet search chasing up some of the more unusual search results. Most of the small charter outfits will have an internet site and you can make further enquiries by e-mail.

Searching yachting and travel magazines may also uncover unusual charters and charter areas. Some areas like Alaska and Canada appeal more to the nearby American market and so feature in American sailing magazines. Others like New Caledonia and Tierra del Fuego (for some reason) appeal to the French market and will be found advertised in French sailing magazines. Eventually you will track down something tangible and finally you will be able to establish what is going on and who to book with.

There are a number of small agencies and brokers with their finger on the pulse of this sort of far-flung charter and if they cannot help directly they may be able to suggest someone who can.

The second option is for the adventurous traveller — just to get on a plane and go and see what is there. This is not a secure option, it may get no result whatsoever, but you will have a grand adventure looking for that elusive charter destination and you may find some exciting options that are little known outside the country you are in. You will of course need a bit of time.

1 USA & Canada:
    Great Lakes
2 Canada: British Columbia
3 USA: Alaska
4 Galapagos islands
5 Tierra del Fuego
6 Belize
7 Honduras
8 Costa Rica
9 Cuba
10 Trinidad & Tobago
11 Mexico: Sea of Cortez
12 Azores
13 Canaries
14 Indonesia
15 Papua New Guinea
16 Vietnam
17 Philippines

USA & CANADA

GREAT LAKES

(See USA East Coast for information on the USA)

The Great Lakes, straddling the USA and Canada, are home to a sizeable resident population of yachts cruising these waters and also support a good number of charter operations. To call these vast inland bodies of waters 'lakes' is something of a misnomer. They are huge and the potential cruising area covers hundreds of miles of coast not to mention the islands dotted around them. Both Lake Superior and Lake Michigan are close to 300 miles long. There are towns and cities dotted around the Great Lakes but what everyone comes here for is the chance to get away from it all. There are huge swathes of wilderness and the scenery is majestic. Autumn (Fall) is especially spectacular, if

cold. There is wildlife aplenty and the fishing is good. The water in many places is crystal clear if not necessarily inviting temperature wise.

The season in the Great Lakes is compressed into a few summer months. It is possible to cruise here, as the locals do, in spring and autumn, but temperatures either side of July and August are on the cool side and at night they can drop suddenly to below freezing. Temperatures of -6°C have been recorded in May and -2°C in September in Duluth, although this is unusual.

Most charter in this area is based near well-known cruising areas like the Apostle Islands or Thunder Bay in Lake Superior or out of the larger cities or their commuter ports like Port Clinton in Lake Erie or Toronto in Lake Ontario. Getting to the charter base is easy enough either through internal flights and a transfer, by rail or

At Duluth (USA)	Av max °C	Av min °C	Highest recorded	Relative humidity	Days 1 mm rain	Wind direction & force
May	13	3	35	60%	12	NW-N/SE-E F4-5
Jun	19	9	36	66%	13	NW-N/S F4-5
Jul	23	12	41	65%	12	N/S F4
Aug	22	12	36	65%	11	N/S F3-4
Sep	17	8	34	69%	11	N/S F4

coach, or by hire car. Most of these charter operations are small affairs, often with two or three yachts operated on behalf of the owners. In many respects this is the best way to go because the operator will have a fund of local knowledge on where to go hiking, fish, or collect blueberries. Most charter is bareboat, but some skippered charter is also available.

Anyone interested in the Great Lakes should do a search on the internet or try American sailing magazines or a charter broker.

BRITISH COLUMBIA

British Columbia has a large number of resident yachts mostly based around Vancouver and Vancouver Island and yacht facilities are consequently well developed. The mainland coast is enclosed by Vancouver Island and further up Queen Charlotte Island. Sprinkled along the coast are a whole cluster of other islands and islets. Most charter is between Vancouver and Vancouver Island amongst the Gulf Islands and also the Anacortes a short distance down the coast in the USA (see USA

West Coast). The large outer islands protect the waters from the Pacific swell and there is wonderful sailing to be had here. The marine life is prolific and there are seabirds everywhere. There are many sheltered anchorages and sufficient marinas and yacht harbours for provisioning and eating ashore in the area.

The season is pretty much compressed into the short summer from June to August. In the spring and autumn it can be distinctly chilly at night and there is a good possibility of depressions coming in across the Pacific. Fog is also a factor to be reckoned with. The other is mosquitoes and midges.

Most yacht charter companies are based around Vancouver itself or on the southern end of Vancouver Island. Most are fairly small affairs with a few boats although there are some larger companies with a good choice of sail and power boats. Getting there is fairly easy with international flights arriving in Vancouver and internal and some international flights arriving at Victoria Airport on Vancouver Island. There are good ferry links to Vancouver Island, particularly from Vancouver to the Anacortes. There are bareboat and skippered yachts available. For

At Vancouver	Av max °C	Av min °C	Highest recorded	Relative humidity	Days 0.25 mm rain	Sea temp °C	Wind direction & force
May	18	8	28	63%	12	11	All dir. F3
Jun	21	11	33	65%	11	14.5	W/E F2-3
Jul	23	12	33	62%	7	14.5	W-NW F3
Aug	23	12	33	62%	8	16	NW/E-SE F3
Sep	18	9	29	72%	9	12.5	W-NW/E F3-4

At Anchorage	Av max °C	Av min °C	Highest recorded	Relative humidity	Days 0.25 mm rain	Wind direction & force
May	12	2	22	49%	5	W-SW F4-5
Jun	17	7	33	57%	6	SE/W-SW F5
Jul	18	9	27	63%	10	NW-W-SW F4-5
Aug	18	8	28	65%	15	W-SW F4-5
Sep	14	4	23	66%	15	W-SW F5-6

contacts and information try the Canadian Tourist Office, the internet, American sailing magazines, or a charter broker.

ALASKA

Yacht charter in Alaska revolves almost exclusively around exploring this huge wilderness. The peaks are capped in snow throughout the summer and glaciers calve into the sea all over the place. The glacial retreat in evidence in most places is a result of the retreat of the Little Ice Age which only occurred here around 1750. The scenery is like little you will see elsewhere. The marine life is close to a cocktail of every coldwater species going. Many go on charter in these waters to watch whales of which you are likely to see Orca (Killer whales), Humpbacks and Minke. Ashore you will see moose, deer and bears. Birdlife includes eagles and gulls. It is a spectacular place and one which impresses everyone who goes there.

The season is obviously short because of the temperatures to be reckoned with. Either side of May and September and the temperatures slump to way below freezing at night and in fact this is still possible between May and September. This means that being prepared for cold weather and biting winds even in the summer is advisable.

Charter here is all skippered charter and usually the skipper (and hostess) are versed in where to look for the abundant wildlife and marine life. For contacts and information try American sailing magazines, the internet or a charter broker.

TIERRA DEL FUEGO/ ANTARCTICA

There are around a dozen or so charter boats operating in this area doing trips around Tierra del Fuego and Antarctica. These range from the sort of charter where you are pretty much a guest and don't have to do much, to charters where you are part of the crew sharing in the duties and crewing of the yacht. Obviously in this hostile bit of the

At Punta Arenas	Av max °C	Av min °C	Highest recorded	Relative humidity	Days 1 mm rain
Oct	11	3	19	65%	5
Nov	12	4	24	65%	5
Dec	14	6	24	67%	8
Jan	14	7	30	68%	6
Feb	14	7	26	64%	5
Mar	12	5	24	69%	7

Seno Pia, Beagle Channel, Tierra del Fuego

world the seasons very much determine where and when you can go and even during the southern summer bad weather can hold a charter up. Itineraries are suggestions of what could happen if the weather permits. Going on charter in this area is very much an adventure into a region which few see. Getting about by yacht is about the only way to do it and the reward is scenery and sights that will astound. There are glaciers, peaks to climb, marine life including whales and seals, seabirds and furry things like beaver ashore.

Trips to Antarctica by yacht are not as unusual as you might think with increasing numbers making the trip every year. While not hazardous it is arduous, not least because of the temperatures and winds in the area.

Yacht charter in the area between the bottom of South America and Antarctica revolves around not only getting there, but trips ashore to climb mountains and glaciers, trekking around the coast, visiting the Horn itself, ice diving (if you are so inclined), and watching the marine life and the flora and fauna ashore.

Charter yachts operate out of Punta Arenas, Ushuaia, Puerto Williams and the Falklands depending on the time of year and intended destinations. There are inter-

national links to Santiago and connections to Punta Arenas, Puerto Williams and Ushuaia, and international links to the Falklands. For information try the internet, general geographic magazines or a charter broker.

GALAPAGOS

Most trips around the Galapagos are on skippered and crewed three- to ten-day trips around the islands, usually with a significant dive element to them. The Galapagos is of course home to the animals that gave Darwin the tip-off for his theory of Natural Selection and the time-bomb of Evolution that was to so drastically change our way of looking at things. Charterers fly in from Quito in Ecuador (to whom the Galapagos belong) and are then ushered onto yachts for the trip around the islands. Everything on the yachts (which are all fairly large) is catered for and either the skipper or another will be on hand to show you around.

For information try an internet search and general travel and geographical magazines or a charter broker. You can also pick up trips at Puerto Ayora on Santa Cruz. 215

TRINIDAD & TOBAGO

Trinidad and Venezuela almost touch each other in the SE corner of the Caribbean. Much of the yacht charter is on cruising boats which have set up in the area for a few years to earn some pennies although the area is likely to develop.

The area is tropical and as such has large coral reef areas for exploration although around much of Trinidad the muddy effluent from the Orinoco restricts visibility and reef development. However on the islands of Tobago and Bonaire there are wonderful dive sites, with that around Bonaire regarded as amongst the best in the world. Ashore things are tropical with a diverse flora and fauna. There is also the wonderful mix of cultures in Trinidad where African, Indian, European and whoever else dropped by are mingled to produce a cocktail of beauty. This inter-mingling of cultures is expressed in the Trinidad Carnival in January, acknowledged by anyone who has been there as the best Carnival anywhere.

There are international flights into Port of Spain. For information on yacht charters try the internet, yachting magazines or a yacht charter agent.

MEXICO

On the west coast of Mexico just under the border with the USA lies the huge Golfo de California which most know by the more evocative name of the Sea of Cortez. It is a huge cruising area with more than enough anchorages to satisfy those who want to put some miles in. The landscape is dramatic and there is much sealife and good fishing. For a flavour of the place read John Steinbeck's *The Sea of Cortez*. Ashore there is Mexico and Mexican food.

The main cruising area is on the western side of the Sea of Cortez. Here there are a number of offshore islands and mainland

SAILING GUIDES AND CHARTS

Cruising Guide to the Sea of Cortez ed. Nancy and Simon Scott/ research Kees Fransbergen. Cruising Guide Publications.

Charlie's Charts West Coast of Mexico

Charlie's Charts Hawaii, Maui, Molokai and Lanai, Oahu and Kanai.

anchorages as well. The attraction of the area is the rugged rocky mountains and clear waters and just being in Mexico. There is bareboat and skippered charter. There are flights into La Paz or it is possible to fly into Los Angeles or San Diego and get connecting flights down to the Baja. For further information try the internet, sailing magazines or a charter agent.

(For climate see the chart for San Diego in USA West Coast.)

HAWAII

In general the Hawaiian Islands are not suited to yacht charter. The prevailing northeast trades blowing across the islands send in large rollers which while welcomed by the surfing fraternity, make many of the anchorages at best uncomfortable and in some cases untenable. There is some skippered charter around the islands and this is the best way to enjoy Hawaii. International flights into Honolulu and numerous internal flights are available.

For information try American sailing magazines or a charter broker.

For unusual Southeast Asia destinations see p205
For unusual Caribbean destinations see p156
For unusual Pacific destinations see p179
For unusual Indian Ocean destinations see p210

INDEX